CW01500000

Preamble

Our purpose has been to record the history of our parish during the second millennium. Clungunford is representative of countless other parishes in the Marches of Wales. It was far from the centre of power, although in the middle of the troubled borderland, where lasting peace came only when the Welsh Tudors won the crown of England and promoted the union of the two countries. During the Middle Ages Welsh wool was the envy of Europe and sheep were the produce of Clungunford, where farmland still constitutes the landscape for miles around.

Documentary references to Clungunford in the medieval period are surprisingly frequent and we have set the recorded local events within the wider national canvas, for people of every manor in England had to support their feudal superiors, whose interests often lay far away. Clungunford was not immune from wars and plagues, taxes and laws. With the spread of local record keeping in Tudor times and particularly following the establishment of parish registers, with details of baptisms marriages and funerals and the making of Wills by people throughout the social spectrum, the problem for the historian can sometimes be a glut of information. We have related much of the developing story of Clungunford during the last five hundred years to the houses in the parish and the people who lived in them, while, through the centuries, St Cuthbert's Church has been the focus of the parish, weathering all the storms. Some of the dates need explanation and this has been included in the Notes on the Chapters at the back of the main text[1] .

In our research for this book, we have received help from a great many people. More than half our neighbours in the parish of Clungunford have provided information, lent us paintings, engravings and photographs and allowed us access to their houses. Particularly useful have been those who have lived longest in the parish or who occupy the houses we describe. From the mass of information supplied to us, it has been difficult to select what should be included in this book and we regret that so much has had to be omitted. To list the names of every one who deserves our thanks would almost equal an electoral roll. Without their help, this book would not have been written and we wish to record our gratitude to them. Many kind friends from further afield have given us crucial advice and several have generously permitted paintings in their possession to be reproduced. We are most grateful to all of them.

Special mention must be made of certain people who have provided expert professional help of a high calibre. Tony Carr and his superb team at the Shropshire Records and Research Centre have been immensely supportive, as has Sue Hubbard at the Herefordshire Record Office. The British Library, the Public Record Office, the Family Record Centre, the Pierpont Morgan

Library in New York and Pearson Print in Craven Arms were of great assistance. Alex Ramsay took some very fine photographs for the book; Eleanor Harris transcribed and translated manuscripts; Madge Moran gave us the benefit of her expertise on timber framed buildings; John Wheatley, the Architect, who has in his care Clungunford church and many others in the Hereford Diocese, provided detailed guidance about the building of St Cuthbert's; Daniel Miles of the Oxford Dendrochronological Laboratory took samples from the timbers of the church and some of the oldest houses in the parish, so revealing invaluable information about their age.

Above all, we are indebted to our Rector, Barney Bell, and the Chairman of the Clungunford Parish Council, Patrick Ramsay. Both of them have been endlessly patient and helpful throughout the long gestation of this book, providing information and suggestions and reading successive drafts of chapters. Patrick has been instrumental in obtaining through the Parish Council a most generous grant from the Local Heritage Initiative, which is a partnership between the Heritage Lottery Fund, Nationwide Building Society and the Countryside Agency, towards the cost of the production of this book, so that, should any profit result, it can benefit the restoration fund for St Cuthbert's.

Finally, we must make it clear that, despite receiving help from so many quarters, the contents of this book are our own responsibility. In a work of this sort, it is obvious that reliance is placed on what can be gleaned from books and manuscripts of previous centuries and from reminiscences. We have tried to check their accuracy as best we can and we trust we have interpreted correctly the narratives of those who have informed and advised us. Any mistakes and omissions will be our own.

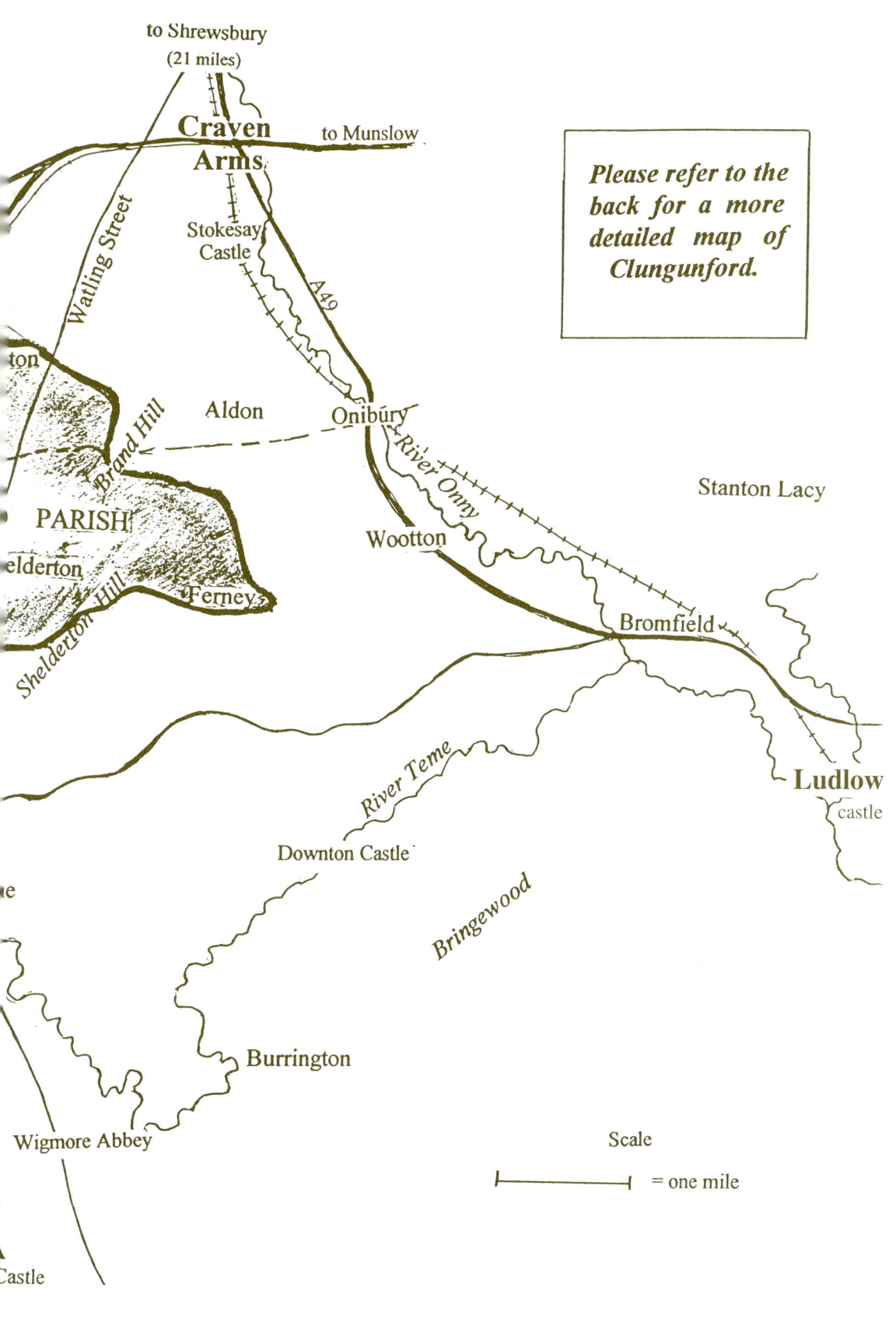

to Shrewsbury
(21 miles)

Craven Arms

to Munslow

Watling Street

Stokesay Castle

A49

...ton

Aldon

Brand Hill

Onibury

Please refer to the
back for a more
detailed map of
Clungunford.

River Onny

PARISH

...elderton

Shelderton Hill

Ferney

Wootton

Stanton Lacy

Bromfield

Ludlow
castle

River Teme

Downton Castle

Bringewood

Burrington

Wigmore Abbey

Scale

⊢————————⊣ = one mile

...Castle

Clungunford

950 Years of a Rural Community

Alick and Fiona Barratt

First published in Great Britain
in 2002 by Alfi Publications.

ISBN 0 9542733 0 3

Printed in England by Livesey Ltd., Shrewsbury (01743) 235651.

Alfi Publications
39 St Petersburgh Mews
London W2 4JT

Contents

Summary of the Medieval Period

Chapter I: Domesday Book. Before the Norman Conquest, Clungunford belonged to an Anglo Saxon thegn called Gunward, who held a ford over the River Clun. It was not Edric's Clun, it was Gunward's Clun or Clun Gunward.

The "tons" or small settlements, which made up the Manor and the parish, were clearings in the forest of Mocktree, which covered the hills from View Edge to Wigmore. The "tons" developed in fertile patches close to the crossing (at "The Crossways") of two ancient roads through the forest (see map in **Fig 2**). Shelderton (the ton by the shelf or cliff) and Rowton (the ton on rough ground) were on the Roman Road (Watling Street). The second road, the ancient drovers road, came from the Midlands down Brand Hill and School Lane and then straight on behind Clungunford Farm and the church, across the ford over the river and on, via Abcott and the Twitchen, into Wales. The church is aligned with this road, as are many of the oldest houses. The bridge over the river was not built for another six hundred years and the "main road", the B4367, did not exist. None of the houses we now see was there in early medieval times but their predecessors probably stood on or near some of the same sites. Beckjay was Bekke's jay and was not on this road system, because it was then an outlying patch of the Jay estate.

The village suffered plunder and burning as the Normans took over and was reduced to one eighth of its Anglo Saxon value immediately after the Conquest. In 1085 William the Conqueror organised an inquiry into the state of the land he had conquered. In 1086 this resulted in Domesday Book (see *Colour Plate 1)*. The entries in the book for Clungunford show that it was well on the way to recovery from the devastation of the conquest and describe a prosperous village, with thirty six labourers and their families, including a dozen slaves. There were two water mills, which suggests a particularly high grain yield and there were fourteen ox drawn ploughs as well as managed woodland (see *Colour Plates 7-10*).

The Normans established the "feudal system" in Clungunford, which meant that every man was responsible to the person on the rung above him on the feudal ladder. He was given land in return for either labour on his superior's farm or military service, not for rent. King William I, the Conqueror, was at the top and below him, as Lord of Clun and Earl of Shrewsbury, he put his friend from Montgomery in Normandy, Earl Roger. He, in turn, gave out the Manor of Clungunford to two Norman lords, Rainald the Sheriff and Picot de Say, who gave his name to Hopesay and Stokesay, which he also held. On the rung below was another Norman, Fulk, who actually farmed almost half the village, letting the Anglo Saxon peasants live there in exchange for their labour. Gunward was never heard of again.

Chapter 2: The Clungunford Knights. By 1165 Clungunford was redivided between three Norman knights. The first was Walter de Hopton, who lived at Hopton Castle, but also held Shelderton, Broadward and later Ferney. The second was Elias de Jay, who lived close to Leintwardine and held Beckjay as an outlying part of his Jay estate and the third was Simon de Halberdyne, who was Lord of the Manor, which may sound grand but in reality he held only a third of the parish. He was the only one of the three who lived in the village and held no land outside the parish. The families of these three knights dominated Clungunford's history during the Middle Ages – the de Halberdynes for two hundred years, the de Jays and de Hoptons for over three hundred years. For the sake of clarity, all the de Hopton land in Cungunford will be called Shelderton, the de Jay land will be called Beckjay and the de Halberdyne land (including Abcott and Rowton) will be called "central Clungunford" in the medieval section of this book (see **Fig 5**).

All these knights had to pay "knight service" to the Lord of Clun, which meant that, notionally at least, they had to ride over to Clun Castle armed and in their chainmail for twenty days a year, or more, and undertake to fight for their lord, whenever they were needed, taking with them men from Clungunford. The de Hopton family actually held so much land in the Clun valley that they had to supply two knights and, when they acquired Coston and part of Mocktree Forest, a footsoldier, too. The Norman rule in the Welsh borders was based on this military obligation and serious fighting was frequent, both by hand to hand combat and with archers using crossbows and longbows (see **Fig 8**). Clun castle was often besieged and occasionally burnt to ashes and there is no doubt that Clungunford also suffered from Welsh raids and cattle rustling. For this reason, the de Halberdynes must have had a defensible fortification, earthworks surmounted by a wooden structure, although nothing of it survives. The most likely site for this fort is under "The Mount" (OS 399 788), where the old drovers' road bends in a loop round the raised site before going down the steep hill into Chapel Road. The motte near the church is an earlier burial mound, not a fort.

The de Hoptons flourished exceedingly, not only in the Clun valley, but also nationally. Almost always called Walter, they were often Sheriffs of Shropshire and one of the many Walters was Baron of the Exchequer in 1275, when he was fined heavily for "Malversion of the office". The kings put them in charge of law enforcement in the Welsh Borders, which seems surprising considering the family's own record. Several of them had to be pardoned for all their own crimes before being made judges, while one of them was behind a cattle rustling episode in 1264 close to Broadward. He kept a dozen oxen, stolen in the raid, to pull heavy carts at Shelderton, which must have been used to move stone from the quarries. He had castle building dreams.

The de Jays and the de Halberdynes led more mundane lives, doing public service in the neighbourhood, especially at the Court at Purslow, on the site of the present Hundred House. The de Halberdynes gave thirty acres of Abcott land to Haughmond Abbey and held the advowson of the church in the thirteenth century and so appointed the Rectors. One particularly pious member of the family had church building dreams.

Chapter 3: Agricultural Boom. The years from 1000 to 1300 were years of increasing prosperity for the village, in which the destruction of the Norman Conquest was only a temporary blip. Records show that sheep farming and the wool trade were the most important activities in the neighbourhood and new farms were carved out of the forest. Sheep runs on the top of Shelderton Rock were close to the country estate of the great wool merchant, Lawrence de Ludlow, who built Stokesay Castle. During the thirteenth century villagers became involved in the cloth trade and there was a fulling mill on the River Clun or on a tributary stream. The sheep were also milked (see *Colour Plate 7*).

After Magna Carta, every "free" man or woman could have a case heard before judge and jury at the king's court and in 1221 a widow from Abcott went to Westminster to accuse Walter de Hopton of the murder of her husband. There was much litigation over land and rights in the forest and it is really through court records that we get the best picture of life in the village. Apparently it was somewhat violent – in 1256 there were three murders in the village within six months.

Markets were established at Ludlow and, at the beginning of the twelfth century, in Clun. Peasants could sell their chickens and eggs, spun wool and spare beasts there and gradually save up enough money to buy their freedom from the "villeinage" which bound them to their lord (see Figs **10 & 11**). From 1200 onwards we begin to find the names of "free" tenants in court records – Roger Bacun and Henry Makelin, for example, and by the end of the century half the peasants in the village were free. However, although feudalism may have been on the way out, there were still a dozen slaves at Shelderton as late as 1300.

The population had probably doubled since the Conquest and most of the forest of Mocktree had been brought into cultivation. There were new settlements with commons and strip fields at Tately and Weo, as well as the de Hoptons' new sheep runs.

Hunting was an essential part of the food chain before the days of abattoirs (see **figs 9 & 21**) so there was great pressure to find new places to hunt and Clun valley records often refer to hawks and hounds in lieu of rent. There was a park at Beckjay for deer and lakes or a series of fish pools at Beckjay, Broadward and Abcott, while the hunting rights over Shelderton were important enough to be mentioned in national records.

Chapter 4: The Disastrous Fourteenth Century. The year 1300 was the high point in Clungunford's prosperity. Had we stood on Clunbury Hill in 1300 we should have seen a very different view from that in 1086. Most of the old forest of Mocktree had gone and there may well have been fewer trees on those hilltops then than there are now. Apart from the new farmland, there was a new road down from Shelderton Hill to the "brade ford" (broad ford) at Broadward, where there was now a mill (see *Colour Plate 9*). There was a road from that ford to Coston, which bypassed the present hamlet of Beckjay (see **Fig 16**). There was a settlement at Broadward.

Soon after 1300 a dramatic climatic cycle of long cold winters, endless rain and gales began, causing a series of disastrous harvests and loss of seed corn. This was followed by epidemics of cattle and sheep disease (probably liver fluke), which caused malnutrition for the villagers and lack of income for the knights. Nevertheless, a fine stone church was built in the first half of the century at great cost to the villagers in labour and to the Lord of the Manor in wages for specialist craftsmen and materials (see *Colour Plates 3– 6*)

The results of all these disasters were the poverty, malnutrition and depopulation of the peasants and near bankruptcy for the de Halberdynes. After two hundred years they handed back their land to the Lord of Clun (the Earl of Arundel) and left the village. The de Jays and the de Hoptons, who had more land and whose tenants had plenty of sheep pasture, survived the crisis albeit with problems. In 1341 Hopton, which included the sheep runs at Shelderton, had a tax bill much reduced specifically on account of a disease of sheep and there are descriptions of many animals lying dead in Shropshire fields.

The man with the most possessions in 1327 was not the Lord of the Manor but the Fuller, who ran a business for finishing off woven cloth. This shows that Clungunford was involved not just in the wool trade but also in the cloth trade, although there is no evidence of the cloth trade continuing after the Black Death.

In the spring of 1349 the Black Death, arrived in the village. This plague was spread by fleas carried by rats but, in the Middle Ages, no one understood what caused the appalling black boils. At least one third of the population died of the plague and much land had to be left uncultivated. Two rectors probably died from it and had to be replaced in quick succession in 1349 and 1351. The plague came again in 1360-2 and 1369, striking at a people already enfeebled by malnutrition and cold, so the population continued to shrink for the rest of the century.

The Earls of Arundel were unable to find anyone to take over the de Halberdynes' former land and consequently it was managed as part of the huge home farm in the Clun valley, where former ploughland had already been turned over to grazing alone. The only animals listed in central Clungunford in 1349 were oxen for ploughing (see *Colour Plate 8*) so it is possible that this land may have been used to grow grain to supply the rest of the estate. After the Black Death the only animal listed was one horse. This village must have been unusually badly hit by the plague.

At the end of the century we begin to hear of individual peasants by name in the records of the Clungunford courts held in the Hundred House at Purslow, as well as in the report on the Bishop's "Visitation". Their sins were sex and alcohol. What else was there to do at a time of no television, or "Flicks in the Sticks"? The descendants of one of these villagers were here over six hundred years later – the Makelins.

Chapter 5: War and Peace in the Fifteenth Century. By 1400 the view from Clunbury Hill had changed dramatically. Not only was the de Halberdynes' fortification crumbling away, but so also were many of the houses. The Lord of the Manor now lived in London so he had no dwelling in the village. The settlements at Broadward and Tately were deserted, as was the fulling mill and many of the fields were no longer cultivated due to a shortage of labour. However, there were still sheep grazing on the hills.

The Earl of Arundel, had been beheaded in 1397, and while the Manor was in the hands of the crown, an ambitious young man in royal employment acquired it. He married the former nanny of the Prince of Wales, soon to be crowned as Henry V. Once his patron was on the throne, William Ryman became powerful and the records of Clungunford Court Rolls show him, extracting every last penny from the peasants, making it impossible for them to renew their leases and insisting on his right to force them to pay to have their own grain ground at his mill (see ***Colour Plates 9&10***). Nevertheless, he managed central Clungunford well and the period between 1411 and 1433 was a brief period of prosperity. Ryman's involvement in the national wool trade benefited his village.

The invasions of the Welsh Prince, Owen Glendower came in the first decade of the century . The local road system was a gift to Welsh plunderers and cattle rustlers. However, the appointment of a Welsh rector may have been the factor which saved the church, for it was not burnt out as so many others were.

Later in the century came those aristocratic skirmishes, given the romantic name of "The Wars of the Roses". Clungunford was in a strategic position close to Ludlow Castle, the Yorkist stronghold, and so was used as a political pawn by scheming politicians. It was also close to important battles at Ludford (1459) and Mortimers Cross (1461) and was certainly not one of the "quietest places under the sun" in the fifteenth century. After 1430, when the Lord of the Manor changed sides, half the ownership ot the village was Lancastrian and the other half was Yorkist, so the peasants must have had to be extremely careful about what they said to whom on political or military subjects. Nevertheless, they probably regarded the chance to fight and earn a soldier's pay as a real advantage. After all, there was a culture of violence anyway during the complete breakdown of law and order in the Welsh Marches. Clungunford records show crimes of violence at all levels of society as well as the presence of highwaymen close by.

Once the original knightly families had moved away, rich absentee landlords became a problem. They were not interested in improvements, nor in selling land to peasants, nor in giving long enough leases for it to be worth a peasant making improvements or building a good house. Ryman sold the Manor to William Burley, Speaker of the House of Commons, in 1433. For a hundred and twenty five years the income from the rents of the Manor was divided between the descendants of his daughters, who probably never came near the place. While in the mid fifteenth century, there was a shortage of male heirs in the de Jay and de Hopton families, so daughters inherited Beckjay and Shelderton. Elizabeth de Jay moved away when she married a Shrewsbury iron founder called Robert Knight, whose family had the forge at Downton two hundred years later. The Knights still owned most of Beckjay into the nineteenth century, thus clocking up over seven hundred years of family connection with that piece of land. Elizabeth, the last of the de Hoptons, married first into the Corbet family, whose descendants kept the Shelderton estate intact until 1656. She led an exciting life and both her second husband, "Butcher Tiptoft", and her third husband, Sir William Stanley, were beheaded She evidently retired to the Clun valley when things got too hot, for she kept Hopton Castle and the hunting over Shelderton as her own until she died in 1499. She may well have been responsible for planting Corbets Wood, some of which was cleared to make space for the first Ferney Hall in the seventeenth century.

Chapter 6: The Middle Class and the Reformation. By 1500 we know from the Purslow Court rolls that brewing was the favourite pastime and that there was at least one pub in Clungunford (see **Fig 24**). We also know the names of many of the peasants – Hinston, Higgs, Shemeth, Gettys and Eyton, for example,– still all Anglo Saxon names, unlike their overlords, who had Norman names like Corbet and Burley. The superiority established by the Normans in 1066 still survived in 1500 but this was about to change.

There is a list of everyone who had moveable possessions of any value in 1524 and this, combined with some Wills, shows us a new middle class developing out of the peasantry. In this group come the Dunnes, the Makelins, the Cornes, the Bores and, last but not least, the Morrises. Some of these people, who had large flocks of fine sheep, were really quite rich. After all, a fleece from one of their sheep was worth twice as much as one from Sussex and the price of wool quadrupled between 1500 and 1550. However, they had a problem, which seems to have curbed their ambition until the end of the century – they could not buy land, because the absentee landlords were not interested in selling. The only man whose family managed to join the new class of the English Country Gentleman was William Morris and this was for a special reason – he rented land in Abcott which had been given to Wigmore and Haughmond Monasteries in the early Middle Ages. After the dissolution of those monasteries, he was able to buy that land and so had the confidence to build himself a fine house on it, which is now called Abcott Manor (see **Colour Plate 11**).

William Morris' Will, which makes delightful reading, shows him grappling with the new protestant ideas for church ritual, or rather for the lack of it, as well as the debts incurred on account of his building works. He was a gentleman with an "overseer" to do the real work, but he still knew every beast on the farm. The question is – how did he make his money?

A few readers may like to dig deeper into the medieval section now, but most will prefer to move on to the second half of this book or to use the Index to look up issues of particular interest to them – names, places or subjects.

1

Clungunford in Domesday Book

Clungunward– Clungunas– Gunnas was that part of "Clonland" which had been the estate of an Anglo Saxon then called Gunward. Since there was a ford over the River Clun at this place, once Gunward was forgotten, the "ward" became "ford". It was Gunward's Clun, as opposed to Edric's Clun. So Domesday Book tells us (see **Colour Plate 1**). Gunward's estate was a considerable landholding before the Norman Conquest. Apart from his Shropshire manors, he held the hill on which Wigmore Castle was later built by the Mortimers.

Had we stood on the top of Clunbury Hill, looking over Gunward's Clun, in 1065 what would we have seen? (see **Colour Plate 2**) The character of the landscape was different in the eleventh century– there was less cultivated land and more "forest". Large, primeval "forests" hung down from the hilltops until they abutted the cultivated areas nearer the valley floor. These "forests" were not like modern ones, always closely planted with trees, but were often uncultivated areas with scattered trees and undergrowth. The cultivated area was far smaller than it is today and would have appeared as a series of cleared areas in the midst of a huge forest.

In the first half of the eleventh century the ancient forest of Mocktree had been traditionally a valuable local facility for landlord and peasant alike. Most of it was available to everyone for hunting but it also contained carefully managed woodland for specific purposes. The forest came down to the east side of Watling Street, then known as "Botstrete", where the old field names tell us there were "bots", that is to say areas of woodland designated for coppicing[1]. The coppiced wood could be used by the peasants for building, for repairs, for fencing or for firewood and the trees were allowed to regenerate for different lengths of time for each intended usage. Domesday Book records that there were also two enclosed areas in the forest, called "hayes", above Watling Street. These were used for hunting red deer or for rearing pigs, which fed on acorns – suggesting that the forest we would have seen from Clunbury Hill would have been largely of oak.

Fig 1: *An Anglo Saxon thegn like Gunward going out to hunt.*

On either side of Clunbury Hill we would have been able to see the cleared hilltops with iron age "castles" at Burrow Fort and Hopton Titterhill, both already ancient, as was the burial mound, known as "The Motte", close to Clungunford church and another below Broadward Hall.

From the description of Gunward's neighbours in Domesday Book, we know that on Clunbury Hill we would have been standing on forested land belonging to Swein, possibly a Danish immigrant, whose estate also included Kempton, Coston and Sibdon. From the hilltop we would have seen in 1065 the land of Edric the Wild, a small part of the huge estates in Shropshire and Herefordshire, which he held as a "free man". To the south west he had Hopton, where there was only a tiny farm in the valley before the Conquest, and most of the land was as yet uncultivated. From Hopton, Edric's land ran west over the hills right to Clun and in the north he held Hopesay, as well. He was a kinsman of the Anglo Saxon king and was a formidable neighbour for Gunward and one who would soon lead him into deep trouble. The last of Gunward's difficult neighbours was Spirtes, the priest, who had already been banished before 1065. Unfortunately, the fall-out from his exile had repercussions for Gunward's peasants. The king had not only banished him but he had confiscated the monastic land which Spirtes had appropriated for himself.

From Clunbury Hill we should have been able to see how the character of the Manor of Clungunford was that of a series of very small settlements spaced out along the valley floor usually just above the flood plain, with Shelderton on rising ground up by the forest. It was then, as now, a widely spaced village, stretching between three and four miles at its furthest extremities. Each small settlement had its own strip field system. In this way people did not have to walk the four miles from one end of the parish to the other in order to start work. The strip field system is discussed on pages 27 and 28.

Clungunford's early history depends to a large extent on its proximity, not only to the ford through the River Clun, but also to ancient roads and particularly to its position close to the crossing (at The Crossways) of the prehistoric drovers' road with the Roman road, which we now call Watling Street. Its course is followed by modern Watling Street, except at Shelderton,, where the ancient road passed to the west of Shelderton House, before going on to Leintwardine. In Anglo Saxon times this road was called "Botstrete" and medieval documents refer to it either as "Botstret" or as "The King's Highway". It is possible that in Anglo Saxon times this road still had much of the hard Roman stone surface left, making it superior to any road in the neighbourhood until the advent of tarmac.

From Clunbury Hill we would also have seen the ancient drovers' road as it came down from Brand Hill and continued on down School Lane. It passed through the site of the bungalows and the Mount and on down Chapel Road. The road then went straight ahead behind Clungunford farm, past Glebe Cottage, leaving the church to its left and so down to the ford. On the other side of the river it continued past the present Abcott Manor and over into Wales via the Twitchen. It was not, of course, modern tarmac road, but rather a rutted track or "green lane".

The ford would have been visible, with the old drovers' road passing through it. You can still just see the remains of its stone foundations on the east side of the river and the remains of the inclined stone approach on the west side. Fred Bason found a roughly paved area of the track continuing on the west side when digging new land drains in the 1980s and remembers that there was still a hard base to the riverbed there in his

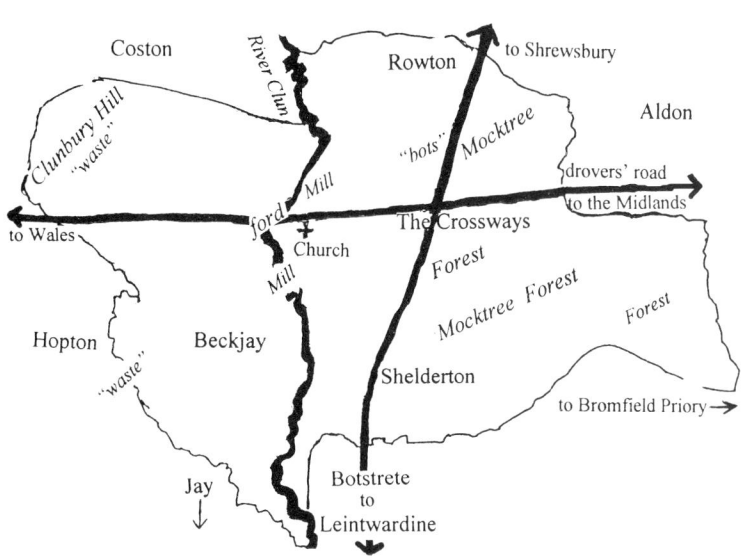

Fig 2. *Sketch Map of Anglo Saxon and early medieval Clungunford.*

childhood. There were obviously paths as well as the two roads. Clungunford Bridge, situated further south, was not built for nearly six hundred years.

We do not know exactly where the houses were in 1065, but it is likely that many were built along the drovers' road, close to the ford, as well as a few at each of the outlying settlements close to Botstret. No building, which stood in the village in 1065, survives today. There were no stone buildings – only houses of wood and daub (mud, sometimes mixed with hair and animal dung), with thatched roofs, standing, in some cases, on raised platforms. The life expectancy of these houses was short as was that of their inmates. There was probably a wooden church with a thatched roof on the site of the nave of the present church. The nearest stone buildings were the churches at Aldon and Leintwardine, which are both mentioned in Domesday Book.

The small settlements of Anglo Saxon Clungunford, which were visible in 1065, survive today. There was central Clungunford (close to the church and the ford over the river), Beckjay (Bekke's Jay)[2] and the "tons" of Rowton and Shelderton, which had grown up as settlements on the old Roman road, Botstret. "Ton "was, in Anglo Saxon times, the word for a small settlement, much more like a hamlet than a town and several such small settlements could be grouped under one "Lord of the Manor". The word was used more often in Shropshire than anywhere else, either in conjunction with a thegn's name , as in Bedstone (Bedgeat's "ton"),or attached to a physical description of the area as in Shelderton (the "ton" by the shelf, that is to say, the cliff under Shelderton Rock), and Rowton (the "ton" originally settled on rough ground). Hopton (the "ton" in the valley) is technically not in the parish of Clungunford, but its history is bound up inextricably with that of Clungunford because it was in the same ownership as part of Clungunford throughout the Middle Ages.

Broadward, known in the Middle Ages as the "brade ford" (the broad ford), was not mentioned until the thirteenth century, nor was Abcott (the cotte or cottage of the "ac", the oak) – these small settlements may not have been inhabited by 1065. The "manor" of Ferney, which forms part of Clungunford's later history, was not cleared of forest for cultivation in the eleventh century and nor were Weo or Tatley. The extent of the old "tons" is sometimes suggested by fields called "Townsend" on the Tithe Map of 1848. For example, "Townsend Field" on the right of the Twitchen road just after the turning off to Abcott Manor.

In 1065 you would have seen two mills on the river grinding grain from the strip fields, one close to Beckjay, where the remains of a later building exist today and another further towards Broome. On the Tithe Map of 1848 there was a field on the Broome road called "Mill Lane Head", which suggests that the mounds and dykes, still visible below it in the field by the river, are the remains of the second mill described in Domesday Book. The double line of very ancient hedge (the continuation of Church Row) was clearly the other end of the same lane. This is, of course, unlikely to have been the exact spot of the Anglo Saxon mill, since it is clear that the river has changed course on its' flood plain several times in the last thousand years. We do not know if these mills were undershot or overshot (see ***Colour plate 9 and* Fig 21**).

The cultivated areas in the view included fields, cultivated in strips a furlong in length, each strip being cultivated by a different person, and pasture of specialised kinds. At a time when all the power for the farming community was provided by animals, particularly oxen, year-round good grazing was of paramount importance. There are still some remains of a weir near the boundary with Coston, which may have been used as early as the eleventh century for flooding the water meadows in early summer to keep the pasture green. There were the commons at Little Common and a big one near Cross Horn, where all the tenants of the manor had the right to graze their animals. The land on the top of Clunbury Hill itself, which became common land later in the Middle Ages, was still "forest" in 1065.

We know from Domesday Book that Clungunford was a particularly good grain producing village in Anglo Saxon times – only seven other villages in the whole county had two mills. Therefore a high proportion of the village land must have been under the plough or reserved for all year round grazing for the oxen which pulled the ploughs. In 1005 Aelfric of Canterbury wrote a description of an Anglo Saxon ploughman's day and the surprising thing about it is how little, not how much, the farm labourer's work changed in Canterbury and Clungunford in the nine hundred years between 1000 AD and 1900AD. The ploughman/slave is asked "How do you do your work? He replies " Oh, Sir, I work very hard. I go out at dawn driving the oxen to the field, and I yoke them to the plough; however hard the weather I dare not stay at home for fear of my master; but, having yoked the oxen and made the ploughshare and coulter fast to the plough, every day I have to plough a whole acre or more.....I have a boy who drives the oxen with a goad and he is even now hoarse with shouting and the cold.......I have to fill the oxens' cribs with hay and give them water, and carry the dung outside".

Fig 3: *Anglo Saxon farming methods, which the Normans found too inefficient.*

Gunward's neighbours, whose land we have just surveyed from the top of Clunbury hill, were disruptive types, whose actions caused Clungunford grief and resulted in the Norman Conquest bringing particularly hard times for the village. Naturally, Edric the Wild, who held his vast estates "as a free man", did not want to cooperate when the Normans arrived because they allowed no one to have land privately owned in that way. Of course he led a rebellion. It is clear from the way in which Clungunford was devastated by the Normans, that Gunward and his peasants, took part in that rebellion. However, lightly armed men from the Clun valley were no match for mounted Norman knights in chain mail. Although the rebels laid siege to Shrewsbury in 1067, the rebellion was a disaster and everyone who had cooperated was given an exemplary sentence. Gunward was never heard of again, presumably killed in action, and Clungunford was "laid waste", that is to say, burnt out so that it was reduced to one eighth of its previous value.

Fig 4: *Norman knights arriving in an Anglo Saxon village to requisition food.*

There cannot have been much of the village left and, although Bromfield priory may have been able to offer sanctuary to some, the impoverished canons were unable to feed a flood of refugees, because most of their land had been confiscated by the crown, on account of the behaviour of Spirtes the priest[3]. He was one of the ten canons at the Anglo Saxon Priory at Bromfield, about whom the king had sent a writ to Gunward and other local thegns in 1060. The purpose of this writ was to explain that the king had given them special privileges as well as grants of land. In the normal course of events this priory would have had a duty of care to give both sanctuary and succour to Gunward's peasants after their crops and homes had been destroyed by the Normans.

The third troublesome neighbour was Wales. The frontier was closer then, at Offa's Dyke, and the Welsh would not have sat back idly watching the chaos caused by the Normans' arrival in Shropshire. No doubt they also had a part in the huge reduction in the value of the Clun valley villages after 1066 and, if nothing else, drove off some of the livestock. Welsh raids had already been a hazard, even before the Conquest. Edward the Confessor had imported a Norman baron, Richard Fitz Scrob, an expert on stone castle building, to advise him on how to keep out the Welsh. It was this Richard who had built Richard's Castle before 1066. Until 1536, when Wales became officially part of England, we can never forget the part Welsh raids played in destabilising life in the village.

The rest of this chapter will concentrate on the detailed description of Clungunford in Domesday Book. In 1085 the Anglo Saxon Chronicle said that "The King had much thought and very deep discussion with his Council about his country – how it was occupied and with what sort of people. Then he sent his men over all England into every shire…. So very narrowly did he have it investigated, that there was no single hide or virgate of land, which was there left out, and not put down in his record; and all these records were brought to him afterwards". From these records Domesday Book was compiled. The two entries in the book for Clungunford are illustrated in *Colour Plate 1* and a translation appears below. These entries describe Clungunford at three stages: as it was immediately before the Norman Conquest, just after the Conquest and in 1085.

THE TWO CLUNGUNFORD ENTRIES IN DOMESDAY BOOK

Holding of Picot under Earl Roger
In Leintwardine Hundred

Picot holds Clun. Gunward held it . 6 hides which pay tax. Land for 15 ploughs.
  In demesne 3; 8 slaves;
8 villeins and 4 bordars with 4 ploughs.
A mill at 54d.
Fulk holds 1 1/2 hides of this land from Picot; he has 2 ploughs (carrucci)in demesne ;
  4 bovars; 3 villeins and 3 bordars with 3 ploughs.
A mill at 32d.
Value of the whole TRE[4] £12; later 30s; now £4 in total.

Holding of Rainald the Sheriff under Earl Roger
In Leintwardine Hundred

Rainald holds Clun. Fulk holds from him. In Leintwardine Hundred.
Gunward held it TRE. 2 hides, which pay tax.
5 villeins and one bordar with 2 ploughs; a further 6 ploughs would be possible there.
  3 hayes.
Value of the whole12s.

The page from Domesday Book, looks incomprehensible. It is, in fact, in a sort of code and in these two tiny paragraphs there is a mass of condensed information on the village, which we can tease out in the next few pages by a little code breaking – only for those readers who fancy ancient documents! Others should move on to the next chapter.

Neither in Anglo Saxon times, nor in Norman times, did people own their land in the modern sense, although, before the Normans came, certain privileged individuals, usually trusted relations of the king, were allowed to hold their land with no obligation other than loyalty to the crown. In Norman times land belonged to the king by inheritance or by conquest. He then apportioned out that land among his friends and relations in such a way as to maintain his power and control over it. In return for what one might call the use of land, each of his "tenants in chief" had to give him military service and ensure that he received taxes ("geld") from the produce of that land. They, in turn, expected certain services from the knights below them on the ladder of feudal society and those knights expected services from the peasants, usually of an agricultural nature but sometimes also of a military nature. In this way every one (except the King) had duties to someone else one stage above them in the social scale, as is implicit in the Domesday book entries for our village. Thus the "feudal system" of government and of land management was established in the Clun valley. No wonder Edric the Wild, the former "free man", did not fancy the new arrangements.

When making the survey, which resulted in Domesday Book, William decided to use the old Anglo Saxon unit of local administration, the "Hundred", as the basis for inquiry. Every hundred had to return certain types of information for three different dates, first from the time of King Edward the Confessor (the TRE of our entries), second soon after the actual conquest of that particular hundred and, third, at the time of the Domesday inquiry in 1085-6. Clungunford was, in 1085, still administered from the Leintwardine Hundred so it comes under that heading in the book. In the twelfth century, it was re-allocated and divided between Purlow and Munslow Hundreds.

Earl Roger, from Montgomery in Normandy, that shadowy figure at the top of both our Domesday entries, was given a huge grant of conquered land to enable him to guard Shropshire not only against the Welsh, but also from anyone who objected to Norman rule. So difficult was his task thought to be, that he was created a "palatinate earl" with powers to act independently of the king, should circumstances require swift action. He was, in effect, a king in Shropshire as long, that is, as he supported the Norman king of England. In his turn, Earl Roger gave land to his friends and relations from Normandy in return for providing fighting men, both mounted knights and foot soldiers. One such friend was Picot, from the village of Say in Roger de Montgomery's estate in Normandy. He is the Picot de Say, lord of the greater part of Clungunford, who appears in the first of our entries, and who gave his name to Hopesay and Stokesay, which were also part of the estate he held under Earl Roger. Small men in Normandy became great men in the Clun valley.

Domesday Book tells us that Picot kept three quarters of the farmland of his manor of Clungunford "in demesne", that is to say for his own use. The other quarter he let to Fulk, another Norman, who also held all of Rainald's land in the parish. Fulk, therefore, in his turn, had depending on him in Clungunford a total of four oxmen, eight villeins and four smallholders. Picot's total land in the village was measured by the Domesday survey at 6 "hides" and a "hide" is thought to have been about 120 acres, so his land in this village was roughly the same size as Geoffrey Rollason's farm in 1999, although Picot's acres were in a slightly different area. Our parish boundaries are not exactly the same as the Anglo Saxon "manors" on which the survey was based, but later patterns of landholding make it clear that Picot's part of the village included the land between the road we now call Watling Street and the river as well as Abcott on the other bank.

However the story is not as simple as that. There was another Norman baron involved – Rainald the Sheriff, who appears as the second big landholder in the Clungunford entry. Major landholders in Clungunford continued to be Sheriffs at intervals for the next nine hundred years (see **Colour Plate 27**). The king needed not only continuing military support in order to hold onto the conquest he had achieved at the Battle of Hastings, he needed trusted administrative officials – to gather in the geld (tax), and keep order. These men had to be given land and manors so that they could move around the territory for which they were responsible, as well as to ensure their loyalty. Such a man was Rainald, who was Sheriff of Shropshire in 1086. He was given a small part of the manor of Clungunford as well as other manors dotted all over the county. Later patterns of landholding suggest that his part of the "vill" was Shelderton, (close up under the old forest of Mocktree), which amounted to about 240 acres, on which he had the same sub tenant as Picot, namely Fulk. In 1086 this section of the village looked the least valuable, but that was to change. Thus in 1086 the total area of the parish under cultivation was under a thousand acres. This changed gradually over the next two hundred years as agriculture expanded and the population grew.

It is clear from Clungunford's two entries in Domesday Book that there had been the most almighty shake-up of the upper classes soon after 1066; Gunward's estate in this village alone had been divided between two new comers. The old Anglo Saxon system of landholding in the area has been revolutionised both in general principle and in detail.

So much for the upper classes in the eleventh century, how about the rest of the people listed in Clungunford? It has been fashionable among historians to say that the Norman Conquest only really changed the lives of the upper class Anglo Saxons, but any consideration of what it must have been like to be a peasant in Clungunford brings one face to face with starvation and terror. Even if they themselves had survived the "harrowing" when the area was laid waste, if their land was burnt, what did they do for seed corn and grazing?

Who were the farmers in the eleventh century and how did they work the land? There were three dozen peasants actually living in Clungunford then, together with their families. Domesday Book tells us that Picot had eight "Servii", that is to say slaves or serfs, on his estate at Clungunford. Fulco also had slaves. His four "bovarii", or oxmen, were almost certainly captured Welshmen, who were generally used as slaves to look after the plough teams. This brings the total number of slaves up to twelve, or one third of the working population of the village. Gunward, would certainly have had slaves, but the nature of their servitude was slightly different. Slaves in Anglo Saxon times were the property of their overlord and as such could be moved about to another part of the country like any other moveable property. If Gunward wished to move men from Clungunford to Wigmore it was his right to do so. Both Anglo Saxon and Norman alike had to provide food and clothing for their slaves and to house them, albeit often with the animals.

However, Norman serfs were tied to their land – their overlord could not move them, nor could they move themselves – the only ways in which the eight serfs in Picot's part of Clungunford could have become free men were to get their lord's permission, or take Holy Orders (also with his permission), or run away to Shrewsbury and hide for "a ycar and a day", after which they were regarded as free men. Shropshire had an extremely high proportion of slaves in the population, and Clungunford had an even higher proportion than the Shropshire norm, probably because any captives from Welsh raids could be kept as slaves to look after plough teams. At this early date, Offa's Dyke was the frontier, and anyone caught on this side of the Dyke, who was unable to speak English, counted as Welsh and could be killed, that is, if you did not want him as a slave. There is a rumour that in Clun at this date, anyone who could only speak Welsh and was caught on the wrong side of Offa's Dyke could be flayed and have his skin nailed to Clun church door.

In the "Manor" of Clungunford as a whole (that is to say in both of the entries) there were sixteen "Villeins" who were not free men, but not slaves either; they were allowed a certain amount of the land of the manor for their own use in exchange for working Fulk or Picot's land for three days a week and "boon work", a polite term for what became compulsory extra work at harvest and sowing time. They could be self sufficient from their own land. Later in the Middle Ages these were often called "customary Tenants". The eight "Bordars", or smallholders, had much the same terms of service as the "Villeins", but the land they had to use for themselves was in the newly cultivated areas on the fringes of he village, unlikely to have been as fertile. The chain of feudal dependency was thus established; the slaves and villeins were dependent on Fulco, Fulco was dependent on Picot (or Rainald), Picot was dependent on Earl Roger and Earl Roger was dependent on the king. In this way, William the Conqueror controlled Clungunford. The "free men" of Anglo Saxon England, like Edric the Wild, had gone.

William's long term aim was to raise the value of the country he had conquered, to make good the devastation he had caused, and improve the farming practices of the subject people. The Domesday assessors were always on the look out for possible improvements. They commented that on Picot's land at Clungunford, although there were already eleven plough teams working, there could be another three. Rainald, or rather his subtenant Fulk, was doing even worse. He only used two ploughs when he had land enough for eight. The implications of this comment in Domesday Book are clear; Rainald's land ran along the edge of the ancient "forest" of Mocktree. He could expect to gain benefits from rights of grazing, pig keeping and wood cutting which were expressed as value in terms of plough teams, although the ploughs were not being used yet. He may also have already been expected to clear land in the forest for agriculture and so increase his acreage as his successors on those acres certainly did.

The ploughs mentioned as being in Clungunford were the"carruccii", that is to say the wheeled ploughs pulled by a team of eight oxen beloved of the Normans – four animals for the morning shift and another four for the afternoon. This type of heavy wheeled plough was unpopular in villages like Clungunford with heavy, glutinous soil, because it was such hard work for the man walking behind, (who was not replaced at mid-day). There are plenty of pictures of later peasants, employing a plough without wheels (See *colour plate 8*) and it is likely that the Normans failed to establish its' systematic use in the Clun valley, however much they advocated it when they first arrived.

Having spent nearly twenty years subduing England, William was extremely short of money and was keen that villages like Clungunford should pay as much tax as possible.

In Norman eyes, this meant using wheeled ploughs to bring as much land as possible under cultivation, the new tax being based on the amount of land that might be ploughed, rather than on the amount which actually was ploughed, so increasing the number of units to be taxed. This tax assessment replaced the more relaxed Anglo Saxon system based on the size of an area of land, a "hide". So from 1086 onwards Clungunford was taxed on the greatest number of ploughs it could possibly have working, not on the number of ploughs it actually had in use, nor on the old "hides". All this is clear from the Domesday entries.

Oderic Vitalis, the English cleric, who was living near Shrewsbury in 1085-6, and whose Anglo Saxon mother would have put him in the picture, had much to say about this change in the type of unit which had paid tax to King Edward the Confessor, which thereby increased the number of taxable units ("shortening" he called it). Later, looking back from Normandy to his Shropshire youth, he complained that "By this shortening of land long since acquired and held, and by the piling up of unaccustomed taxation, he (William the Conqueror) shamefully oppressed the common people of the kingdom, impoverished them by taking away their goods, and reduced them to extreme poverty from a state of great plenty." He was describing exactly what Domesday Book shows had happened in Clungunford.

In addition, we know that, whereas since 1021 the king's taxation had normally been assessed at two shillings per "hide", in 1084 William had demanded a tax at the equivalent of six shillings per hide. So Clungunford would have had to pay nearly two and a half pounds in tax on its' total of eight hides (about 960 acres) in 1084, whereas before the Conquest it had to pay one third of that sum. No wonder Oderic wrote of the king's impoverishment of the people.

2

The Clungunford Knights

Three knightly families dominated Clungunford during the early Middle Ages. One of these families, the de Halberdynes, left just before the Black Death. Descendants of the other two, the de Jays and de Hoptons, although they had left the village itself several hundred years ago, were still living in South Shropshire at the second Millenium. As their descent is through heiresses, they have different surnames nowadays. However, reading about their medieval forebears is tough going – many people, having looked at **Fig 5**, might prefer to move on to Chapter 3 immediately!

Standing on Clunbury Hill the year after the Battle of Hastings, in 1067, we would have seen a devastated landscape. The hill itself was hardly touched but Edric the Wild's land at Hopton was still smoking – laid completely "waste". Clun and Hopesay were little better. The prosperous village of Clungunford was in ruins, with many of the houses burnt and much of the population dead or starving and so unable to till the scorched fields or care for such animals as the Welsh had not removed. The manor had been valued, before the Conquest, at over twelve pounds but in 1067 it had been reduced to one and a half pounds.

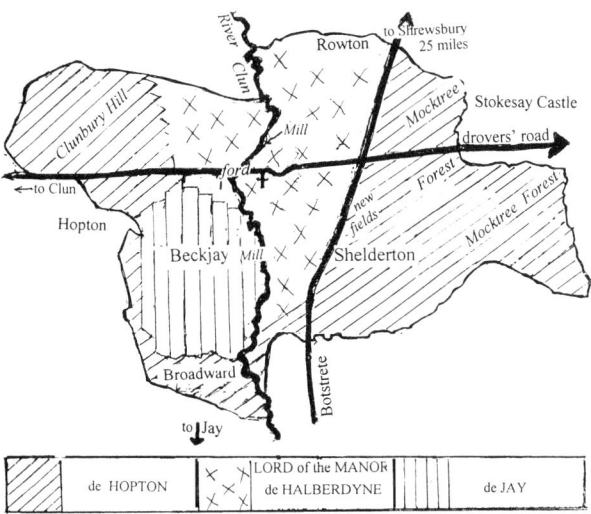

Fig 5. *Sketch map showing landownership during the Middle Ages. The land of the Lord of the Manor will be called "central Clungunford" throughout this book. In the medieval chapters, all the land of the de Hoptons in the Parish of Clungunford, including Shelderton, Broadward and Ferney, will be called "Shelderton", unless there is a need to be more specific[1]. The feudal overlords of these knights will be called "the Arundels".*

If we had looked again nearly a hundred years later, in 1165, the year in which this description of the Clungunford knights begins, we would have found the view broadly similar to that in Anglo Saxon times. There would have been slightly less forest and more fields than in 1065, as well as more houses for the growing population, but the changes would not have been dramatic. The devastation and burning of vegetation that occurred as the Normans conquered the land in the late 1060s had regenerated and the houses had been rebuilt and the population increased. The landscape changed slowly over a period of two hundred years, whereas the pattern of landholders changed quickly, and sometimes violently, as we have seen. The rest of this chapter is concerned only with the leading families in the district.

It is easier to appreciate the dramatic changes in the pattern of landholding in the parish of Clungunford by looking at a sketch map, than by looking at the view from Clunbury Hill. In Anglo Saxon times the pattern looked much like an interlocking jigsaw puzzle – each landlord being represented by one, or several, pieces. Immediately after the Norman Conquest a completely new jigsaw was created, bearing little resemblance to the earlier one. This second jigsaw was described in Domesday Book. A third jigsaw was created in the twelfth century and this jigsaw survived in the main until the seventeenth century and is illustrated by the sketch map.

The state of affairs at the time of the third jigsaw is described in the Liber Niger of 1165, which was compiled to show the king how landholding and military obligations had changed in the eighty years since Domesday Book. This shows us Clungunford as a fully fledged "feudal" village. Earl Roger's descendants had been replaced as "tenants–in–chief" by the FitzAlan family. This had come about because Earl Roger's son had rebelled against King Henry 1, in 1102. The rebellion was unsuccessful and therefore the vast estates of the Montgomery family were taken away and re-divided between the Mortimers in Herefordshire and the Fitz Alans in the Clun valley. The FitzAlans, first Lords of Clun, then Earls of Arundel from 1244 and finally through their heiress, Dukes of Norfolk, remained overlords of Clungunford until the end of the Middle Ages and so played a major role in Clungunford affairs.

Even after they had moved their main residence to Sussex in the fifteenth century and acquired a Dukedom, they kept the title of Lord Clun and, when the people of Clun were planning a fete in the 1930s, they wrote a letter addressed, not to the Duke of Norfolk, but to "Lord Clun, Arundel Castle", asking him if he would come to open their fete. Back came the reply, signed "Clun".

By 1165, in the next rung down the feudal ladder, Picot's family and that of Rainald the Sheriff, who had taken over from Gunward straight after the conquest, had been replaced in Clungunford by the three Norman knights – Simon de Halberdyne, who was Lord of the Manor, Elias de Jay, who held Beckjay and Walter de Hopton, who lived at Hopton and held Shelderton as part of his estate. Whereas the land in Clungunford held by the Lord of the Manor was all that he owned, the land in Clungunford of the last two knights constituted only a small fraction of their estate. All these men held their land in exchange for "knight service", that is to say for the promise of military service when their overlord needed them. They were expected to ride to Clun Castle armed and in their chainmail for twenty days a year (or forty days in the case of Walter de Hopton), or for one day every three weeks. They were also expected to take with them men from their estate to fight in any combat in which their overlord, or his overlord, the king, chose to engage. Usually these were battles with the Welsh, which would have seemed a good cause, but sometimes the king required their presence in Scotland or France. These grants of land in exchange for military service were called "fiefs". Nine knights had to do "knight service" at Clun Castle and three of these had land in Clungunford. Fighting was part of normal life throughout the twelfth and thirteenth centuries. The "knight service", by which these three families had to provide mounted officers for the army, was crucially important for Norman survival in England.

The first of our knights is Simon de Halburdino (variously spelt but called de Halberdyne throughout this history), who was the Lord of the Manor of Clungunford. Although the title of "Lord of the Manor" notionally went with the area of farmland in the centre of the modern village and survived right down to the time of the Rocke family, in fact this description distorts the picture because Simon de Halberdyne and his successors on that farmland were the least important of the knights who had land in the parish. In 1165 Simon owed the service of one mounted knight to the Lord of Clun Castle for twenty days a year. "The Manor" did not mean the kind of house we now think of as a manor house, but was a small administrative area of farmland involving a military obligation.

It seems that in 1165 Simon had recently come over, not from Normandy but, as was frequent in later Norman settlements, from Flanders. There is still a district on the outskirts of Lille called Haubourdin, which was probably his home village. His was described as a "new enfoeffment" because he had recently been granted the land, so he was still using the name of his French village. It has been suggested that his name came from a "halberd", a combined spear and battleaxe. This is possible, but it is more probable that he was "of" a place in the way that his neighbours were. In 1165 he had recently been granted his fief, when Picot de Say's granddaughter and heir in Clungunford, Isabelle, married the Lord of Clun, so moving up a rung on the feudal ladder and leaving a space below for Simon from Flanders.

He was, therefore, a parvenu by comparison with his neighbour Walter de Hopton, who owed the service of two knights to Clun Castle by an "old enfeoffment" and already considered his family to be "of Hopton". Some of the land which the de Hoptons held for several centuries was in what we would now call Clungunford, namely Shelderton, Broadward and Ferney. In fact, throughout the Middle Ages, the de Hopton family and their successors, the Corbets, actually held more land in the Parish of Clungunford than the Lords of the Manor, the de Halberdynes., and their successors, the Barkeleys.

The de Hoptons' family record, the "ffroma Canonica", quotes a grant supposedly from William the Conqueror, but surely from William Rufus, as follows:-

To the heyrs male of the Hopton Family lawfully begotten
To me and to mine, to thee and to thine,
While the water runs and the sun doth shine,
For lack of Heyrs to the king again,
I, William the King, the third of my reign
Give to the Norman Hunter.
To me that are both Line and deare

The Hoppe and Hoptune
And all the bounds up and downe............

In 1065 Hopton Castle had been described as being mainly "waste" with only about two hundred and forty acres under cultivation, unlike Clungunford, which had nearly a thousand acres of arable and pasture. By 1165, most of Rainald's part of Clungunford, that is to say Shelderton, and Broadward, had been re-allocated to the "Norman Hunter", described in this verse, together with the "waste" and other land at Hopton Castle. Whether or not you are convinced by the authenticity of this charter as an eleventh century document rather than a Tudor one, it is clear that Fulk's family had been replaced by the de Hoptons well before 1165, when theirs was described as an "an old enfeoffment". The third year of William II's reign was 1090, so it is possible that that was the date at which the de Hoptons arrived in the Clun valley. Their land was a large feudal holding, which is why they were responsible for providing two knights to Clun Castle.

The third of our knights, Elias de Jay, held Beckjay as an outlying part of his estate. To use the feudal jargon, he was also "enfeoffed" by an "old enfeoffment" of the Manor of Bedstone for the service of one knight to Clun in 1165. This manor had been completely "waste" when the Normans arrived, and the de Jay family usually lived at Jay, close to Leintwardine, until the fifteenth century, while gradually developing their land at Bedstone.

These three families were to run Clungunford throughout the early Middle Ages. The de Halberdynes for nearly two hundred years and the de Jays and the de Hoptons for three hundred, only ceasing to be big names in the neighbourhood when they failed to produce sons and their daughters married out of the village in the mid fifteenth century. Even after that, the heirs of these daughters remained absentee landlords of large parts of the village several hundred years more. The oldest son of the de Halberdynes was usually called Simon and later on Roger, that of the de Hoptons, Walter, and that of the de Jays, Elias to start with and then usually, but not always, John. This can lead to confusion between the generations, to say the least.

This picture is complicated by the fact that the Lord of the Manor, Simon de Halberdyne and his descendants, held only one third of the land in Clungunford parish, that is to say of the land being discussed in this history. As is clear from the sketch map, most of the remaining two thirds were held by the Lord of the neighbouring Manor of Hopton Castle, while the Lord of Jay (adjacent to Leintwardine) held Beckjay as an outlying patch of his estate (**Fig 5**). The Lord of Hopton Castle held Broadward and Shelderton, and from the thirteenth century onwards, the land uphill from Watling Street as well as the land over the top, later known as Ferney.

This confusing situation is complicated even further by the fact that, by the thirteenth century, the Lord of the Manor had obtained the prestigious advowson of the church. This meant that, although he only farmed a small area in the centre of the village, he appointed the Rector. The tithe income may often have been nearly as big as the income from the small estate which went with the Manor. The apportionment of tithes at this early date is not certain, but by the fourteenth century, the holder of the advowson had to hand over to the bishop a third of the tithes, but this still left him with considerable power over the third which was intended for the poor of the parish as well as the final third due to the Rector, whose appointment he controlled. We see the Lords of the Manor holding onto the church advowson for over eight hundred years and frequently appointing members of their own family as Rectors until the late nineteenth century. The last Rocke Rector died in 1945.

There was another major survey of the knightly classes in the 1240s, the Testa de Neville, and we find the same three families still dominating Clungunford. John de Jay holds a knight's fee in Jay, Bedstone and Beckjay. So he is liable for knight service at Clun Castle for twenty days a year, whereas Walter de Hopton, for his land at Hopton, Broadward, Coston and Shelderton owes not only two knights for twenty days, but one footsoldier all year round. He has clearly made good, whereas poor old Simon de Halberdyne has been reduced to half a knight! That is not quite as bad as it sounds because it really meant knight service for ten days a year instead of twenty days. By 1279 the Hundred Court records show that the Simon de Halberdyne of that time had dropped out of the knightly class altogether, although he remained Lord of the Manor of Clungunford.

Leading members of our knightly families had positions of importance at the Assize Court: for example in 1221 Simon de Halberdyne was an "elizor", in charge of choosing the jury. The main aim of Magna Carta was really to stop the king acting outside the law and one of the benefits the barons had insisted on before sealing the Charter in 1215 was the right to have their claims concerning dispossession of their land heard immediately. By 1233 Simon de Halberdyne had risen to the job of judge for the county, specializing in cases where people were claiming that they had recently been wrongfully dispossessed of their land. Simon's grandson was one of the county Coroners at the end of the thirteenth century when, among many other duties, the job of such men was to check that the court fines were actually paid to the Crown and not pocketed by the barons. The de Halberdynes' jobs were all of a local, Shropshire nature.

The de Jays held similar posts in the county. For example, Walter de Jay was Chief Bailiff at Purslow Hundred Court in 1272, with the duty of summoning people to court. In 1279 the Purslow Hundred Rolls record the de Jays as having maintained their position at Jay and Beckjay. They took advantage of the growth of sheep farming and added Bedstone Hill (which had been described as "waste" in 1086) to their holding. Unlike Simon de Halberdyne they still owed the service of one knight to Clun castle in 1279[2].

Although the de Jays became far more prosperous than the de Halberdynes, only on one occasion do we hear of them being involved outside the county at a national level. That is when a junior member of the family, Brian de Jay, joined the Knights Templar, which was a celibate Order, founded to protect the Christian buildings in Jerusalem. The Arundel family, the overlords of Clungunford in the years of the great crusades, certainly approved of the Order and gave much land in Cardington and Corvedale to the Templars, who also had plots in Ludlow. There is even a carving of a lamb and flag in Clungunford church, which may well be a Templar emblem, but since nobody knows where it came from and there no record of a Templar knight in the village, it cannot be taken as proof of a Templar connection actually in Clungunford itself.

You could hardly expect the heads of our knightly families to join this celibate order but junior members of their families evidently did. In 1295, at a time when the head of the family was Walter de Jay and the Hundred Court records tell us that his son Thomas was to inherit the manor, Brian de Jay became Master of the English Templars and in the Close Rolls there is a writ from Edward I to the Constable of Dover Castle directing him to aid Brian de Jay's progress in a journey to Cyprus in order to talk to the Grand Master. This same Brian certainly got around, because he was killed fighting for the English king against the Scots at the Battle of Falkirk, two years later. He may well have taken foot soldiers from his family's land at Beckjay to fight with him, but this is mere conjecture – we have no record of peasants going to war, although they obviously did so.

Unfortunately for Brian's memory, the next king, Edward II was weaker and less belligerent. He was more interested in the material possessions of the Templars than in the glory of battle, so he joined in the movement to supress the Order on a series of trumped-up charges, which were pursued with great cruelty. Stephen de Stapelbrugge, a former member of the order was captured and confessed under torture that he had been initiated by Brian de Jay, then Master of the Templars in England. He recounted that 'a cross was brought in, and then, in the presence of two brothers with drawn swords, the receptor (Brian de Jay) told him, "It is necessary for you to deny that Jesus Christ is God and man, and to deny Mary his mother", and to spit on the cross'. The reception had taken place at dawn and he believed that such receptions were general in the Order. He also admitted that he had been told not to believe in the sacrament at the altar, that the Grand Master (Brian de Jay) gave a general absolution from sins, and that homosexuality was allowed. In the reign of Edward II the Templars were abolished and their land in England was given to The Knights of St John (the Hospitallers) or to private individuals. No one knows where the lamb and flag carving, now in Clungunford church, originated but it may well have been a Templar emblem. There were several Templar foundations in Shropshire and the Arundels favoured the Order, but there is, as yet, no evidence for any such foundation in Clungunford itself.

Fig 6 . *Effigy of a thirteenth century knight in the Temple church, looking much as the Clungunford knights would have done.*

Meanwhile, the main branch of Brian de Jay's family were leading more mundane lives, building up the family fortunes at Bedstone and Beckjay, so that in 1272 the de Jays, unlike the de Halberdynes, were included in the list of the Knights of Edward I. Only those with property worth more than twenty pounds were included.

The de Hoptons were operating on a different plane altogether by the thirteenth century. Once they had gathered part of the small Manor of Coston into their estate, their land surrounded the apparently rich farmland of the de Halberdyne's in a pincer action, which allowed the de Halberdynes no room for expansion.

The de Hoptons understood the growing importance of sheep farming and they were able to develop this source of riches by adding more land above Shelderton, at Hopton Titterhill and on the east side of Clunbury Hill to their estate. Records from the Purslow and Munslow Hundred Courts and from the Inquisitions after the deaths of various family members show that they had procured the right to "assart" land into the forest of Mocktree – that is to say to bring it into cultivation for the first time. In 1255, in the Hundred Court Rolls, Walter de Hopton is recorded as paying two shillings a year for a licence to develop the forest and, whereas in 1240 he held Hopton, Broadwood and Shelderton, by 1279 he had added to these places, not only Coston, but also Tately and Weo. The last two places were cleared of forest between 1240 and 1272.

This expansion is recognized in their increased feudal obligations– from the provision of two knights to Clun castle in 1165 to the provision of two knights and one permanent footsoldier in 1240. Clearly by that date they were employing substitutes to do their knightly duties or, more probably, paying "scutage" instead. In fact, a "fief", which in the early twelfth century, had meant a grant of land in exchange for personal military service, had by the thirteenth century become an annual money payment – £10 per year in the Clun Valley at this date. This was somewhat closer to our idea of rent, except that an element of military obligation was still included.

With increasing frequency, national records, such as the Patent Rolls, record royal pardons given to the head of the de Hopton family. Not only did they get away with murder, but at that very moment when you would have thought they deserved beheading, they were given new powers of jurisdiction and of searching out criminals in the Marches and even in Wales itself. The kings were so desperate to stop total anarchy developing in the area that they would enlist the services of any local knight with good connections in the neighbourhood, however corrupt or violent he might be in his personal life, to try to establish law and order.

The personal standards of the Walter de Hopton who was head of the family in the 1260s are illustrated by the following story. Rees's Ancient Petitions Concerning Wales describes an incident in 1264, when twelve oxen, three heifers and a steer, the property of a widow from Lydbury, were being driven along "the King's Highway" to Wigmore Abbey for sale. When they came to Walter de Hopton's fishpond on the road between Hopton and Jay, three thieves (Walter son of the Chaplain, the Forester and Robert le Monner), stole the beasts and took them to the wood at Hopton. After the raid, Walter de Hopton sent the oxen over to Shelderton to pull his carts, so receiving stolen goods. In view of the fact that he was to be Sheriff of Shropshire in 1267 and held judicial positions in many other counties, frequently being employed to look into murders all over the country, Walter de Hopton's part in this cattle rustling episode is interesting. The widow, Alice, is petitioning the King for compensation of £20. She says that the reason that she did not take her case to the Assize Court in the right year was that Walter was the King's Justice there in that year, but she was ruled out of time. Heavy ox carts were used at this date for moving building materials, so Walter de Hopton was probably developing the quarries at Shelderton to provide stone – and possibly having castle building dreams.

However, less than ten years later he got his just desserts. In 1273 the Court Rolls show that Walter de Hopton took to court at Westminster, John FitzAlan, soon to be Earl of Arundel and Walter's overlord in the feudal system, and Peter de Jay, his neighbour, for stealing his cattle. Presumably even Walter felt that justice would not be done if the case were to be tried at the Assize Court, where his feudal overlord, in this case a member of the Arundel family, had influence.

Walter de Hopton functioned on a different basis from our other two knights, not only on account of his larger estate and greater military obligations, but also because he himself and his descendants were increasingly absent from the Clun valley on business of national importance. Of course he, unlike Roger de Halberdyne, was included in the 1272 list of the knights of Edward I. A class of professional lawyers grew up in the thirteenth century. This was the new way to power and riches. This Walter de Hopton was no longer only a soldier, but, following the national trend, a professional lawyer, who was owed as much as 40 marks in salary by the king in 1278. When he died, early in the next century, the annual income from his land in the Clun valley was slightly less than that sum, so clearly his professional career was of great importance to the family fortunes. No doubt it was this, which made him able to find such a bride as the Baroness of Wem.

After his marriage to the Baroness, Walter was one of the most important landholders in the county and was set on a successful career in the king's service. By 1275 he was Baron of the Exchequer and a figure of national importance. He is recorded as a witness to the homage of Alexander, King of Scotland, at Westminster Abbey in 1278. And this was despite the fact that the Patent Rolls record him being fined 2000 marks, for "malversion of the office" the year before! The whole annual value of his two Shropshire estates was less than an eighth of that sum in 1305.

In spite of holding such high office, he appears to have kept his estate in the Clun valley as his family seat. This is confirmed by the fact that he built the "tower house" at Hopton Castle towards the end of the thirteenth century, probably using the stone from his own quarries at Shelderton. The castle was based on the same plan as that at Clun and always had good living quarters and windows. As his Inquisition Post Mortem shows, the family kept a considerable garden there shortly after 1300 and a fishpond at Broadward to provide food for such times as Lent and Fridays, when they ate fish rather than meat. The head of the family may have been moving round not only the county but also the country, but his wife and children still needed a home and it seems that the Clun valley provided that, as well as the right to hunt over Shelderton and Hopton Titterhill, so that there was plenty of food for them and for their retainers.

On the rung below the knights were their major subtenants – the de Rowtons and de Costons. In the late thirteenth century the de Costons even had to provide knight service at Hopton Castle for three weeks a year in the manner that their overlord, Walter de Hopton, had to provide knight service at Clun Castle. The de Hoptons were beginning to ape the Lords of Clun. The de Coston family survived as lesser tenants for many generations, but their story is not part of this history.

The de Rowton family appear as free subtenants of the de Halberdynes and their successors between the twelfth and the fifteenth centuries, holding lesser posts in the public life of the locality. For example, Ivor de Rowton was a juror at the Assizes of 1256, Lucas was a witness in 1279 and a juror in 1292. Richard and Alice bought a house in Ludlow for Agnes, daughter of Roger de Rowton. The rent for this house was one rose. In Kirby's Quest of 1284 The de Rowtons were expected to provide a quarter of a knight's fee at Clun Castle. They were still acting as jurors as late as 1415 but a Will, listed in Hereford and dated 1445 shows that the senior branch of the family had no male heir.

By the thirteenth century feudal dues may have been commuted for a sort of early rent called "scutage", but "knight service" was not yet simply for fun and games or for the public display of wealth and jousting, as it became in the later Middle Ages. There was still a very real danger of fighting in the borders of Wales. While Richard I was away on crusade in 1199, the Welsh invaded Shropshire and, according to the Welsh Chronicles, laid the land waste and besieged Clun castle. No doubt Clungunford suffered then and again when there was another Welsh invasion in 1234 led by Llewellyn ap Gryffyd. The suburbs of Clun were burnt in 1264, though the invaders failed to take the castle.

The need for protection against Welsh raiders meant that even minor landholders, like the de Halberdynes, needed fortifications in addition to the feudal arrangements of their overlords. No remains of their earth ramped fortification survive, but there must have been one and the most likely site for this structure is underneath The Mount , where the drovers' road does a distinct loop, suggesting that its original course has been altered. It was probably similar in layout to the remains of the earthworks belonging to the Lord of the Manor of Coston, which trains on the Central Wales line bisect.

Fig 7. *Lightly armed foot soldiers were vulnerable to both mounted knights and archers.*

Fig 8. *The crossbow, which shot two arrows a minute and the longbow, which shot ten arrows a minute.*

The de Hoptons were replacing such a fortification when they built Hopton Castle. Speed, writing in 1611, records that, of the 186 castles in all England, 32 were in Shropshire. Clearly there was an exceptional need for defence in the county. Speed was, of course only recording proper castles, which had survived into the seventeenth century but, in the early Middle Ages, every manor house in the Clun valley had to be able to withstand a sudden Welsh attack.

The knights were heavily armoured and fought in close combat with swords, while the peasants were lightly armed and fought with any implement they could lay hands on, unless they were trained archers. It was from the Welsh that the English learnt about the effectiveness of the longbow. Made of yew, it was able to deliver ten to twelve arrows per minute, whereas the crossbow, could only deliver two arrows a minute. Once the English had been converted to the longbow, the story changed, and in 1264 there was a major battle, at which there is no doubt that our local knights, or their substitutes, followed by their villeins, fought their best. The result of the hail of arrows produced by the English longbows was the total defeat of the Welsh. Certainly this battle seems to have led to a period of comparative freedom from Welsh raids in the Clun valley, so that by the 1290s the king could expect the inhabitants to pay heavy taxes to enable him to fund a crusade or to fight the Scots, to whom he had turned his attentions now that the Welsh were quietened for a while.

It has been relatively easy to discover something of the fortunes of Clungunford's three feudal knights during the early Middle Ages, but it is only when feudalism begins to break down in the thirteenth century, that the lesser tenants become real people to us and begin to be named. We shall follow the fortunes of some of them in the next chapter.

3

Agricultural Boom before 1300

The years 1066 to 1086, although devastating and terrifying for the people of Clungunford at the time, had been, in fact, only a temporary blip in the graph of agricultural expansion in the three hundred years after the first Millenium. Oderic Vitalis, as we have seen, described the years just before the Conquest as a time of great plenty. The Normans, who seem to have produced a population explosion wherever they went, be it Denmark, Normandy, Sicily or Clungunford, confidently expected to be able to feed the increased population by expanding farms into primeval forest and by insisting on the most productive farming methods known. After all, the tax assessment for Clungunford had been based on using the maximum number of ploughs possible, not on the more relaxed Anglo Saxon system of land measurement. However, not even the demanding Norman settlers foresaw the impact of sheep rearing on the Clun valley. The farming methods described in this chapter will be illustrated by illuminations from the Luttrell Pasalter, which was owned by the Tenant-in-Chief of Clungunford.

Encroachment on the Forest of Mocktree was one of the major factors in the agricultural expansion of the twelfth and thirteenth centuries. Although there are still references to individual foresters, such as Henry in 1266 and John as late as 1272, during the thirteenth century the "assarts" (newly developed fields) caused Mocktree to lose its character as one large forest and come to be regarded as three separate woods – La Haye (at the Shelderton end), Kingswood (presumably remaining part of the crown's land at Leintwardine) and Whychwood (towards Wigmore).

The boundaries within the forest were finally determined in 1277 when Walter de Hopton gave up his claim to the "rights of common" which he had claimed on the Wootton side "as appurtenant to his lands in Shelderton". The Munslow Hundred Rolls record that both parties agreed to a perambulation of the "bosc" to establish the boundary between the estates of the de Hoptons and the de Lacys on the far side of the forest. So at that date the furthest extent of the Shelderton estate was established (the boundary was just below the present Ferney Hall) and in this way the land that was later to become the Ferney Estate became definitely part of the parish of Clungunford, while Duxmore belonged to the Manor of Wootton and so to Onibury parish. The later royal perambulation of the forests in Shropshire in 1300 does not appear to outline this boundary, because it did not directly concern the king.

Hunting, although often depicted as a sport, was essential for food at this period and the reduction in the size of the forest near Clungunford had a serious impact on the food chain. The frequency of rents being paid in either hunting dogs or hawks shows how important hunting was to the lords, far more important than the modern equivalent, a shotgun. Two of the knights of Clungunford did their best to compensate for the loss of hunting possibilities in the forests. In 1180, the Munslow Hundred Rolls record a grant to the de Hoptons of the right of "Free Warrender" over Shelderton and Broadward. This allowed them to hunt rabbits, which had recently been introduced to England from Normandy, and other small game, such as hares, pheasants and partridges, as well as vermin like foxes. The downside of this was that their subtenants were not allowed to do anything to control these animals ranging over their crops and eating their chickens, nor could they stop the huntsmen riding through their crops.

Fig 9 *Hunting with a hawk and with dogs of the sort used for the "free warren" hunting over Shelderton*

The de Jays solved the problem of hunting in a different way. One of the documents copied by the Herald records that in 1250 Gilbert of Bucknell gave back land called "Le Paroc" to his father in law, Walter de Jay. A paroc was a park and in 1846 there was still a large field called "Beckjay Park" next to the old drive gate to Clungunford House on the corner of the road to Beckjay. As the old forests ceased to be hunting grounds for the barons, it became fashionable for individuals to create their own parks, where the fallow deer, imported from Normandy, could graze among cattle in a way in which the native red deer would not. It seems the de Jay family were creating a place at Beckjay to keep game for hunting, not a great park as at Powis Castle, but a small, Clungunford style, park. We expect meat to come to us via a slaughter house, but we should remember that in the Middle Ages meat came more frequently from hunting with dogs and hawks, and bow and arrow. Both Beckjay Park and the de Hopton's right of "Free Warrender" over Shelderton were a necessary part of the food chain for the upper crust, who had to support a bevy of retainers as well as their own families.

The peasants also wanted to supplement their diet by hunting, but it was a brave man who set out with bow and arrow in Beckjay Park – they used snares, traps, catapults and even nets to catch birds as well as, of course, fish traps (see ***Colour Plate 9***). Just before 1200, when the Norman forest laws were beginning to bite and when the forests were anyway being reduced in size, there is the following entry in the Anglo Saxon Chronicle:- "He (the king) made great protection for game, and imposed laws for the same, that who slew hart or hind, should be made blind" and have his testicles removed. That, of course, applied only to royal forests, but it does give the flavour of the competition for hunting rights.

Markets established at the newly "planted" towns like Ludlow needed feeding and the market established there in Henry II's reign was a good outlet for spare produce from the two mills at Clungunford, as well as providing a market for the lesser peasants' eggs, chickens and so on. A tax was levied on every horse load taken into Ludlow market. The fair at Clun followed in 1205 and, timed at Martinmas in November, it gave the peasants a chance to sell their animals for salting down for the winter. The "salter" was to be one of the richest men in Clungunford in the 1327 tax assessment. Soon the Lord of Clun had to give the king two greyhounds a year for the privilege of holding two markets and later in the thirteenth century, three fairs a year are recorded at Clun. The amount of coinage in circulation in England rose sevenfold during the fifty years surrounding 1200, due in part to the increase in the wool trade and in part to the sale of peasant produce as well as to a developing labour market. During this period, Clungunford was able to move gradually towards a money economy.

Money in the eleventh and twelfth centuries, in the sense of coinage, had been more of a nuisance than anything else in village life because the smallest unit, a silver penny, was too valuable to have much relevance. At a time when a whole sheep's carcase was worth four pence, if you wanted to give small change you had to cut up a penny. However, by the thirteenth century, when the markets were being established, coinage was becoming useful, not only for knights, such as Walter de Hopton, who wanted to pay "scutage", (that is money– instead of doing service at Clun Castle), but also for wage earning free peasants, who could hire themselves out for four pence a week and could pay money rent rather than just provide free labour. In the thirteenth century the villeins began to escape from servitude, so that by 1300 half of them were free and were working as tenant smallholders, who might hire themselves out as labourers. Others were engaged in some sort of craft, such as masonry, carpentry, blacksmithing or cloth making.

A garden and an orchard were part of nearly every peasant "messuage" and were an important part of the village economy. These "messuages", which are referred to in the documents about

Fig 10. *Woman feeding hens and spinning with a distaff at the same time*

Haughmond Abbey's land at Abcott, for example, usually consisted of a simple house, one or two outbuildings and between ten and fifteen acres. There the peasants grew, not only food for their families, but also extra to sell, as well as a pig or two and on the bigger "messuages", some cows. They might even raise a spare ox, which they could sell for four shillings in 1300, twelve times a labourer's weekly wage. Wheat could be sold in town for a penny for about two and a half pounds. Hens were not killed for eating until their egg laying years passed, and the sales, at Clun or Ludlow market, of eggs and occasionally a cow or pig, as well as some sheep kept on common land, enabled the hard working to save up enough cash to buy their freedom. It was largely out of profits from these sales that the widow Agnes from Abcott and Roger Bacun from Shelderton, who both appear later in this chapter, were able to buy their freedom.

Women, particularly widows, appear frequently in Clungunford documents, as they do in the Luttrell Psalter and we should not underestimate their importance in the development of a money economy in the village. Although, in reality, they formed a large part of the work force, they were not usually part of the "customary labour" deal whereby a villein held his house and a small patch of ground, in exchange for labour. Thus an industrious woman could add greatly to the chances of her family being able to buy their freedom. Women appear in the Luttrell Psalter involved in hen and goose keeping, sheep milking, cheese making (see *Colour plate 7*), as well as spinning and weaving. No doubt they pursued these activities in Clungunford, too. These jobs, although they were subject to the "small tithe", were outside the control of the Lord of the Manor, so that any profit was kept by the family, as cash, or as value for barter.

Fig 11: *Women carding wool and using the recently invented spinning wheel.*

Grain prices quadrupled between 1180 and 1220 and the area of the parish under plough expanded. Although some of this expansion may have been necessary in order to feed the increased population in the village, there would have been spare grain to sell at the local markets, particularly from central Clungunford (see *Colour Plate 10*)

Sheep were the most important facet of local agriculture and, when land on the top of Shelderton Hill and Brand Hill was cleared, large areas were used as grazing for the sheep whose fleeces were bought by merchants like Lawrence de Ludlow. He became so rich on the proceeds of wool that he could afford to build the magnificent Great Hall at Stokesay Castle in the 1270s. By 1294 he was head of England's consortium of wool merchants. The Victoria County History describes the wool trade and stresses the pre-eminence of Welsh Border sheep at this date. They could be used to produce milk as well as fleeces; one ewe produced about sixty pints of milk per lactation and this could be used for cheese (see **Colour Plate 7**).

Fleeces were tiny compared with modern ones, weighing only one to two pounds each, but the profits were excellent from a beast, which could be grazed on the common land of the village. The profits for big merchants could be huge – when Lawrence de Ludlow's goods were impounded in Flanders in the next century one load of 330 sacks of wool were valued at £1,828 at a time when the rents of the whole of Walter de Hopton's Hopton estate were valued at £22 a year. Of course, this was not all profit for the merchant, he had to pay the de Hoptons and also their free tenants for the fleeces from Shelderton and Hopton Titterhill and probably the de Jays for theirs from Bedstone Hill. Not that he, personally would have bought and sold – he worked from a base in Shrewsbury. These figures give some idea of the scale of his turnover and explain why the family were able to build such a fine house as Stokesay Castle and why the people who supplied them with fleeces became rich, too.

The fact that the de Hoptons became the most powerful of our knightly families arose out of the exact position of the land they happened to acquire in the early days after the Conquest– that is the land along the edge of Mocktree Forest, which was ripe for development in the push for agricultural expansion. This provided good grazing for sheep and therefore income from wool. The large area of sheep-run and common grazing all along the top of Clunbury and Shelderton Hills, which remained seven hundred years later, was probably established for the use of the de Hoptons and their tenants in the thirteenth century; a Ferney Estate Map of 1782 luckily includes large parts of the former de Hopton land. On that we can see not only the commons, but also the strip field system in the three "Brock up" fields above Watling Street. These were part of the new assarts made by the de Hoptons once they had obtained the lease of part of Mocktree Forest from the king in 1195. The fact that they also expanded in the same manner over the former "waste" at Hopton Titterhill may lie outside the scope of our history, but it adds to our understanding of the wealth and upward social mobility of this family at a time when the English wool trade was in its heyday. . Walter de Hopton may not have been able to equal Stokesay Castle, but he did build himself a prestigious "tower house" in stone in the late thirteenth century, modelled on that of the Arundels at Clun.

In the two hundred years after the Domesday survey the relative value of arable land and pasture in Clungunford completely reversed; the Manor of central Clungunford, which had seemed so valuable in 1085 on account of its high grain yield and its two mills, had fallen back until it lagged far behind its neighbours, who were able to expand their pasture. Of course, in 1066 Shelderton had been part of the central Clungunford estate, but the changes which, as we have seen, came about in the eleventh century reduced the size of this holding to about 600 acres. We cannot yet find any detailed documentary evidence concerning grain yields, animals or even rents for Clungunford specifically until it came into the accounting system of the Arundel estates in 1346. However, some of the Arundels' estate surveys of their neighbouring farms for the period around 1300 do give a general idea of what was happening in the Clun valley. For instance, arable land was valued at between two pence and six pence an acre, whereas pasture was worth six times as much and the Earl's bailiff turned the whole of the Clun valley home farm over to grazing some time in the thirteenth century. By 1349 the Earl had 3,500 sheep on his Clun valley farms.

We can see how a sheep farmer flourished on a lesser scale on the other side of Clungunford, by looking at the accounts of the vicar of Stokesay, where the land belonged to Haughmond Abbey. The Abbey records show that the vicar's income in 1252 consisted of ten shillings from fleeces, ten shillings from lambs and only two shillings and six pence from all his other agricultural produce put together. There is no doubt that sheep were the most valuable commodity in this neighbourhood.

Many former arable fields in Clungunford were changed to permanent pasture, the word for such a piece of land being a "leasow". A glance at the Tithe Map which gives field names, shows Clungunford as being littered with "leasows" on land which is described in Domesday as being ploughland. Admittedly, the assessors in 1085 had under-reported pasture, or at least had only seen its potential as part of an arable system, but there is no doubt that Clungunford took advantage of the burgeoning wool market and the richer members of village society were heavily involved in sheep rearing before 1300 while the poorer ones and children found work as shepherds. Although the strip fields were divided by hedges from pasture and small secure enclosures were made out of woven hazel fences, this was not practical for large areas. The commons were not fenced and the flocks needed constant watching before the days of the easily erected wire fence.

Although the long staple fleece was not developed until the next century, the presence of a particularly fine breed of sheep in the Clun valley contributed greatly to the relative wealth of the parish of Clungunford. Hardy Old Shropshire sheep flourished on the high ground and on the "commons", rarely needing shelter or extra feed and each fleece from the Earl of Arundel's Shropshire flock was twice as valuable as one from his Sussex flock by the turn of the century. The Lord of the Manor himself may not have been able to benefit as greatly as his neighbours from sheep rearing on his own central Clungunford farm, but we should remember that the tithes came from the whole parish, including the parts which belonged to the de

Fig 12. *Shepherds watching sheep on common land with no hedges.*

Hoptons and de Jays. It was for this reason, that at the time of Pope Nicholas's Taxation in 1291, Clungunford appears as one of the richest villages in the neighbourhood, its tithe being valued at six pounds per annum compared with Bedstone's at two pounds.

Apart from sheep, oxen were the staple beasts of village life because they cost less than a cow to pasture, could be shared with neighbours, were the strongest beast for haulage in heavy clay soil, and could ultimately be eaten. (see **Colour Plate 8**). As we have already seen, there were ox drawn carts at Shelderton and these were probably soon used to cart stone from the quarries there for the building of Hopton Castle and, some years later for St Cuthbert's church. Such vehicles would also have been necessary for the carting of millstones, which is recorded in the Clun valley villages, although most everyday goods transport was by packhorse and mule. Cows, on the other hand, known as "lazy beasts", might be good to eat, but a medieval cow only gave one tenth as much milk per lactation as a modern cow, so there were not a great many cows in the village and most of those were probably feeding the knightly tables.

Fig 13. *A horse drawn harrow.*

Horses, smaller beasts than today, were also expensive to keep but were used for harrowing, for pack animals and for getting around – a reasonable day's horseback journey was estimated at about forty miles. In times of emergency, such as delivering the king's writ to the Sheriff, a messenger could cover up to sixty miles in a day, provided it was summertime and there was a full moon and a good road like Watling Street, which may well still have had the remains of a hard Roman surface in the Middle Ages. Warhorses were raised at studs like the one at Clun, not in Clungunford.

While sheep flourished on the high ground and pasture, the strip field system remained the basis of village food production, with its joint sowing of winter wheat and a little rye for bread and spring sowing of barley for fodder and for that all important feature of village life – brewing – as well as oats (for man and beast alike) and peas and beans as a field crop. The names "lower, middle and upper" fields, on the Tithe Map suggest that a three field system was in operation in Clungunford in the Middle Ages This was better than a two field system because the animal diseases left in the ground after a year of grazing could survive for one year, but not for two. There is evidence, either on the ground, or on old maps, of strip fields at Shelderton, Broadwood, Beckjay, Tately and close by Hope Dingle.

However, to assume from this that there was always a perfect three-field system in each of the "tons" of Clungunford and that they remained the same throughout the Middle Ages, would be to over simplify a constantly changing situation. The ebb and flow of both the human and animal populations had its influence on land use. The field names on the Tithe Map provide evidence of this fluid situation; the many "Tindings" (ie burnings) at Hopton Heath provide a description of the method of heath clearance used there, probably by the family called "de la Hethe" who only appear in late medieval documents. Whereas the "Brooches" (and possibly, the "Brock-ups" at Shelderton), suggest a different, manual, method of clearing the forest to make space for fields. They were probably cleared before Tately, in the mid thirteenth century. It is not certain whether Brand Hill (burnt hill) was so named because the forest was burnt off there in the thirteenth century, or because it was full of charcoal burning pits and platforms in the seventeenth century and possibly earlier. The sites of some of these are still visible when a field is ploughed near the top of Shelderton Hill, to the north of the road to Wetmore

By the thirteenth century much attention was given to fertilizers and there was competition to have animals pastured on your land for manuring on the hoof. Marl was much used, too. This was a mixture of lime and subsoil, which were dug out of pits in the fields and, on Brand Hill. Even if sheep farming was the most profitable occupation, the peasants still needed to eat and grain could be sold to people from the villages higher up the Clun valley, where the Lord's land had been turned over to pasture alone.

In the last chapter we followed the fortunes of the Clungunford knights. In this chapter we shall try to discover something about the peasants, whose lives were intimately bound up with the expanding agriculture. Only "free" men were allowed to appear at any court other than that of the lord, and since twelfth century Manorial Court Rolls for Clungunford have not survived (like those of most other villages in the country), it is hard to discover the names of "unfree" peasants, the "customary tenants". However, we can discover quite a bit about the "free" villagers.

What we do know is that everyone was dependent for his land on the person directly above him in the social scale. He had to pay for it by knight service, labour or rent, depending on his social status. There were other unattractive customs for the feudal peasant, such as the "heriot", which obliged the family to give the best beast to their lord when the head of the family died. This could bring disaster to a family. Another unpopular custom was the "droit de seigneur", by which the lord had the right to sleep with a peasant girl on the night before her marriage. This right was only discontinued in Clungunford in the sixteenth century, when the Earl of Arundel renounced his right in the whole Clun Valley for £60. It would have been a long way to travel once he had moved to Sussex. How often it was enforced we shall never know.

We may have few records of named individuals in the parish before the end of the fourteenth century, but we can gain remarkably detailed information about the types of lesser tenant in Shelderton at the end of this period of agricultural expansion from the Inquisition Post Mortem of the Walter de Hopton, who died in 1305. We are extremely grateful to Bob Milner for giving us a copy of his transcript of the document. Apart from the four "free tenants, there were still thirteen slaves in this part of Shelderton, while at Broadward there were still fifteen "customary tenants", that is to say tenants who paid for their land largely in labour. Whereas the "free tenants" at Shelderton paid four shillings and two pence a year in rent, the "customary tenants" there paid only five pence a year, or one tenth of the "free tenants'" rent. The reason for this was that most of the rent of the "customary tenants" was paid in labour on three days every week and more if necessary. Even though we are not necessarily comparing like with like exactly, this does, nevertheless, show that certain aspects of feudalism were still alive and well in Clungunford as late as 1300. It was a mixed economy, based partly on feudal obligations, and partly on modern rents and careers.

Although there is little evidence for Clungunford itself as yet, we do have some information concerning the occupations of people in neighbouring villages, which were part of the Earl of Arundel's home farm. He had started to keep estate records by the late thirteenth century and the Sussex Record Society has published a survey, including those for the Earl's home farm in the Clun valley, in 1301. From this we learn that Agnes Taty, a married woman at Hopesay, "carried the Earls' letters" anywhere in the county and was a free tenant, as was the man at Aston Pound who raised a falcon a year as his rent.

Hopesay also had a reeve (farm manager), a clerk (priest), "a parsonman," and among the list of "bondmen" there were a mason, a tiler, a mercer and a "corviser" (boot and shoe maker). At Acton there was another mason and at Kempton a miller and "le bagger" (beggar). The tenants of Barlow had the duty of carrying millstones from the Clun to the mill at Kempton. At Clunton there was another reeve as well as two millers and a fuller – clearly the Clun valley workforce included people involved, not only in the production of fleeces, but also in the cloth finishing trade. Fulling was particularly important as a means of strengthening cloth before a long staple fleece was developed. We know that before 1327 the richest man in central Clungunford was a fuller.

Fig 14: *Falconer. Before the advent of the shot gun, the privileged hunted with hawks and such birds were highly sought after.*

Clunton also had a clerk, a belward (presumably to ring and look after the church bell), a smith, a beggar, Richard le Hunte (huntsman) as well as a "wodewarde" (forester), who had to either look after woods at Radnor, or pay a shilling rent and cart flour anywhere in Shropshire. There is every reason to assume that occupations in Clungunford were similar.

The question of the types of rents paid by the new, unfeudal, tenants is not clear. Some, like those at Shelderton in 1305, paid in coinage, which was by now much more practical and common, but equally, some paid in kind. There are no records for Clungunford, but an Inquisition Post Mortem shows that rents paid in kind by Walter de Hopton's wife's tenants at Wem in 1290 included "fowls, ploughshares, works, reaping, six quarters of oats, woodland honey and sparrow hawks", while a free tenant higher up the Clun valley paid his rent in cumin and all bondmen in Kempton paid "hawk money". There is every reason to believe that some Clungunford rents came in similar forms. They might even have come in as exotic a form as those of Minsterley in Richard II's reign when "four greyhounds' collars, 2lbs pepper, 2 lbs cumin, a barbed arrow and a park with deer" were the rent for the manor. One annual rent for grazing in Clungunford is still a turkey at Christmas.

It is in the detailed records of the courts, both local and national, in criminal matters and in civil ones, which follow, that we find most of the hard evidence for the effect on Clungunford itself of the rise of a money economy, as well as the new freedom of many peasants and the position of women. In these years of agricultural boom, land was at a premium and the history of the courts and of agriculture is thus so inextricably bound up that for the rest of this chapter they will be treated together. It is through court records that we begin to discover the names of villagers other than our three knights soon after 1200. Clungunford was (just) under English law. Most of Clun itself was under Welsh law, but the Court Rolls of Clungunford, when they do survive from the late fourteenth century, are all headed "Hallemot Anglicoram" – hall court of the English. At a higher level, the great barons of the Welsh Borders were literally a law unto themselves. In order to ensure their help against the Welsh, the kings had granted these "palatinate" earls immense powers, which they came to regret. The later medieval kings, in order to claw back some of this power, had to give major subtenants, such as the de Hoptons, sweeping powers to keep order where the "palatinate earls", like the Arundels, were failing to do so.

The village sometimes reacted surprisingly quickly to national events and trends. For example, we know that all over the country during this period a struggle went on between the kings and their barons over the control of court cases; justice could be a good source of income and both kings and barons wanted to get their hands on it. Thus Magna Carta in 1215 was not an improvement for the barons alone. It clearly stated that "No **freeman** shall be seized or imprisoned, or stripped of his rights or possessions………..except by lawful judgement of his equals or by the law of the land." From now on every freeman (and woman) of Clungunford had the right to trial by jury in the king's court for a serious crime or for redress if wronged. At this time, when more and more of the inhabitants of Clungunford were buying their freedom and selling their labour to the people whose serfs and villeins they had recently been, this right to a hearing in the king's court was sought after.

Eight years after Magna Carta, the widow, Agnes from Clungunford, appears in the Curia Regis Rolls. She went to the High Court in London to accuse Walter de Hopton and others of his family and friends, of murdering her husband. Clearly she was confident of her worth in society, had money and felt she could stand up against any man – even a local grandee. However, when she got to Westminster, the cross questioning forced her to admit that, although she believed other members of the de Hopton family were guilty, Walter de Hopton, himself was not. So she was thrown into prison for perjury and told that, later on, the case must be heard at the local assizes. No doubt she had hoped for more impartial justice if she went to Westminster, because in Shropshire the court was more likely to be under the influence of the local magnate, Walter de Hopton. Of course, it must be admitted that she probably also hoped that nobody at Westminster would know that she was accusing the wrong man! Simon de Halberdyne is recorded as having been in charge of choosing the jury at the local Assize Court in 1221 and Agnes must have been aware that in that very year another widow, Matilda from Abcott,[1] had lost her case for recovery of her dowry at the local court at a time when her Lord of the Manor, that same Simon, was influential. Widows in Clungunford in the thirteenth century were not going to let themselves be downtrodden.

The Assize Court, sitting at Purslow Hundred Court in 1256, with twelve jurors from the Hundred, gives the flavour of life in the neighbourhood. In the space of the six months since the last court, there had been fifteen murders – three of them in Clungunford. This represents a higher rate of murder per head of population than that of New York City in the year 2000. One of these murders has already been well described in the Gunnas Gazette and here is a translation of the record of that double murder direct from the Assize Roll: "Simon miller of Broadward stabbed William son of Philip of Abcott right through the body with a lance, and William instantly struck back at Simon and then cut his throat, so that they both died on the spot.........The townships of Clungunford, Jay, Beckjay and Abcott buried the body without the coroner's view", (for which they were fined). From this we know that there was by now another mill at Broadward, probably just downstream from the present bridge – evidence of the boom in agriculture and the growth of the population.

Millers were evidently violent folk for another record from the same session reads "Hugh miller struck Will son of Redwy with a stake which did not draw blood, but from which he died eight days later. Hugh fled and is of ill repute, so let him be exacted and outlawed.....". The third murderer was Phillip son of Jordan from Rowton, who took a Danish axe to the head of his victim and then fled. He was also outlawed. The possessions of a murderer were confiscated and, in all these cases, the townships were fined for burying the corpse without showing it to the coroner, and in the last case, Aston, Hope and Hopesay were fined because they had not given chase, that is to say, set up a " hue and cry".

We have already discussed in theory the expansion of cultivated land into the forest but it is in the court rolls that this development becomes a reality. As early as 1207 the man who held land in Mocktree Forest on the opposite side from Clungunford – William de Wodeton (Wootton) – appears in the records of the Assize Court because he had been caught out "for that he had made waste of Mocktree Forest...." while he was in theory the guardian of the forest, the Forester. In 1274 the widow of the de Lacy tenant in chief on the Stokesay side did not dare to pursue her rights of "free chase and free warren" in the forest because of "Sir Roger de Mortimer and his men", according to the court records of Stanton Lacy! There was clearly pressure on rights in the forest at all levels of society and for a variety of purposes. We know from the Hundred Rolls of 1255 Walter de Hopton was paying the king two shillings a year for a licence to develop his part of the forest of Mocktree (and also towards the guarding of the road on the edge of the forest, called Botstrete) and we also know that Henry III liked to sell off forest land to raise money. At some stage around this time Walter must have actually bought that part of the forest which he developed at Tately and also at Weo, and it was probably then that the large commons and sheep-runs right over the top of the hill were established for the de Hoptons' tenants.

There are quite a few court cases involving Shelderton, which show how jealously land up against the forest was guarded because it was a prime site for agricultural development. "Boscs" were areas fenced off within the forest for grazing, or in order to keep out deer and so allow natural re-growth. According to the Assize Rolls, the de Hoptons had three such enclosures in Mocktree as part of their land at Shelderton and Richard FitzHenry insisted that he had "estovers" (the right to take timber for building and brushwood for fencing) from them, which Walter was denying him in 1256. The remains of these fenced areas can still just be made out way up in the relatively recently planted woodland to the south of the present road up Shelderton Hill, where among the trees, you can still see the remains of ancient coppiced and laid oaks, bark-less and half buried. One can imagine Clungunford dwellers collecting their wood from them "by hook or by crook" in the thirteenth century.

It was not only the knightly classes who sought to benefit from the development (or otherwise) of Mocktree: We hear in the Assize Court records, in the middle of the century, of a new type of man, Richard Bacun. He must have been a freeman or he could not have appeared in the king's court. He had clearly bought his freedom and the Shropshire Eyre Roll records him demanding privileges in the forest as "his by right as a free tenant of Shelderton". Anyway he was not afraid to take the local grandee, Walter de Hopton, to the Assizes in 1256 . He won his case against Walter for "estovers" at Shelderton, provided he agreed to take "estovers" in Hopton instead should Walter want to make "assarts" (new fields cut out of woods) in Shelderton– quite a complicated arrangement which left Walter able to develop further should he so wish– at Tately and Weo, for instance. A new pushy type of peasant is beginning to appear in the records. Unlike the Domesday feudal tenant, he is named and demands rights because he rents his land in a more modern manner. The same Roger Bacun appears again on the other side of the forest near Wootton trying to get rights on common land there "as appurtanent to his tenement in Shelderton", but failing, in the Assize Court of 1267 . He may have been a new type of peasant, but he wanted the best of both worlds and claimed old rights with Anglo Saxon names as part of his new type of tenancy. The problem for these new small farmers was that they did not have enough variety of land to be truly self sufficient and yet they had to raise money for the kings' increasingly frequent taxes.

Court records show how much litigation there was over the fringes of the forest, but the centre was being opened up too. It was wise of Walter de Hopton to keep the right to push Roger Bacun's "estovers" across to Hopton, because by 1272 he had developed agricultural land at Tately and at Weo. After the quarries were developed, many routes were used to drag stone from them over centuries – the hillside is riddled with paths. Both Tately and Weo are first mentioned as settlements in the Inquisition Post Mortem of the Earl of Arundel, which was taken in 1272.

The end of the thirteenth century was one of the high points of Clungunford's history and the confidence, which that prosperity engendered, is reflected to this day by two fine stone buildings. As we have noted, the owner of Shelderton built a "tower house", which was not only defensible, but from the beginning had elegant living rooms, namely Hopton Castle. The Lord of the Manor of Clungunford could have built himself a fine house on the proceeds of the agricultural boom but, instead, he soon decided to build a house of God, namely St Cuthbert's church.

4

The Disasters of the Fourteenth Century

The century started well and the view from the top of Clunbury Hill in 1300 was very different from that in 1085. The population had, following national trends, probably doubled, making seventy labourers and their families in the enlarged village, so that the pressure for agricultural development had eaten into the wild land surrounding the village (see **Fig 16**).

The old forest of Mocktree was no longer a single entity but had been bitten into, leaving only a few areas of woodland visible, for example, those "boscs" under the steep edge of Shelderton Rock. There is probably more woodland running along the hills above Watling Street today than there was in 1300. Where there had been trees, or at least "forest" in the medieval sense of the word in 1066, there was, in 1300, common land on the top of the hill, heavily grazed by sheep. The parish actually ran alongside the land of that great wool merchant, Lawrence de Ludlow and was clearly part of that phase of the English wool trade, which depended on the production of fleeces, rather than of cloth.

The landscape had altered, not only because the forest had been displaced by agricultural land, but also because the percentage of arable land had shrunk and the percentage of pasture had grown. There were more animals, particularly sheep, and less grain per cultivated acre.

Apart from the increase in the number of sheep, the greatest change in the view was that the trees had been cleared for agriculture right along the east side of Watling Street. As we have seen, this was the moment when the "Broc up" fields named in the Tithe Map, and now known as "The Block-ups", came into being. These may have been called "Brooches", which was, in various forms, an ancient word for newly cleared land, or they may have been so named on account of their very large badger population. Broc was the Anglo Saxon name for badgers and it is good to think of the ancestors of the animals we still see on the road at Shelderton living in the same setts in 1299. Maybe their homes are older than any of the houses in Clungunford.

The number of millers committing murders suggests that there would have been several corn mills (see *colour plate 9* and **Fig 20**). There must have been a fulling mill also, either on the river or, possibly, on one of the streams, such as that at Broadward. Central Clungunford was evidently still producing good crops of grain.

Fig 15. *Threshing, with a specialised tool.*

The fact that the Earl of Arundel definitely had fulling mills higher up the river in 1300, combined with the fact that the richest man in Clungunford was the fuller in 1327, suggests that Clungunford was already involved in the cloth trade as well as the wool trade by this date and that there was a fulling mill.

There was far more "managed" water in general in the view then. Many of the new fields "assarted" out of the forest had ponds from which animals could drink and the landscape glittered with small pools. These have only been allowed to silt up since the arrival of piped water in the twentieth century and there are the vestiges of many to be seen at Shelderton and along Watling Street as well as at Weo and Tately . There are the remains of larger pools at Beckjay, formed by damming a stream. These were referred to as "Beckjay Lake" on the Tithe Map. There are also the remains of three pools at Abcott Manor, which were fed by the stream running down from Clunbury hill, which has now been diverted. The fish pool of the de Hoptons is pin-pointed on the map in the description of the cattle rustling episode in the 1260s and we can see the remains of one of them in front of Broadward Hall today. These pools were established in the early Middle Ages when most manor houses dug their own ponds for fish for eating.

The means of food production for the locals, in an age when shopping was not a possibility, formed a prominent part of the view over the village. The quantity of managed water showed what an important part fish played in the diet of rich and poor alike. No doubt the peasants managed to collect a few trout from the unpolluted river and there would have been traps for fish and eels close to the mills (see *colour plate 9*) The knightly families had pike, bream, perch, roach and soon carp from their ponds and lakes. There was a fenced park, no doubt with fallow deer and cattle grazing together, at Beckjay, but the medieval pleasure gardens which had recently been laid out at Clun and Hopton Castles were out of sight. There was good hunting at Shelderton, we know from the de Hoptons' grant of "Free Warrender". Each of the peasants' "messuages" had a garden and an orchard.

Broadward, which is not specifically mentioned in Domesday Book (the references to a place of that name refer to somewhere further south), had by the thirteenth century become quite a sizeable settlement. It is described as a "hamelett" in 1305 and had houses as well as a mill. The Shropshire Archaeological Records pin-point the deserted medieval settlement as being at National Grid Reference OS 394 768. The site of the new small settlement at Tately is marked by the foundations of a more recent barn behind Doctor's Coppice. There was a new strip field system there. Weo, established as a settlement in the thirteenth century, is now outside the parish.

These new settlements, as well as the quarries which had been recently opened up, necessitated new roads, which would have been visible, for those with good eye-sight from Clunbury Hill in 1300. It is impossible to date the exact moment when each path came to deserve the name of "road", but let us assume that that occurred when it was first used for ox drawn carts going to and from a new settlement on a regular basis. Whereas in Anglo Saxon, times Botstrete (Watling Street) and the prehistoric drovers' road down to the ford had been the only roads of any importance, by the thirteenth century a road running diagonally, north east to south west, had been developed. It joined the new settlement at Tately and the quarries on Shelderton Hill to the broad ford at Broadward. We can see it today, running in a cleft as it comes down from Shelderton Hill. It then follows the course of the modern road for a short distance before moving into the wood on the west, where it continues round the curve of the hill for some distance, so avoiding the steep incline, finally runs in a deep channel, before rejoining the modern road, between steep banks, on its way to Watling Street. At this point it becomes the narrow lane, sunken between the hedges, joining Shelderton to the Leintwardine road, which it crosses, before running through the field at the Lynches and down to the river, which it crossed, probably diagonally, so making the ford broad.

Soon after the river crossing it divided, one half running straight on out of the parish and the other half turning right and following the same course as the modern road, through deep banks, for some of the way to Beckjay. We can still see the straight course of the old road where it takes to the fields and bypasses modern Beckjay, before rejoining the contemporary main road to the Rocke Arms. The medieval road then passed behind the present tearooms and on towards Coston, via a cross roads at Abcott. The road through Beckjay had obviously been an ancient track but in 1264, the widow, whose cattle were stolen at Broadward, had preferred to use the longer way round, on The King's Highway, rather than use the shorter route via Beckjay, which was evidently not a good road then.

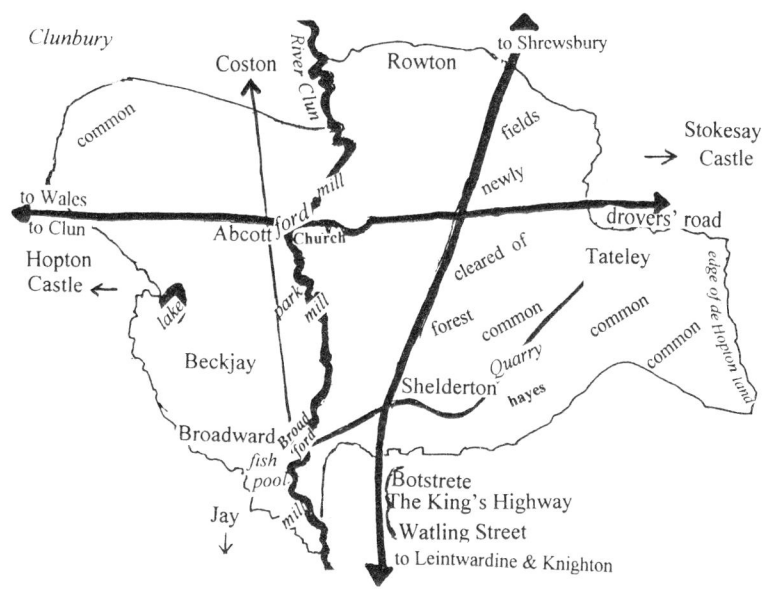

Fig.16. *Clungunford circa 1300. Forest had been changed into farmland and some of the footpaths had became roads. Often our deeply buried lanes follow these medieval roads.*

The appearance of the buildings in central Clungunford, which were grouped along the village street running down to the ford, as well as in those in the other "tons", is still problematical. There was a church on the site of the present one, probably built of wood and very soon to be replaced by a stone structure. The only things still standing today, which witnessed the building of the church are three veteran oaks in the field to the right of the Twitchen Road, just after the railway bridge. They were probably there in 1300 and may have been part of the boundary between the de Hopton land and central Clungunford. They are close to "townsend field" on the named Tithe map.

Fig 17. *A veteran oak, which may have been planted to mark the boundary between the de Hopton and de Halberdyne land before the stone church was built.*

Since the population had doubled, there must have been many simple "wood framed" peasants houses, most of them with the one or two outbuildings expected of a "messuage". At this early date, many of them would have been "long houses" with animals living at one end and people at the other. These houses have not survived probably because their foundations were "earthfast" and simply rotted away. There may have been a few single storey "cruck" houses, although none has survived the change to two storey buildings, which came to the village between 1550 and 1650. The eagerness of Walter de Hopton to have heavy oxcarts at Shelderton in the 1260s suggests that the quarries were opening up then, so there may well have been some such carts in the view, dragging stone for foundations. We know there was a good house at Abcott but we do not yet know what it looked like. The prestigious new "tower house" at Hopton, would have been just out of sight.

As we have seen, there must have been a good residence for the de Halberdine family, probably a defensible, moated house, at least as good as the one at Coston, the site of which one travels through in any train on the Mid Wales line. It is likely that, in the thirteenth century, this defensible "manor house" stood on the high ground now occupied by The Mount. Certainly, a glance at a detailed map makes it clear that the drovers' road, the original "village street" was diverted round this site, although subsequent building works in the area have removed all traces.

This would have been the obvious site, well above flood level and beside the road coming down from the King's Highway (Watling Street). It is impossible that the tiny Motte close to the church can have fulfilled that role and it was found during nineteenth century digs to be a prehistoric burial mound.

As we have seen, the year 1300 marked the high point of Clungunford's medieval development. After this, the Bishops' registers show it as being unable to pay it's tithe all too frequently for the next two hundred years. There were, of course, some better years but the general trend is towards poverty. When considering this trend, it is best to divide the century into two sections– before the Black Death and after the Black Death.

Before the Black Death came the weather. An adverse climatic cycle soon set in and there are reports from all over Britain of storms and floods. In 1312 the burgesses of Shrewsbury petitioned King John to give them money for repairs because a large part of the city wall had collapsed due to floods and the Welsh Bridge was about to fall. The Severn, like the Clun, must have risen to the level it did in the winter of 2000 – 2001. National records show that the harvest of 1315 was a total disaster due to the rain in that summer, and for the next seven years the winters were exceptionally long and fierce, the land often flooded so that seed corn rotted in the ground and winter feed for animals was almost impossible to find.

As if that was not enough, a "murrain" of cattle and sheep swept the country in the 1320s. This was probably "liver fluke", which flourished in the streams, which were swollen after heavy rain. Usually, at this early date, we have to rely on the records of the church (where a high rate of literacy prevailed and an accurate system of accounting had been developed), or on the records of royal manors, such as Ruyton in north Shropshire, for our information. In 1319 all 17 cattle on the demesne farm at Ruyton died and 60 out of 190 sheep. In the following year 117 bushels of wheat sown produced only 296 bushels at the harvest. Oats were even worse– a sowing of 332 bushels produced only 466 bushels. There were similar reports from all over the country and Clungunford seems to have followed the general trend.

In the midst of all these troubles, a new warfaring king, Edward III, demanded a "Lay Subsidy" in 1327. This tax may have been a disaster for an impoverished village, but it is a blessing for historians. It tells us who lived in the village and had a reasonable amount of possessions and how rich these people were in relation to each other. Thus we can discover how Clungunford society was changing.

For Clungunford dwellers it was yet another extra tax designed to take a fifteenth of the value of the moveable possessions of country people (a tenth for the urban populations). People whose possessions were worth less than ten shillings were exempt, as were the clergy and, more surprisingly, all the armour, riding horses, jewels, robes and silver or pewter plate of our three knights. The argument for the last exemption was that it was expensive either to do knight service at Clun every three weeks or to pay someone else to do it.

You would expect that the largest landowner would also be the richest man for tax purposes, but the de Hoptons somehow always seem to have had an eye for the main chance and Walter de Hopton had a scam going whereby his stepbrother or possibly even his step nephew, the son or grandson of the Baroness of Wem by her previous marriage, had to pay the tax at Shelderton![1]

Roger de Halberdyne, the Lord of the Manor, paid more than the de Hoptons at three pounds and eleven shillings. His tax bill was almost the equivalent of employing two labourers for a year to cart stone for the church. He was probably able to pay this particular tax because, as both the owner of the advowson and "acolyte" of the church, he may, with the Bishop's permission, have been able to appropriate to himself that portion of the tithe income from the parish, which was normally due to the rector. There is no record of a rector at St Cuthbert's then and, after all, he was building a new church. His role is dealt with more fully in the chapter on the church, suffice it to say here that he seems to have been the first of a long series of "squarsons".

The really surprising thing about the assessment for tax in 1327 is that Walter the "fuller" paid more tax than the lord of his manor, and more than the lords of Hopton and Jay. He paid over four pounds in total in both parts of the village. Fulling was part of the cloth manufacturing process and involved either cleaning the dirt and grease from the wool before weaving or pressing the woven cloth to finish and strengthen it. This was an essential process in the production of strong cloth before sheep with a long staple fleece had been bred. Evidently there was a fulling mill here, as there was in most villages on the Clun. As grain production on the feudal lords' farms and those of their tenants suffered from bad weather and sheep disease and rents went down, the professional fuller overtook the former land owners in a new type of wealth based on moveable possessions. It was, of course impossible that he could really have overtaken the owners of Hopton Castle, but his taxable wealth was mostly caused by the possession of rolls of cloth, which would have been difficult to conceal, had he wished to conceal it. This tax return makes it clear that Clungunford was heavily involved in the cloth trade shortly before the Black Death.

Another big taxpayer was the farm bailiff, Richard le Graunger, who at two shillings and four pence paid only slightly less than Walter de Huggeford, who was one of the county tax collecters. We cannot be absolutely sure whose bailiff Roger le Graunger was, but his relative wealth suggests that he was working for the Walter de Hopton of the day, who was too busy with national affairs to keep a close eye on his own land at Shelderton. Various subtenants are listed as de Coston, de Eweldon and de Broadward and there are several relations of the main landowners, who are quite rich. Among the lesser tax payers there are listed several people with what we should consider nowadays as proper surnames– Oldape, Houwel, Bercar. So there were about two dozen people in the village in the mid fourteenth century who had a reasonable number of personal possessions. About half of them were certainly connected to the old feudal families, but society was changing and professional men like farm managers and fullers could earn a good living, while those with the new surnames were probably villeins who had been able to buy their freedom.

What this tax return does not do, unfortunately, is to tell us anything about the really poor in Clungunford. We have to rely on William Langland, the poet born in Cleobury Mortimer for that. His description later in the century of the diet of the cottager in " Piers Ploughman" shows how seasonal was their ability to eat properly:

> *I have no penny, quoth Piers, pullets for to buy,*
> *Nor neither geese nor piglets but two green cheeses,*
> *A few curds and cream and an oaten cake*
> *And two loaves of beans and bran to bake for my little ones.*
> *And besides I say by my soul I have no salt bacon'*
> *And by this livelihood we must live till Lammas time*
> *Nor no little eggs, by Christ, collops for to make;*
> *But I have parsley and leeks and many cabbages,*
> *And besides a cow and a calf and a cart mare*
> *To draw afield my dung the while the drought lasteth.*
> *And by that I hope to have harvest in my croft,*
> *And then may I prepare the dinner as I dearly like.*

The "cow and calf and cart mare" were not valuable enough to bring him into the taxable class.

There were yet more taxes and, in the Lay Subsidy Roll for 1334, while Jay had to pay one pound sixteen shillings and Hopton three pounds and Hopesay over four pounds, there is no sum at all entered after central Clungunford or Shelderton, which suggests that they were considered too poor to pay anything.

In 1341 the tax assessment, although it does not tell us about individuals, does show the generally deteriorating situation. Whereas, at "Pope Nicholas's Taxation" in 1291 the income from Clungunford's tithes had been assessed at £6, at the assessment for 1341 the tithes were worth only £2. It is true that the tax was calculated in a slightly different way, so that some "small tithes", such as the peasants' chickens, were not included in 1341, but, nevertheless, the value of the village produce had dropped nearly two thirds. The Assessors noted that much of the land of the parish lay fallow, "the tenants being poor and the king's taxes frequent". Hopton's tax was reduced specifically on account of "a murrain of sheep" – an outbreak of sheep disease.

Here is a picture of a struggling population already unable to till all their fields, due, no doubt in part, to the death and enfeeblement from starvation of many labourers. This was a time of social mobility and some went to the towns to look for work.

Joining someone's army was another way of moving to avoid starvation. The only recorded example of a man leaving the immediate district to fight for the king comes, not surprisingly, from the knightly class – Brian de Jay who was killed fighting in Scotland. The Earl of Arundel was a commander at the Battle of Poitiers in 1346. There is a record of Edward II demanding 200 men from Clun for his Scottish wars, which surely must have meant some men from Clungunford. They were probably glad to get away from malnutrition at home and have the chance of a soldier's pay.

Despite all these difficulties, these were the years during which the church was being built. There is nothing surprising about the fact that a church was started in the prosperous early years of the century. What is surprising, seen from a modern point of view, is that the building work continued during the years of privation clearly indicated in the 1341 tax assessment. The fate of the de Halberdynes, whose forbear began the building programme, may have been a direct result of his patronage. The fact that the Earl of Arundel, not a de Halberdyne, presented the new rector in 1349 tells a tale. In 1346 Roger de Halberdyne finally gave up the struggle to keep up with his knightly neighbours and handed back his "fief" to the Earl of Arundel[2]. He could have died leaving no heir, but that is unlikely in that he had at least two sons. More probably he formed part of the drift into the towns, which occurred at this date.

It is tempting to romance and suggest that the descendants of the de Halberdynes were the Ludlow family called Clungunwas, who lived in "The Great House", that fine medieval building next to Stone House in Corve Street, Ludlow. Unfortunately there is as yet no hard evidence to connect the two families and the one Clungunwas Will which survives intact from 1543 does not refer to any Clungunford connection, although there must originally have been one. The de Halberdynes just might have felt it more appropriate to lose their Norman name, which would not have been fashionable in cloth manufacturing circles. But this is pure speculation.

The extra taxation, combined with the building of the church, was the last straw for the de Halberdyne family whose farm had been steadily decreasing in value even before it was hit by the bad harvests and cattle murrains. It is clear that, throughout history, the central Clungunford Manor has only been a really viable entity if the Lord of the Manor also owned land elsewhere or had some other source of income. It was also desirable that the Rector be a close family member, if not the squire himself, so that the squire, or his family, received a portion of the tithes due to the advowson. These tithes came from the whole parish and not just from the lands of the manor, which was, as we have seen, only a small part of the parish. The fate of the de Halberdynes in the fourteenth century foreshadowed that of the Rockes in the twentieth century.

The Black Death in 1349 struck a village already so depressed that it did not recover its former prosperity for a hundred and fifty years. First a disease of corn, then a disease of cattle and finally a disease of men. The Black Death arrived in Shropshire in the spring of 1349 and approximately one third of the population died in that year. It was a terrible death. A description from a Welsh song describes it as "death coming into our midst like black smoke, a plague which cuts off the young, a rootless phantom......Woe is me of the shilling in the arm pit.....Great is its seething like a burning cinder....a grievous thing of shy colour......A mixed multitude, a black plague like halfpence, like berries". It was spread mainly by fleas from rats arriving on ships from the Middle East but people living in 1349 did not understand this and often believed it was an evil spirit. The fleas abounded in the straw with which people covered their floors. The rich changed their straw four times a year, but the poor only once. No one saw the connection between hygiene and disease.

We may no longer believe that animals can catch the bubonic plague, but it is certain that through neglect, many animals did die, just as many mills ceased to grind. The chronicler

Henry Knighton reports 5,000 dead animals in one Shropshire field alone "their bodies so corrupted by the plague that neither beast nor bird would touch them" so leading to an appalling stench. Even if we are sceptical about the accuracy of this description, local records do show that many animals did die for one reason or another during the plague years.

Arundel estate records tell of the animals in this village in 1349, just as the Black Death arrived and again in 1351, just after the first wave had finished. Of course, individual peasants would have owned a few animals of their own, like the "cow and a calf and a cart mare" of Piers Ploughman, but these were not listed in the estate records. In 1349 the only animals the Lord of the Manor, now the Earl of Arundel, had in Clungunford were twelve oxen for ploughing. This indicates that he may well have been using central Clungunford as a breadbasket for the rest of his home farm, which, as we have seen was turned over to grazing alone. The same survey shows that the Earl had 3,500 sheep on the pasture of his home farm. Two years later there were no oxen at all in Clungunford, only one workhorse. Apparently there were not enough labourers left to work the ploughs on the farm. Agriculture in Clungunford was clearly devastated by the Black Death.

We have more information about the animals in the village than about the humans during the Black Death. There are no secular records of plague deaths in Clungunford because the parish registers had not started then, but it is likely that it was the plague which caused the abandonment of the settlements at Broadward and at Tately, where Bob Milner's findings of pottery shards stops after the mid fourteenth century. Three archbishops of Canturbury died of plague in one year in 1348-9. The Rector of Clungunford probably died of it and had to be replaced by John Vincent in 1349, who in turn was replaced by Sir Roger Pyard within two years – perhaps John Vincent had died of plague, too. There are records of people refusing to go near even their own children when they were suffering from the disease and it was getting hard to find clergy to minister to dying parishioners.

After the Black Death, there was, obviously, a sharp drop in the population, which led to an acute labour shortage. There were a series of statutes passed by Parliaments aimed at keeping down the price at which labourers were allowed to sell their labour to the four pence per week current before the Black Death. However the legislation was not effective; labourers simply would not work for that sum any longer.

Rents began to fall and it was difficult to let land. Again we have to rely on church records for information; in1353 the rents of Lilleshall Abbey were down 60% on their 1330 value and in 1375, after the third bout of plague, they were down 60% on their 1353 value. Lack of demand for produce combined with the difficulty in getting fields tilled and the drop in rental value drastically reduced the value of land. The ordinary people of the village, who had begun to feature in the records of court cases concerning land in the times of agricultural boom, no longer went to court aggressively at this time of agricultural recession, when land became less, not more, desirable. It is, therefore, harder to find information about individual peasants in the fourteenth century than it is in the thirteenth century, though we do know that over England as a whole, this was a time when the peasants began to move around from estate to estate looking for the best deal. The lack of continuity in the surnames appearing in Clungunford documents over the next hundred years suggests that there were many changes in the peasant families living here. There is, however, one deed of 1373 concerning land at Tately, which shows that land transfers were being settled in coinage and that there was a professional lawyer in the area. This complicated legal document involves two generations of the Makelin family, whose forebear had signed a de Jay document a hundred and fifty years before – not everyone was on the move[3].

In this time of recession the Earls of Arundel found it impossible to find a tenant for central Clungunford and it was thrown into their huge Clun valley home farm where it remained until the end of the fourteenth century. It was divided into thirds (in value, rather than on the ground) and given as part of a dowry to daughters of the family and so is sometimes recorded as belonging to their husbands. An Inquisition Post Mortem, held soon after Roger had handed it back to the Earl of Arundel in 1346, states that it has been divided between the Ladies Ufflet and Bergaveny, sisters of the Earl, and Richard Leinthall, widower of a third sister. William, the current earl is unlikely to have been interested in it himself, since he was not only Sheriff of Shropshire at the time, but also one of the commanders of the English forces at the Battle of Poitiers in the same year.

At the other end of the social scale, Piers Ploughman described how he had to plough with half starved heifers and we know from the Arundel Estate Survey that there were no oxen on the central Clungunford farm in 1351, so the situation was broadly similar:-

> .....*I saw a poor man by me on the plough hanging.*
> *His coat was of a clout that clary was called;*
> *His hood was full of holes, and his hair cut,*
> *With his nobby shoes patched full thick,*
> *His tongue peeped out as the earth he trod,*
> *His hosen overhung his gaiter on every side*
> *All beslobbered with mire as he the plough followed.*
> *Two mittens so scanty made all of patches,*
> *The fingres were worn and full of mud hung.*
> *This fellow wandered in the muck almost to the ankle,*
> *Four heiffers before him that weak had become;*
> *You could count all their ribs, so wretched they were;*

Fig 18 . *Breaking up clods. The hard labour shown here is more representative of work on a peasant holding than the ploughing for the lord shown in Colour Plate 8.*

Such people could not leave a positive record of their individual lives. However, the Court of their overlord, held at Purslow Hundred House every six months, recorded their misdemeaners – alcohol and sex mostly. What else was there to do in the evenings with no television and only a rush lamp to read by – on the extremely unlikely chance that you knew how to read? The "Hallimote Anglicorum" of the Earls of Arundel records that in 1388 half a dozen Clungunford villagers had been caught brewing illicit ale, for which they were awaiting sentence, and that John Allen, the chaplain, was in deep trouble for selling their concoction.

Brewing was a big issue, as the peasants could hope to make a little extra on the side by selling ale from their homes, but the ale had to be passed as suitable by a "conner", a local official and, only after this, was a sign put outside the house to indicate that ale was being legally sold. Apart from its use in swelling peasant incomes, the "Church Ales" were the chief means by which money was raised for repairs to the fabric and nave of the church. At the "church house" (possibly a predecessor of Glebe Cottage, (see *Colour Plate 15*) ale was brewed legally several times a year for a big, fundraising, knees-up in the church itself, attended by the whole village. The last trace of this medieval use of Clungunford church for partying was when the Easter Feast, given by the Rector, was stopped in 1636.

It is frustrating, but not surprising, that there are no Clungunford documents relating to Lollardy, that early attempt to reform the church and circulate the Bible in English. We know that it was rife in the diocese but, since the bishops did not approve, it had, of necessity, to be kept secret. When the Bishop of Hereford made a "Visitation" to the parish in 1397 there was no mention of Lollardy. It must have been a strain for the Rector to entertain the Bishop and his entourage at Glebe Cottage (see *Colour Plate15*), if that truly was the rectory then, but he was duty bound to do so on such occasions. However, only the laity were allowed to bring matters to the Bishop's attention. This was a great chance for village infighting because everyone had the chance to grass on his neighbour (or on the clergy). The bishop recorded that on this occasion "The parishioners say that Thomas Atkyns is fornicating with Constance Note. Also that David Taelour is commiting adultery with Alison, whom he keeps. (The man appears: he asserts they are married: the woman asserts the same: they have a day to bring letters of attestation), also that Reynald Tresser is fornicating with Katherine who he keeps ... Also that Isobel Harrys is commiting adultery with Bady, the rector's servant." Apart for an intestacy, the Bishop had nothing else to say about Clungunford.

Clungunford was not involved in anything as high profile as the Peasants Revolt of 1381 and, in fact, the revolt was over before news of it could have reached the village. However, it is certain that, after the Black Death and the resulting rise in the status of the labouring classes vis-a-vis the knightly classes, society in Clungunford was never the same again.

5

War and Peace in the Fifteenth Century

No one looking at the view from Clunbury Hill over prosperous Clungunford in 1300 could have guessed how dramatically different it would look in 1400. Not only had expansion ceased but also the area of cultivated land had actually shrunk considerably, so that many of the field strips were fallow or waste. The peasant population had almost halved due to malnutrition, The Black Death and the drift into towns. Many of their "earthfast" houses were collapsing back into heaps of mud and wood.

There were fewer houses in the view than there had been when the population had been nearly twice as big. The recently "assarted" settlement at Tately was no longer inhabited, although some of the fields were farmed, and the settlement at Broadward was deserted, never to be re-colonised in the same way.

Instead of being farmed as a near self sufficient entity, as it had been until 1346, central Clungunford had been worked for the last fifty years as part of a huge farm, which included the whole valley between Clun and the present Clungunford bridge (except for Clunbury), as well as Hopesay and Barlow. This had inevitably affected land usage so that the proportion of arable to pasture had changed once more. As we have seen, there is some evidence to suggest that central Clungunford had been used as a breadbasket for the Clun valley home farm. If so, this change of land usage would have been clear in the view, resulting in fewer animals, except for oxen, and more land under plough below Watling Street.

The pattern of landholding was broadly the same as it had been since 1165 (see **Fig 5**), except that central Clungunford had been part of the tenant-in-chief, the Earl of Arundel's estate between 1346 and 1397. After the eleventh Earl was beheaded in 1397, it was held, as we shall see, by an absentee landowner. His farm had the same boundaries as that of the de Halberdynes in 1300. The roads must have been similar to those in **Fig 16**.

Village society was beginning to change fast by this time and a system of social organisation known as "Bastard Feudalism" was fully developed in Clungunford by 1400. The Earls of Arundel were still the paramount overlords of the Clun valley. They were the "tenants in chief" of the king. The next tier down in the feudal hierarchy, that is to say, the knights, the de Hoptons, de Jays and the Lord of the Manor of central Clungunford (by now an absentee man of business), still held their estates as "fiefs" from the Earls of Arundel. The difference in the late Middle Ages is that, instead of riding to Clun to do "knights service", or employing someone else to do so, the knights simply paid rent – ten pounds a year for each knightly holding.

Below the knights came their free tenants the de Rowtons, de Broomes and de Costons whose names had been appearing in lists of jurors for two hundred years. There were some other free tenants in 1400, but none of them were leading members of the community. Some names describe their own or their forebear's job i.e. Taylor, Carpenter, Salter. These are the clues we get as to the kinds of crafts which had been carried on in the village, although by now the descriptions had usually become merely names passed down from father to son and may not have originated in this village. It is noticeable that the fuller is no longer prominent in 1400. Some surnames obviously originated as "son of"– Richard, Thomas and even Davies, but some, like Unche, Atcokes, Smallbache, Makelin and Bore have no obvious origin although it is clear they are not Norman. The names of the free men who paid tax in 1327 have disappeared. Many must have died of plague but others had simply moved – gone into a town, joined the army or even gone to sea. The court records imply that there were still some old fashioned "customary tenants" in the village, or at least people who paid part of their rent in labour.

The Lord of the Manor of central Clungunford lived in London in 1400 and so there was no good house for him to inhabit, although the earthworks of the de Halberdyne's defensible fort would still have been visible. The de Hopton family were still living at Hopton Castle, which was, of course, out of sight, although it was possible to see their fish pools below the present Broadward Hall. The de Jays lived in the manor at Jay and their small park was visible near Beckjay Mill. There was one real improvement showing in the view for everyone to rejoice in– a fine stone church had been built, with a bell to sound out the Angelus across the valley. There is more information on medieval St Cuthbert's in the chapter on the church.

Having set the local scene at the beginning of the century, it is necessary to look at those events in the national scene, which impinged on the village. Whereas the miseries of fourteenth century Clungunford had been unavoidable, those of the fifteenth were largely man made. There were two different civil wars during the century, each with the same underlying cause, namely uncertainty as to the rightful occupant of the throne. One was the Welsh insurrection under Owen Glendower, which devastated the whole county of Shropshire and the other was that series of aristocratic skirmishes, part of which was later given the romantic name of "The Wars of the Roses." Clungunford was no longer one of the "quietest places under the sun" but was, for once, close to the centre of national affairs. Men from the village clearly formed part of the armies of the warring factions and their families were often on the receiving end of the violence, which was the fallout of warfare. However, it must be said that, in the fifteenth century, war was viewed differently, and many Clungunford men probably welcomed the chance to join an army, even if their families rued the accompanying violence in the neighbourhood.

The Welsh Wars started with an order from the King; "Cease every excuse, and without delay repair in person and in his best array to the person of the King, with knights, esquires and men at arms and archers of the county.......to repair to him in all haste, with their whole power in such force as they may, as Owen Glendower and other rebels of Wales have newly made insurrection, ……..purposing by main force to invade the realm, to destroy the English and other liege subjects of the King". This message to the Sheriff of Shropshire shows Henry IV, having underestimated Glendower's power to unite the Welsh the year before, panicking in the spring of 1401. He had just realised that Glendower was seen, by the Welsh, as the true descendent of three royal Welsh dynasties and as such, the rightful Prince of Wales. He, Henry IV of Lancaster, was seen as the usurper with a weak claim to the English throne. He had deposed Richard II, whom the Welsh preferred and they saw no reason for his son, the future Henry V, to be Prince of Wales. Their anger over his appointment erupted. Under Owen Glendower they waged war against Henry IV, passing frequently through the Borders on the way, plundering as they went.

Another writ (preserved, like the first, in the Close Rolls) demands that a proclamation is made in Shrewsbury " that no man of whatsoever estate, degree or condition shall for any cause upon any pretence take into Wales any corn or other victuals or armour............under pain of forfeiting double the value thereof." From now on, even if the Welsh had been willing to pay for the produce of Clungunford, the villagers were unable to sell it to them without risk of a prohibitive fine – so the Welsh could just help themselves.

Glendower won a decisive battle in 1402 against the Mortimers of Wigmore at Pilleth, three miles south of Knighton. There was a pitched battle at Shrewsbury in 1402 at which Hotspur, son of the Earl of Northumberland, hoped to seize the throne from Henry, helped by Glendower's army, which he expected to march from Wales to join him. However, Glendower did not turn up and Hotspur was killed. A "Commission of Array", designed to raise troops in places like Clungunford for that battle, says that "Owen Glendower and other rebels from those parts, for want of victuals, intend to come suddenly with no small posse to the Marches of the

Fig 19 . *Owen Glendower pursued by English knights*

country to seek victuals and to waste the country". This warned of plans for a terrifying thing called a "chevauchee", which was the means by which both sides used to pay for a war. It involved marching your army through a tract of land with instructions to plunder and especially to take animals to feed the troops.

There is no evidence for Clungunford specifically, but south west Shropshire took the brunt of the Welsh depredations and the king and the (English) Prince of Wales, consequently concentrated much of their energies on this part of the Welsh Border. In April 1404 the burgesses of Shrewsbury petitioned the king for relief because the Welsh had destroyed a third of the town, while Clun was devastated and in 1407 all sheep round Shrewsbury were either killed or driven away by the Welsh. Villages anywhere on the route between Wales and these towns were either "distruitur" i.e. completely burnt out, or had all their stock stolen, or both. Later it was said that a third of the whole county was devasted.

In 1406 Bishop Mascall's register records that fifty two churches west of the Long Mynd were burnt out. Clun and Bucknell were in the list, but not Clungunford. Bishop Mascall's register mentions a commission being set up to report to the Dean of Clun on the delapidations to "the chancel, to all things belonging to the church and to the rectory" in Clungunford in 1405. At first sight this seems to link St Cuthbert's in with the destruction of the fifty two churches, but it was really probably only a demand for repairs after a period of neglect. As we see in the chapter on the church, the timbers of the chancel roof had been put up in 1330 and, since they show no sign of burning, we must conclude that Glendower did St Cuthbert's only minimal damage, if any at all. The clue to this reprieve may well be that Clungunford had a Welsh Rector, Phillip ap David. He applied for a year's leave of absence in order to study in 1406 – presumably while his rectory had the builders in. It could well have been the presence of this Welshman which preserved the church from firing by Glendower's men. This does not necessarily mean that he also protected the secular buildings.

Soon after the war began, there is a description in the Petitions Concerning Wales of a cattle rustling episode at Ludlow. A thousand head of cattle had just been sold to pay for the victuals of the king's army against Glendower, when the herd was hijacked just outside the town by a crowd of more than two hundred men. The cattle were all driven into Ludlow market place, where the thieves "cried havoc" (the medieval call for an army to plunder), and all the cattle were driven off by bands of Ludlovians. In this case the citizens of Ludlow were the beneficiaries of the raid but this was not always the case. Ludlow had town walls, Clungunford did not.

Certainly the stock of Clungunford was vulnerable, because it was close to unusually fine roads (see **Fig 2**). It is true that Edward I had pushed the frontier with Wales back from Offa's Dyke to more or less its present position. Nevertheless, it was too close for comfort unless you could make an accommodation with the Welsh. There is still a track from the west, known as "Glendower's Way", which passes south of Knighton. From there it was a short step for the Welsh to reach the beginning of Botstrete (Watling Street), which led through Clungunford and Stretton and on towards Shrewsbury. The burgers of Shrewsbury complained to Parliament that two thirds of the stock in the suburbs of Shrewsbury had been stolen by the Welsh in 1408.

How much more of the Clungunford stock could have gone? The old drovers road, which passed through the de Hopton's sheep runs, crossed Botstrete at the Crossways and ran on down to the ford on its way to Wales, was also a gift to Welsh stock rustlers. Given the vulnerability of the village, it is possible that Clungunford was one of the border villages which paid protection money to Glendower. Unfortunately, again there is no evidence as to whether this was the case – probably no written record was kept.

Unless you count the very absence of surviving written records as evidence of chaos in the Purslow Hundred, it is hard to know how the village fared during Glendower's War. The records of the local courts, which exist for the late fourteenth century, but are lost for the duration of the war, do start again in 1411. This break in the records is, of course, only circumstantial evidence for chaos in the neighbourhood.

We do know, however, that the Clun valley was certainly deeply infiltrated by the Welsh and the Peace Roll for 1408 records that the miller at Clunbury "commonly received Welsh rebels". He was accused of guiding a group of "rebels" to Purslow, where they had kidnapped John Bloke and taken him off to Wales. It was wise to sit on the fence in a place like Clungunford if you had your ear to the ground and knew about the groundswell of Welsh support for Glendower. After all, back in 1387 Glendower had been a retainer of the Earl of Arundel and therefore may well have had friends in the neighbourhood. The king was right to be suspicious. In 1409, the ravages on his Shropshire estates were so dreadful that the Earl of Arundel joined with other Shropshire barons in asking the king to grant permission for them to make a separate treaty with the Welsh. Permission was refused, but the violence in this part of the Marches did, in fact, die down even before Glendower died in 1415.

The Lord of the Manor of central Clungunford was, as we have seen, the Earl of Arundel himself for over fifty years after 1346. However, when the eleventh earl was beheaded in 1397, the land returned to the crown. Before it could be restored to his son with the rest of the estate, a shrewd man of business in the king's employ seized his chance. Blakeway records that a certain William Ryman was given a tenancy of the Manor and Advowson of Clungunford in 1399 and he remained the (absentee) Lord of the Manor for over thirty years. He was to be given something else instead should he be "disturbed" by a member of the Arundel family. However, their attempts to disturb him failed. So, for the first thirty years of the fifteenth century whatever rents Clungunford was able to produce, went to this stranger from London. Although as late as 1431 "The Feudal Aid" records Clungunford as still "belonging" in the feudal sense, to the Arundels, William Ryman was, in practice, the Lord of the Manor during the first third of the century.

He appears often in the Close and Patent Rolls, so we know quite a bit about him. He married a woman called Elizabeth, who, being born in the 1360s, was probably older than he was and bore him no children to inherit the lease of Clungunford. But his marriage was a shrewd move. She had been nanny and probably wet nurse to the future King Henry V. William Ryman was therefore trusted totally by Henry V as the husband of his beloved old nanny. He had acquired the lease of Clungunford and another small property in Shrewsbury under Henry 1V, but once Henry V came to the throne Ryman's rise was meteoric.

Among many other jobs, he was employed at Chichester as "Controller of the petty custom, the subsidy of the wools, hides and wool-fells" in 1413 provided he executed the office in person. This posting was not renewed, but it shows how useful his experience with a wool producing Clun valley village had been; he had become a wool expert among his other talents and it is possible that he had wanted Clungunford because he could see that its sheep farming potential had not been fully exploited under the Earl's bailiffs. The fact that he had property at Calais, where the Company of the Wool Staple was usually situated in order to police the wool trade, does suggest that he had more than a passing interest in wool production. However, no evidence has come to light to suggest that the cloth making industry, which had existed in the village before the Black Death, was revived while Ryman was Lord of the Manor.

In 1415 he was one of the "Auditors of the accounts of the Exchequer to audit the accounts of the King's chamberlain in North Wales and Chester, and to place the King's farms there at an advantage". The Purslow Court rolls for these years show just how good he was at placing his own farm at an advantage. He was soon called "Esquire" and was to audit the accounts of "Chamberlains, receivers, bailiffs, ringilds and other ministers." He was to be paid six shillings and eight pence a day for wages and expenses from the day of his departure from the City of London until his return there "as well as a ten pound yearly fee with full power of charging, allowing and demising forms and selling casual profits." This certainly proves that he did not live in Clungunford, although he no doubt found it to have been on the route to North Wales when claiming his expenses from the King. With such powerful royal connections he must have been a formidable figure when he appeared in Shropshire

Once the worst of Glendower's depredations were over, local records begin again and cases appearing in Ryman's Manorial Court show his bailiff ruling with a rod of iron. The villagers are no longer in trouble merely for illicit brewing or failing to appear in court as they had been under the Earl of Arundel's bailiff. In 1411 they are all in disgrace for not using the Lord of the Manor's mill for grinding their grain (for which privilege they had to pay), and for grinding their own at home, as they said they had always done before under the Earls of Arundel. Ryman was determined to extract every last penny.

The picture of village life given in Ryman's court rolls shows how a clever businessman could manipulate the manorial system, always making it work to his own gain. Where it still existed, the old Norman system of villeinage, that is to say payment of rent by days of labour on the lord's farm, could be used to the landlord's advantage, while newer systems, like copyhold leases, rent paid in coinage or kind, could also be made to work in his favour. These records clearly show both old and new systems working at the same time in Clungunford.

In 1411 Thomas Atcoke had apparently died since the last court was held and not only was his heir to pay "heriot" (a kind of feudal inheritance tax) in the form of a heifer, which was Atcoke's only animal, but also the new tenant, Richard Unche, had to pay an entry fee of seven shillings. These men were still "customary tenants" and therefore could not build up much capital. If the heifer was truly Atcoke's only animal and there was, as we are told, no money left to pay the remaining tax bill, then any son Atcoke may have had would not have been able to afford the entry fee for the house and half virgate of land (30 acres), even though the rent was merely the "labour owed by custom " to the lord. Ryman was thus able to prevent peasants inheriting land and so becoming relatively powerful.

In 1414 we find, in the Roll of the Court Leet for Clungunford, that a long list of villagers are fined from two to four pence because they had not given to Thomas Atcoke a quantity of corn. The main problem was not that the deceased Thomas or his heirs were lacking in corn, but that he should have handed over half the said corn to Ryman's bailiff. The fines levied at this court, of course, went into Ryman's pocket and they more than compensated for the corn. At the same court Philip (ap David), the Rector and John de Rowton were fined two pence because they had failed to close their fences or gates on the due day. Within a system of strip farming it clearly was extremely detrimental to the whole community if one or two members failed to abide by the rules and let their stock wander over other peoples' winter wheat in January (the date of the court). In some ways this court was a facility for the villagers, not only for their lord.

In the Roll of 1416 Roger Symes is recorded as surrendering into the hand of the lord two houses and a virgate and a half of land (90 acres) and paying two shillings for the privilege. This land was held by "copyhold", a new form of tenure by which the deeds were held by the Manorial Court and the rent was paid in coinage rather than labour. It was said to be the responsibility of "the villata" to discover about the dilapidations to Symes' houses and they are given only one day to do so. It is interesting that, while Ryman gets the rent, the peasants have the responsibility!

A tough landlord had some real advantages for the village. Although the "unfree" tenants, who had to come to Ryman's court, were punished for their petty misdemeanors, the records for the Assize Court show far more violent crime for all the surrounding villages. Even when the Welsh were not around, there was much cattle rustling by the locals at Kempton and Edgton, "laying in wait" in order to kill all over the place and Ludlow was a very murderous town. But no violent crime or stock thieving is recorded for Clungunford itself at this time although it is quite clear that the rest of the neighbourhood was alive with highwaymen and stock rustlers.

It is noticeable that the Ryman years constituted the only long phase between 1341 and 1513 during which the parish is only once in the Bishop's list of parishes exempt from the tithe on account of poverty. Of course much of the tithe was due from de Jay and de Hopton land so he cannot be given all the credit. What it does show is that, once the Welsh Wars were over, it was perfectly possible to manage the farmland of central Clungunford well in the fifteenth century and it was merely that, for the rest of the century, nobody took the trouble to do so. The de Hoptons, of course thrived, but it can no longer be said that their income depended on the Hopton estate alone. The de Jays clearly recovered from the traumas of the previous century for Sir Rowland was able to build a particularly fine house, now known as Manor Farm Bedstone, just before 1450, but that is outside the scope of this history.

William Ryman's use of the advowson of the church was creative to say the least and may in some important ways have worked to the advantage of the villagers. Although, Welshmen were not allowed to work in England until 1536, sometime before 1405, Ryman in his capacity as Lord of the Manor and owner of the advowson, somehow managed to appoint a Welsh Rector.

As we have suggested before, this may have been crucial in protecting the fabric of the church. An even more mysterious fact about his ownership of the advowson is that he managed to keep the Bishop away. Bishops Mascall, Lacy and Spofford had "Visitations" to all the surrounding parishes but, for a reason nobody can understand, not to Clungunford.

While he was Lord of the Manor a second bell was given to the church. Bearing in mind that the de Hoptons and de Jays had the advowsons of Hopton Castle and Bedstone churches, who else would have had enough money to commission such a bell for St Cuthberts? There is more information about this bell in the chapter on the church.

.

Ryman was Lord of the Manor of Clungunford during the early skirmishes leading up to the "The Wars of the Roses". The two factions, now known as the white rose of York and the red rose of Lancaster (rival claimants to the throne), were both represented in the neighbourhood, and at one stage even within the parish itself. Even if there was no "Battle of Clungunford", the armies passed along Botsrete, often pillaging as they went, while Ludlow Castle, the bastion of the Yorkists, was less than ten miles away.

From 1430 – 1455 there was only political jockeying around the village between supporters of the Yorkists and Lancastrians, but serious fighting broke out in 1455 at the Battle of St Albans and finished only when Henry Tudor gained the throne in 1485 at the Battle of Bosworth Field. One of the two battles which most affected Clungunford, was the Battle of Ludford Bridge in 1459, when Ludlow was pillaged. The other was the Battle of Mortimers Cross in 1461, where Sir Walter de Hopton took men from his estates to fight. Sir Richard Corbet, heir to Shelderton, fought at Bosworth Field. Such was the culture of war in those times that it may well be that the villagers actually welcomed the chance of joining an army, with its promise of pay and plunder – that might have seemed better than the life of a ploughman.

The Earls of Arundel supported the red rose of Lancaster, that is to say the Kings Henry IV, V and VI. Therefore Clun was a Lancastrian stronghold and the Lord of Clungunford Manor, William Ryman, was also a keen Lancastrian for as long as Henry V promoted his interests, so central Clungunford supported the red rose during that reign. The de Hoptons, were Lancastrian, too, although they did occasionally marry into Yorkist families, so Shelderton was usually supposed to support the red rose. However, Ryman changed sides in the 1430s and after that, Clungunford dwellers must have had to be extremely careful over what they said and to whom, since half the parish was Lancastrian and the other half was now Yorkist in the run up to the real fighting.

Ryman was a political person and was soon involved, playing one person off against another and central Clungunford became a pawn in this game. The land, astride that good road, Botstrete (Watling Street), and close to Ludlow Castle, which became the Duke of York's headquarters, was in such a strategic position that the ownership of the village became a political issue. Having become deserted by Henry VI, who had turned a deaf ear to pleas in favour of his father's former nanny and her husband, Ryman became close not only to the great Yorkist, William Burley, sometime Speaker of the House of Commons, but also to the Duke of York himself. He is shown in the Patent Rolls by the early 1430s as still hanging on to the centre of the village and the advowson against counter claims from the Earl's sisters and their heirs, the Lady Bergevenny and Sir Rowland Leinthall, as he had done in 1416. In 1432 Sir Rowland claimed the advowson of the church, but in the following year he was routed in court by Ryman. We do have to ask why such a rich man as Sir Rowland bothered to argue over the advowson and a fraction of the rents of a small part of such a village. After all, he had already made enough money, from the ransoms of the French prisoners he had taken at the Battle of Agincourt, to enable him to build a house the size of Hampton Court in Herefordshire. Clungunford rents were peanuts to him. He was a Lancastrian and he wanted the manor and advowson for political reasons – it was conveniently close to Ludlow Castle.

The row in 1432 between Sir Rowland and Ryman was over the appointment of the Rector, each favouring a different candidate. There is obviously far more in this than meets the eye, but the details of what lay behind the row are frustratingly obscure. It is clearly a story of political intrigue, rather than of religious belief. Thirty years earlier, we might have considered the question of one clergyman approving the bible in English as an issue in the appointment of a new Rector, but by 1430 this was not of interest at Sir Rowland's level in society. Suffice it to say that the issue went to court at Westminster and was decided in William Ryman's favour. By now a Yorkist, he could whisper in the Duke of York's ear in Ludlow and annoy Sir Rowland by holding on to his rightful inheritance – a "moitie" of Clungunford and the right to appoint the Rector.

Soon Ryman transferred the Manor of Clungunford into a trust, with himself, William Burley, and the Duke of York as trustees. Having deserted the Lancastrian cause, he was now moving in the highest possible Yorkist circles. The jockeying for position was happening, in the 1430s, not just in the neighbourhood but actually within Clungunford itself. The Lancastrian de Hoptons had part of their estate within the parish of St Cuthbert's church, of which the newly Yorkist William Ryman had the advowson of the church.

In 1433 the trustees sold the Manor of Clungunford to William Burley, no doubt at a price favourable to Ryman, who had, after all, been only a tenant himself, as the "Feudal Aid" of 1431, which includes it in the Arundel fief, proves. For over a hundred years this part of the village belonged to William Burley, sometime Speaker of the House of Commons, and to his heirs, none of whom were closely enough involved to foster its prosperity in the way earlier owners had done. Perhaps it is for this reason that there is no record of any one living in the village being actively involved in the cloth trade. Such a cottage industry, which flourished as close as Ludlow, did need organisation and more constant supervision than would interest an absentee landlord. The only record of the involvement in the cloth trade (as opposed to merely the wool trade) of anyone from Clungunford comes in the records of the Clungunwas family, weavers, who lived in the fine medieval house next to Stone House at the bottom of Corve Street, Ludlow, in the fifteenth century. They must, surely, have come from Clungunford originally. Unfortunately, the Will of Thomas Clungunwas of 1543 makes no mention of any cousins in the village.

The lawlessness, which was rife in the neighbourhood, was not limited to peasants, vagabonds and paupers. The upper classes behaved outrageously by our standards. The Walter de Hopton who held Shelderton in the early fifteenth century, is noted in the Peace Rolls as having been pardoned by the king for all his crimes, except murder and rape, before being given the job of seeking out criminals in the Welsh Borders in 1408. However, by 1460 his descendent, another Walter, was pardoned of all his crimes, (without excluding murder and rape), before being given the same job by Henry VI, so desperate was the king to enforce some sort of order in the neighbourhood. This same Walter, the following year, took soldiers from the Hopton estate, which of course included Shelderton, to fight the battle at Mortimer's Cross, which divested Henry of his throne and gave it to Edward IV.

The father-in–law of Elizabeth de Hopton (to whom we shall return soon), Sir Thomas Corbet, is described in the Assize Roll of 1412 as being accused with others of going "armed and arrayed in warlike manner to the number of forty men" and to have "entered the house of the parson of Edgmond and carried away his clothes.... and his maser cups bound with silver, and gilt cups of silver and gilt, his oxen and 200 sheep". And this was at the time when his father was Sheriff of the county. A court appearance for such a crime did nothing to harm his career. He became Sheriff in 1428 and was Member of Parliament for the county in 1429

There is no doubt that the tenants of these violent families experienced the rough side of their lords' characters. It would be interesting to know whether the inhabitants of central Clungunford, managed so strictly by Ryman, envied or pitied their neighbours at Shelderton, whose lord was a lawless knight. True, much depended on the character of the bailiff, but bailiffs got their orders. As late as 1482, the Patent Rolls record a general pardon for Robert Corbet, "late of Hopton by Clun", for all offences committed by him before November 18th, whereas one of his tenants, "Richard Bugell of Shelderton, Knave" had his pardon revoked in 1477.

Nor did this lawlessness stop at the gentry – in 1414, there is a letter from the king saying that some King's Bench judges have been dispatched to Shropshire to "reduce affrays and riots" and in particular they are to settle the disputes between Lord Furnival and the overlord of Clungunford, the twelfth Earl of Arundel. The lawlessness in the neighbourhood continued throughout the century. The establishment of The Council of the Marches in the 1470s may have helped a little, but the neighbourhood was not really well controlled until the next century. This may well be the reason that there are no surviving manorial rolls from 1422, when the Arundels moved to Sussex, until 1500.

Another effect of all the war-mongering was, obviously, an increased death rate in the male population. We have no specific records of individual peasants fighting in specific battles, as we sometimes do for their lords, but they did form the greater part of any army and were killed in the fierce battles such as Mortimers Cross in 1461, where they were lightly armed and far more vulnerable than the mounted knights (see **Fig 7**).

They are likely to have formed part of the Lancastrian army, which defeated the Yorkists at Ludford. Cannon were drawn up by the Teme, possibly for the first time in the neighbourhood, but there was no serious fighting and the reward for joining the army was to be allowed to pillage Ludlow. "Havoc" was cried again in the market square and the town was pillaged "to the bare walls".

The Clungunford peasants involvement in this event and in much other fighting in the neighbourhood, as well as further afield, can be assumed, but no list of a muster survives.

Add to death on the battlefield, the movement of people into the towns to escape rural poverty and the demographic downturn which had begun after the agricultural disasters a century before and had been accelerated by the death of a third of the population during the outbreaks of the Black Death and you have a real change in society. Bob Milners' pottery finds at Tately are material evidence of the decline in population: he has found nothing there dating from after the Black Death until after 1500. Presumably that settlement was abandoned for the whole of the fifteenth century, as was the one at Broadward.

It is possible to trace, in the Patent and Close Rolls, the shortage of male heirs among the gentry. It is true that we rarely know the cause of the death of their sons, but families, who had dominated life in the neighbourhood since a generation or two after Domesday Book, and whose importance in village life is explained at the beginning of Chapter 2, undoubtedly died out in the fifteenth century. Their land is divided between their daughters, who, although born and brought up in the village or close by, usually moved away when they married and, of course, changed their names. Luckily following their "blood-lines" is not

Fig 20. Knight in the kind of armour he would have worn at the Battle of Ludford Bridge in 1459.

a serious problem because the Clarenceaux Herald was dispatched to prosperous Shropshire in 1623 to look into the rash of requests from local families to be considered as gentry now that they had made their fortunes. They were eager to tell the Herald about their ancestors. These families had to provide documentary evidence to support their claims going back several generations and some of these pedigrees traced the families back to Clungunford in the Middle Ages. In "The Visitation of Shropshire" of 1623 we see the histories of the girls who had left Clungunford in late medieval times as well as the family trees of their husbands, who usually decided not to live at the property of the heiress they had married. They were too involved in their trade in Shrewsbury, or their life as leading London lawyers to do so.

Elizabeth, only child of the last de Hopton of Hopton Castle, who was born before 1422 and died in 1499, married in the mid fifteenth century, Roger Corbet, the son of Thomas Corbet, whom we have met before as the leader of the gang who beat up a rector in 1412. The Corbets had needed to marry into money and Elizabeth was the heiress of the Lucy family as well as the de Hoptons, so she brought with her two estates. It could well have been Elizabeth who was responsible for the re-afforestation of the other side of Shelderton Rock, "Corbet's Wood". This plantation stretched from Ferney Dingle over to Green Lanes and from below Tately down to the boundary with Wetmore. Part of this wood was felled in the seventeenth century to allow for the building of Ferney Hall and to allow space for its pleasure grounds. Part of it is still shown as standing on eighteenth century maps. Thus the Corbets, unlike the other families into which Clungunford heiresses married, did make a positive mark on the landscape, even if they never allowed any tenant to buy land or build a good house.

Elizabeth de Hopton outlived her first husband by thirty two years and married twice more, leading a hazardous life, since both her second and her third husbands were beheaded, the last one, unfortunately, before he could see his brother pluck the crown of England from a thorn bush and set it on the head of Henry Tudor, so ending the Wars of the Roses. Her second husband, the Earl of Worcester, was known as "Butcher Tiptoft", on account of the unusually cruel ways in which he had his enemies put to death – the Earl of Oxford, for instance, was disembowelled, castrated and then burnt while still alive. She was clearly a stalwart lady, but even so she may have felt the need to retire to Hopton Castle occasionally. The Hopton estate, including Shederton, remained in her name until her death in 1499.

Fig 21. *Nobles hunting with hounds and hawks in about 1430 – the year in which the de Hopton's Right of Free Warren over Shelderton was confirmed.*

Hopton was an extremely small part of the Corbet estates, but it seems that someone took particular care of it and, since it remained in Elizabeth's name until she died in 1499, it is likely that she used it as her dower house. In 1430 her father had arranged for Parliament to reconfirm the right of "free warren" over Shelderton and Broadward, which had been granted to his forbear in the twelfth century. Evidently there had been some objections. This right of "free warren" extended over Hopton Titterhill as well as over the newly afforested area at Shelderton, which must have provided good cover for game. It was a fine hunting estate in the fifteenth century. In 1482 her son, Sir Richard Corbet, was described as "late of Hopton", so we may assume that he had moved away, and that Hopton Castle was not the main home of the senior branch of the Corbets. They probably used it and the land at Shelderton as the equivalent of a modern shooting estate, just as the Arundels used Clun Castle after their move to Arundel Castle – as a holiday home. We shall never know if "Butcher Tiptoft" ever went hawking at Shelderton. Sir Richard died before his mother and never inherited Shelderton, which went to his son Sir Robert Corbet in 1499.

Fig 22. *Tomb of Sir Robert Corbet, owner of Shelderton. Moreton Corbet church.*

The two de Jay girls, Eleanor and Elizabeth, whose father, Sir Rowland, had married in 1451, were last of their surname. They married and moved away before the end of the century. Eleanor married Thomas Jennings of Walliborne. Elizabeth married the Shrewsbury iron founder, Robert Knight. It seems that the advowson of Bedstone Church was left to both daughters because descendants of both are recorded as having continued to present the Rectors there. Elizabeth took the possession of the land at Beckjay with her. Elizabeth and Roberts' daughter, Katherine, married into the Ireland family, who still claimed their half share of the Bedstone advowson in 1708. It was relations of Elizabeth de Jay's husband, the Knight family, iron founders of Shrewsbury, who moved to Downton and worked the forge there and finally in the eighteenth century built Downton Castle and established the "picturesque landscape". The Knights still owned most of Beckjay until 1863, although the land was, of course, farmed by tenants in the intervening centuries.

Sir William Burley, who was born at Broncroft Castle and bought central Clungunford in 1433 from William Ryman, was Sheriff of Shropshire and Member of Parliament, eventually becoming Speaker, as well as being a successful London lawyer. As his fortunes prospered he sought to enlarge his Shropshire estate, first by buying the Manor of Wistanstow and then that of Clungunford as well as other land.

He died in 1461 and his heirs in Clungunford were his daughter, Joanna and his grandson William Trussel, son of Elizabeth Trussel (nee Burley). It is probable that the Clungunford rents and advowson had already been part of his daughters' dowries when they married their lawyer husbands, Sir William Trussel and Sir Thomas Littleton[1].

Thus for a hundred years, from the mid fifteenth until the mid sixteenth century, the central part of the village belonged to successful politicians and lawyers (either directly or through their wives' estates) and they, of necessity had to work elsewhere. Ease of access along Botsrete clearly contributed to the desirability of Clungunford as a bit of real estate for any absentee landlord. Sir William Littleton, who inherited half the village through his mother, was a Knight of the Bath and wrote the "New Tenures", one of the great legal books of all time, which clarified the types of landholding which had grown up in a disorganised manner as the feudal system collapsed. However, he does not seem to have shared his expertise with the tenantry of Clungunford; one of the reasons that the village was slow to prosper was that the leases were too short to make investment in time or money worthwhile.

However, at the end of the fifteenth century we do find in Clungunford a new group of people who, even if we cannot describe any of them as rich, did form the beginnings of a middle class. The absence of a Lord of the Manor meant no doubt, that then, as now, a greater number of the inhabitants felt themselves able to hold a responsible part in village life. Also depopulation had resulted in lower land values, so that more people could afford to pay a modern type of rent for their properties, even if the leases were unsatisfactory and the land was not for sale. The names of these people appear among the lists of jurors at Purslow. These lists no longer contain only the de Costons, de Rowtons etc. There are Fillys and Mattes and as well as Makelins representing Clungunford. There were also a dozen people of some substance from Clungunford, who had their wills proved at Hereford. Unfortunately, all these wills were destroyed when they were stored in the cathedral at the same time as Oliver Cromwell's hungry horses. We only have a list of the names: William Longfield, the tenant at Abcott, Richard Voler, John Smallbache whose descendents lived at Broome, Sir William Hopkins, the Rector, as well as John Rowton, Geoffry Clement, Agnes Dunne, Thomas Bebbe, Thomas Mattes and a group of people whose forbears may have been village craftsmen – all called John – Wever, Turner and Taylor. Some of the people who we might call middle class in the next century came from these families.

The diminished population, was another of the causes of the prolonged poverty of the central area of the village, as described in the Bishop's register. In 1435, 1445, 1461, 1474 and 1492 the parish is listed as being too poor to pay its taxes to the Bishop. Henry VII forced it to pay the Great Royal Subsidy in 1489, but at six shillings and eight pence, its assessment was lower than that of all the surrounding villages. However, the problems caused by depopulation were exacerbated by the fact that the lawyers and politicians, who were the absentee landlords after 1433, had little interest in good farm management, or in encouraging small scale cloth manufacture. The manor was merely an investment for them. Even for the Corbets, Shelderton may have been of interest only as a hunting ground and the newly planted "Corbet's Wood" would not have brought employment to the village once it was planted up. For this reason Clungunford was slow, by Shropshire standards, to take advantage of the revival of farming fortunes which accompanied the relatively settled Tudor times at the end of the Wars of the Roses.

6

The Middle Class and the Reformation

The first half of the sixteenth century saw Clungunford begin to recover from the low level to which it had sunk during the preceding two centuries. The violence, which had been such a problem in the in the previous century, was gradually brought under control by the Council of the Marches, based at Ludlow Castle. The last time Clungunford is listed in the bishop's register as being too poor to pay tithes is in 1513, when it was said to be "depauperata" on account of floods and fires. The village does not seem to have been still deeply involved in the English cloth trade, which so enriched areas like East Anglia and the Cotswolds in the fifteenth century. In the surviving sixteenth century Clungunford Wills there is no mention of any equipment connected with the cloth trade. Before the Black Death, Clungunford, with its rich fuller and good grazing, was involved with both wool and cloth trades but it seems that the absentee landlords never encouraged this cottage industry but rather preferred the farmers on their land to concentrate, either on producing grain or raising sheep and, to a lesser extent, cattle. It is, however, not impossible that it was through some aspect of the cloth trade that the only country gentleman to appear in the village in this period made the money to start his family's upward movement.

Once agriculture became profitable again and the market for the long staple wool of the Clun sheep was assured in the more settled Tudor times, the village began to thrive. The price of sheep everywhere is said to have quadrupled between 1500 and 1550, and records of the sheep sold from the Clungunford flock suggest that the rise was even greater here. The village was no longer too poor to pay its tithes. This was a period of great social change, when the peasants escaped almost entirely from the feudal system and a middle class developed, several families building up large farms.

It is interesting that the peasant names in sixteenth century court records are, mostly, different from those a hundred years earlier. Although the knightly families remained the same for hundreds of years, after the Black Death, many of the peasant families seem to have moved around so that only the Makelins, Bores, Marets and Bebes and a few others remain constant and, of these, only the Makelins appear for several hundred years. This is in marked contrast to their landlords. Another thing suggested by the names in these records is that the Anglo Saxon and Norman populations remained separate in Clungunford for over four hundred years after the Conquest, one as peasant and the other as lord. This early form of apartheid changed in Tudor times.

Starting at the bottom of the social scale, we can discover the names of the peasants, or at least those who were in trouble with the courts. The records of the Purslow Hundred Courts survive sporadically, in legible form, from 1500 to 1520; the names which most frequently appear in the Clungunford section are Hynston, Higgs, Shemeth, Don and Eyton. William Eyton's crime is always non-appearance! In fact this was an increasing problem at Purslow, as the feudal lords' courts held less respect in Tudor times. People with Anglo Saxon names like Hegys, Gettys and Shemeth were in trouble for illegally slaughtering meat, which was now becoming an important part of the peasant diet. Brewing, as ever the favourite pastime in the village, was held against John Shemeth and Richard Higgs. Women, as is usual in Clungunford, appear in court, as well as men. In 1513 Esabel Holland was fined four pence for assaulting Margaret Bronton. In October 1500 the whole "villata" of Clungunford was fined twelve pence for falsely accusing Thomas Watters. The jury of twelve local men heard the trial and found him not guilty. Slander was unacceptable.

The court held at Purslow Hundred House dealt with a mixture of village business on the same day so that we find items concerned with the regulation of normal village life appearing on the same piece of parchment as crimes, for example, arrangements were made for animals from "the flock" to be sold to raise money for the common cause, sometimes sheep, sometimes a pig and once "a mare from the herd", which was valued at twenty pence; evidently the villagers were breeding horses in 1520. As late as 1519 we find Huw Rawling's heir having to pay the old inheritance tax of a "heriot", that is to say, his best cow. Pockets of feudalism were still alive.

Unfortunately we do not hear much more about the poorer peasants, out of court, until the Parish Registers start, but in the next bracket up we find a group of people rich enough to have moveable possessions worth over ten pounds and thus having to pay tax at the Lay Subsidies raised in 1524-5 to pay for Henry VIII's extravagances, such as the Field of the Cloth of Gold and war with France. In this group is John Bebbe, the tax collector from Broadward and William Maret from Abcott, as well as a John Davyes, who is probably the man who left an interesting Will in 1544. Roger Page, the juror, paid at a lower rate still, as did Roger Rowton, a somewhat impoverished descendant of the original Rowton family, who now lived at Broadward, the senior branch of the de Rowton family having died out in the fifteenth century.

Fig 23. *A parchment roll from Purslow Hundred Court 1519. Although court rolls for Clungunford exist from the 1380s, the earlier rolls are very fragile[1].*

John Bore had more possessions than anyone else in Clungunford in 1524, for he was assessed at seven pounds – two pounds more than John Cornes. To put this in perspective, he paid a third of the sum paid by Thomas Vernon, who owned the Stokesay estate including Stokesay Castle. John Bore may not have been a major landowner, but he was a peasant working his way into the new middle class. He may possibly have lived in the previous building on the site of the present Church Farm, although it is unlikely that he owned it. Had he done so, he would have rebuilt it, but the dendrochronologists' tests, show that the rebuild on that site did not happen until the end of the century. There is no evidence as to what his other valuable possessions were but a large flock of sheep is the most likely thing. Sheep were worth two shillings each if they were fine animals bred in the Clun valley and the price was always rising. To qualify as a taxpayer at all in 1524 he would have needed a flock of a hundred but he must have had a far larger one to justify such a big tax bill. This John Bore may, or may not, have been a member of the Baugh family of Aldon who came to prominence later in the century and have appeared occasionally in earlier documents, but he certainly was the man found guilty of assault at the Purslow Court in both 1513 and 1514. He had an on-going feud with his neighbour Huw Cornes, which was fought out on The King's Highway (Watling Street). Huw was always fined twelve pence, that is to say one and a half times the value of the sow he was keeping for the village and four times as much as his neighbour, so he no doubt started the fights. When Huw was in court for the same offence six months later he was fined sixteen pence for re-offending. The implication of all this is that Huw was the aggressor and John merely fought back.

The Cornes family lived at Rowton in the predecessor of the present Rowton Grange. The cellar of the earlier building remains under part of the western cross-wing. It was a smaller, lower building than the one which stands today. The exterior weathering high on the hall gable suggests that the roof of the 1571 hall stood higher than the older building, against which it was built, for at least twenty years. Again, although the Cornes family were thriving, they did not rebuild their house until later in the century, which suggests that they were still tenants until the middle of the century. John Cornes, who paid five pounds tax at Rowton in 1524, was probably Huw's father. In 1556 their land to the west of Botstret (Watling Street) is referred to in a marriage settlement of the Dunne family. Huw did leave a Will, but although it was listed, it evidently did not survive the weeks during which it was kept in Hereford Cathedral at the same time as Oliver Cromwell's horses.

Fig 24. *Medieval Publican like William Longfield of Abcott*

Unfortunately, the same can be said of the Will of William Longfield. The Longfields were tenants at Abcott from about 1490 until they died out in 1530, paying tax at a lower rate than the Bores or the Cornes. William was the chief brewer in the village and seems to have been keeping a pub at Abcott. By 1520 the fines recorded at the Hundred Court for brewing were, in reality, a licence fee. William Longfield was fined twice as much as William Morris and Roger Page and the

Maret brothers, who were probably only selling ale from their own houses, as opposed to running a pub.

John Makelin, the Corbets' tenant at Shelderton, paid over five pounds tax and therefore was one of the richest men in the village, second only to John Bore. The first record of the Makelins in Clungunford is in 1230 and the last in 1990, when John Makelin was buried in the churchyard, followed by his wife, Nancy, a year later. However, they moved out of the parish (although not far out) from the latter part of the seventeenth century for two hundred years. It is surprising that one of the two most ancient families in the village did not make a permanent mark on the landscape. The clue to this puzzle, in Tudor times at any rate, is the lack of freehold land available in the Shelderton part of the parish, where the richest member of the family was then living. The Corbets descendants did not sell off any of their Shelderton estate until the 1650s and John Barker's Will shows that, in the mid sixteenth century, they were giving their tenants only the unpopular twenty one year leases, rather than the preferred leases, which lasted until the last survivor of three named people died. In addition, there was no church land to be sold at Shelderton when the monasteries were dissolved. Therefore, the Makelins could not buy a freehold of former monastic land as the Morrises did at Abcott. Thus there was no incentive for them to build a good house, since there was no certainty that their descendants would be able to live in it. The best that could be hoped for there was that the Corbets would waive three years' rent, provided the tenant built a house on the land he was renting. This would only pay for the building of a modest dwelling at a time when skilled labour was becoming increasingly expensive to hire.

There is no mention in the Lay Subsidy assessment of the Listers of Rowton, who were well connected people, marrying into the leading Shropshire families. They are described in Hardwick's pedigrees as having bought Rowton in 1482, but they must have bought that part of Rowton which lies outside the parish of Clungunford, namely Rowton Manor. Nor is there mention in the Lay Subsidy assessment of the Dunnes. Perhaps they had not arrived by 1525, but they were certainly well established by 1556, the date of a marriage settlement with the Smallman family of Broome. Apart from the complicated land swaps recorded in the Marriage Settlement[2], Edward Smallman was to give to "Edward and Elizabeth on the day of their marriage twenty pounds and her array, her bedde and borde, covered after the custom of the countrey" (see **Fig 25**). Although some of their land lay outside the parish, the Dunnes evidently felt themselves to be connected with Clungunford because they left money "for the poor of Clungunford" in later Wills.

The most interesting of all the families mentioned in the Lay Subsidy assessment of 1525 were the Morrises. They lived at the house now known as Abcott Manor (see ***Colour Plate 11***) and were unique in Clungunford because they were the only rich peasants who aspired to become English Country Gentlemen in the sixteenth century. A more detailed account of this house comes in the chapter on Abcott Manor. There are many puzzles about Abcott and the Morrises. How did William Morris make his money and where did he come from? At what stage did the family build up the three hundred acres, which belonged to them in the next century? Hardwick has William coming from Clun in his "Pedigrees", but he provides no evidence for this. Certainly a William Morris came to live in Abcott between the 1524 Lay Subsidy, in which he does not appear, and the 1525 one, in which he does. However, he is not a rich man because he was assessed for tax at only just over two pounds – much the same as the handful of other tax paying peasants at Abcott that year. If this is the same William Morris who built Abcott Manor, he must either have had a rich father or made a great deal of money between 1525 and 1540. "In the cloth trade" would be the obvious answer to the question about his newly acquired wealth, but there is no mention in his Will of either sheep or equipment for making cloth or yarn, although many other sorts of possessions are mentioned. It would be mere conjecture to say that he had a huge flock of sheep and many looms, which he left to his son, Thomas, his residuary legatee, and therefore did not need to describe in his Will, and that his "overseer", William Page, was overseeing a local cottage industry and organising piecework carding, spinning and weaving. It is safer to assume that he had a huge flock of sheep. So far, there is no certain answer to the question of how he made his money, nor of exactly when the family were able to buy the additional land, which they definitely owned in the next century.

The Will of William Morris, who died in 1549, is worth quoting at length. Unfortunately, he does not describe his new house, nor its furnishings, nor the farming or business enterprises which underpinned his rise in society, because he leaves everything not specifically mentioned to his eldest son, Thomas. Either this Thomas, or his son, who was also called Thomas, is noted in the Parish registers as dying in 1596. We get a full description of all the possessions which William did not leave to his son, as well as some idea of his concerns. He leaves two pence "to the poor men's chest" and four pence to the "mother church at Hereford" before going on to say "Also I bequeath to my ghostly father (i.e. to my confessor), Sir William Shingler, two shillings and four pence to pray for me". Evidently he had not heard, or would not accept, that "chantries", saying prayers for the souls of the dead, had been abolished two years before, nor that Confession was frowned upon by the new Protestant authorities. He must have had mixed feelings about the Reformation. On the one hand it had allowed him to buy his land, but on the other hand, he had doubts as to whether the new type of sacraments (or rather the lack of them) would work. It was extremely hard for a devout old man like this to have all his beliefs turned upside down by the Protestant Reformation.

Fig 25. *Interior of a late medieval house including a bed, such as the one mentioned in William Morris's Will and in the Dunne Marriage Settlement.*

He goes on to describe some of his worldly possessions:- "I bequeath to Anne, my son's daughter, a red cow, a pot and a pan with six pottery dishes and a wild bay mare with a star on her forehead. Item, I bequeath to Thomas, my son's son, a great pot, with a mild heifer and two silver spoons (which are) at pledge with Cock's of Ludlow for 2s 6d. Item, I bequeath to William, my son's son a mare and a yearling cow. Also I will that Thomas, my son, shall recover from Joan, my brother's wife, the following parcels: a bed covering with a fustian blanket, a silver spoon, a pair of warming irons, a brass basin with 2 candle sticks......."

You can just see him finding out which animals were the favourites with each grandchild and you can begin to imagine what the inside of his house would have looked like with these furnishings. His is the only Clungunford Will of this date which mentions silver and he must have owned a reasonable amount if, having left the majority of his possessions to his son, he still had some left over for his grandson. It is noticeable that he left no books, although printed books were in existence seventy years before he died.

He was a great one for borrowing money against pledges, for example:- in addition to the debt to the pawnbroker in Ludlow, he says "I owe for pledge of a brass pot to Richard Morris 8s....I owe John Barker in pledge of a pot 17d ..." John Barker had already received a bushel of rye in part payment of the original loan of two shillings and four pence.. The galloping inflation of the 1540s must have complicated his finances and the debasement of the currency may have had some bearing on the logistics of his building project at Abcott. He had obviously needed ready cash, probably in order to complete the new house, and had hoped, where possible, to repay with his farm produce. Between 1500 and 1550 the cost of hiring a carpenter rose from four pence to nine pence a day, the same sum as the fleece from one of his sheep. He may have been, by now, a gentleman with Roger Page as his "overseer", but, unlike the Lords of the Manor across the river, he was still closely enough involved with his farm to know each animal individually.

John Barker may never have received his seventeen pence because he died in the same year, leaving another very Catholic Will. He left his soul to "Almighty God and to the blessed virgin Mary", who was not at all politically correct in the midst of Edward VI's Protestant purges. He left "4d to the high altar of the parish church". As you would expect from their different tax assessments twenty five years before, he had hardly any possessions available to scatter round his family, unlike William Morris – only a pot and a pan are mentioned. His bequests are almost entirely animals:- to his younger son he left "six young beasts, three ewes and three lambs, a wether sheep and two hog sheep, a hog swine, two suckers and a pan". To his wife he left "an ox, two kine, a heifer and a weanling calf, one hog swine, two suckers, a whether sheep and two hog sheep." He was a middle ranking tenant, who had paid at the lowest level for the Lay Subsidy and the greater part of his Will is spent explaining how the lease of his house, rented from "the Lady Corbet" , will work and how his widow is to live in one half of it and his elder son in the other half.

The Will of John Davies, who died in 1544 at Shelderton, shows how important sheep were in the village economy now that a long staple Clun breed had been developed; his main possession was a flock fifty sheep.

There is no doubt that drinking ale was the most popular activity in the village and the evidence for liquor licensing at Purslow suggests that there was at least one pub in Clungunford by 1520. We know about the "feasts" in the church at Easter, only from the fact that such things were closed down in 1636, but St Cuthbert's must have been used as a village meeting place in the way that was normal until the Reformation. No doubt such "feasts" and "Church Ales" were an important part of village life until the climate of the Reformation frowned on them. As the only large building in the village the church had to be used as a venue for many such village activities before the advent of Clungunford House lawn or the Village Hall. The "Church Ales" also helped to finance the maintenance of the fabric of the church, as their modern equivalents do today.

A novelty in village life was the appearance of property dealers such as "…. Harford, esquire and John Farley, yeoman", who bought up the monastic land at Abcott[3] and Richard Stringfellow[4], who dealt in land in central Clungunford. Men like this jumped at the chance to make money by collecting up remnants of monastic property, which were too small for the Exchequer to bother about, like that at Abcott. They also took advantage of the impending collapse of feudalism which made it easier for people who had inherited the income from small, divided parcels of land (as part of women's dowries for example) to sell these inconvenient assets .

Now what of the absentee land owners? They were remote from Clungunford, and not interested in the village but we hear about some of them in the Patent Rolls and the State Papers. Half the Burley inheritance of central Clungunford had come down through the female line (via the Trussels) to the Earl of Oxford. He did not want to be bothered with the rents of such a small inheritance (a half share of probably less than six hundred acres). Sir John Littleton, the distinguished London lawyer, who had inherited the other half, felt the same, so the property dealer, Richard Stringfellow was able to help them out, by arranging for a newcomer, William Barkeley to buy both halves[5]. Thus both shares in the small manor of central Clungunford were reunited after a hundred years and the Lord of the Manor became an important figure in the village again.

As we saw in the last chapter, the Knight family, heirs of Elizabeth de Jay, lived in Shrewsbury, and in the fifteenth century, let their land at Beckjay to various farmers and successive millers.

Once the redoubtable old Elizabeth (nee de Hopton), who had been born before 1422 and brought up at Hopton Castle, had died in 1499, the Hopton estate was such a tiny fragment of the huge Corbet inheritance that it only gets a brief mention in their Wills. Elizabeth's grandson and her heir in Shelderton, Sir Robert Corbet died in 1513 and there is an effigy of him in Moreton Corbet church (**Fig 22**). However, John Barker's Will shows that the family were still involved to some extent with Clungunford and in 1534 another Robert Corbet presented the new rector, Thomas Haywarde – presumably by some arrangement with William Burley's heirs, who are most unlikely to have minded who was Rector of Clungunford.

Not only did the Tudors, those clever administrators, make Clungunford take care of its own poor, but they also ordered that each parish should keep a record of every person who was christened, married or buried in the church. Thus the Parish Registers were begun in Clungunford in 1559. Not everyone living in the parish came into these catagories, but the Registers give more detail than had ever been recorded about individuals before. From this moment, the history of the village has to be researched and written up in an entirely different way to allow for the assimilation of the vastly increased number of facts, names and houses that are available to research.

7

St. Cuthbert's Church, Clungunford

Clungunford church is dedicated to St Cuthbert, who was the most loved saint in Anglo Saxon England. "Now Cuthbert had great numbers of people coming to him not just from Lindisfarne but even from remote parts of Britain, attracted by his reputation for miracles. They confessed their sins, confided in him about their temptations and laid open to him the common troubles of humanity they were labouring under – all in the hope of gaining consolation from so holy a man. They were not disappointed." So wrote Bede in his "Life of St Cuthbert", written about thirty years after the Saint's death in 687 – based, in part, on evidence from a monk who had known Cuthbert. Pilgimages to the shrine at Durham continued throughout Anglo Saxon times. Is it too fanciful to believe that one of those pilgrims came from a remote part of Britain, now called Clungunford, and returned home to found a church dedicated to this lovable and holy man ?

Although St Cuthbert was famous in Anglo Saxon times chiefly for his ability to perform miracles to heal people, in later times he has been remembered as the Saint to whom the Lindisfarne Gospels were dedicated and who was closely involved with the environment – with the elements and particularly with the animal world. Bede records him praying all night standing in the sea, being spied upon by another monk, who saw, as the saint returned to the beach, "two otters bounded out of the water, stretched themselves out before him, and tried to dry him on their fur. They finished, received his blessing and slipped back to their watery home". There are other tales of his rapport with birds, such as that of him asking ravens, in the name of Jesus, not to eat his roof. One of those birds then returned to apologise to him and none of them ever did it again. Other birds were asked not to eat

Fig. 26. *Statue of St Cuthbert on the church porch.*

his barley unless God had given them permission – they also never did so again. Some of these stories are illustrated in the post medieval church decorations in Clungunford church.

The existence of a church within the Manor of Clungunford in Anglo Saxon times has been deduced by the most respectable historians despite the absence of any archeological remains or documents actually mentioning it. The fact that it is not mentioned in Domesday Book merely proves that, unlike the church at Stanton Lacy which still has late Anglo Saxon masonry, it was not built in stone by 1086. The Normans rarely bothered to record churches not built in stone.

The dedication to St Cuthbert would be most unusual in a Norman foundation, whereas the saint was extremely popular in Anglo Saxon times. This points to a preconquest date for the the dedication of the church. In addition to the evidence of the dedication there is the evidence in Domesday Book that Clungunford had been a very prosperous village in 1066 – one of only eight in the whole county producing enough grain to merit two mills. Surely such a village would have had its own church.

However, the advowson of Clungunford church is conspicuous for its absence in the document handing over the manor to Simon de Halberdyne in the mid twelfth century (recorded in the Liber Niger). Nor is it mentioned in the list of surrounding churches given to Wenlock Abbey by Isabelle de Say later in that century (recorded in the Monasticon), which does imply that she did not own the advowson by the late twelfth century.

The first definite reference to the parish found so far comes in the Cartulary of Haughmond Abbey between 1235 and 1245, when Radulpho, "Parsona" of Clungunford, witnessed a document at the Abbey. In 1277 the Rector, Stephen de Clun, is recorded as having applied for a licence for a year's leave of absence. The next reference is in 1302, when Roger de Halberdyne, the Lord of the Manor, is said to have been "acolyte" at the church. These documents help to prove that there was a church here before the present building.

Roger de Halberdyne was still acolyte in 1327. An acolyte was the lowest of the ecclesiastical orders, usually involved in assisting an ordained priest at the communion service, so he either had a priest on the strength, or he had a visiting priest. By being merely an acolyte, he was allowed to marry, as indeed he did, producing two sons to inherit his estate.

Clearly he was a very devout man and it can be no coincidence that the present church (see *Colour Plates 3-6*) was built largely during his lifetime. Dendrochronological analysis has revealed that the trees from which the chancel roof was originally made were put in the roof, green, in 1330. These trussed rafter couples are now hidden above Victorian boarding. The roof resting on these timbers would have been slated, probably with sandstone slates, the material supported by rafter couples, as at Clunbury and other local churches, and it is interesting to find Hugh the Tiler of Clungunford mentioned in the Bishop's register for 1333. No doubt it was he who had put on those slates.

What a project it must have been for the village! Most of the material with which the walls are built is "silt stone", from local quarries such as those on Shelderton Hill, where, some years before, there is a record of a heavy oxdrawn cart suitable for carrying stone. This "rubble work" with local stone was surely done by the villagers themselves and in places, such as the curving lines of the stones north of the altar, we can see areas of work done by their unprofessional hands. In other places the "rubble work" is good and speaks of skill and experience on the part of the builders. Other Clun valley manors were farmed directly by the Arundel estate at this date and therefore are included in the estate surveys. These records mention professional masons specifically and some of these would have been available to work in Clungunford. There were probably masons here, too, but we have no record of them.

In other areas, particularly round the windows, old red sandstone was used. This was a "free stone" which could be accurately shaped and was cut to angles and used as a framework or skeleton against which irregular rubble stone could be built. This red sandstone also came from a Shropshire quarry, but one further afield than Shelderton. The windows were made entirely out of this sandstone and the carving of the stone, especially for the east window, as well as the window design, involved specialist craftsmanship. John Wheatley, the Architect in charge of the 1999-2001 repair work, has suggested that it was done by the same team of itinerant stone masons as some work in the transept of Hereford Cathedral as well as at Worfield and Alberbury churches. The windows in those churches are of about the same date and use the same type of "spherical geometry" in their design. Carting stone from afar and paying specialist craftsmen must have cost the patron much money, just as the labouring work on the stone must have cost his tenants much in energy at a time of great agricultural distress

It is probable that the chancel was added on to the east end of a lower, existing church, which was subsequently replaced when the present nave was built. There is evidence that this was a practice used elsewhere. It would also explain the "extra" buttress at the west end of the chancel, which would have been necessary to support the south wall of the chancel until the new, higher nave was built and might go some way to explain why the chancel arch is off-set. John Wheatley has pointed out that the system of roofing was altered between the two parts of the roof, the chancel having single timber wall plates and the nave double. The greater height of the new chancel would explain why its west facing roof timbers show exterior weathering.

Fig. 27. *Chancel of Church seen from the nave.*

In the summer of 2001, dendrochronological sample cores were taken from the chancel, nave and vestry. Those from the chancel produced a felling date of 1328-9, which implies that the roof was put up, green, in 1330. The nave only produced one timber suitable for dating and the core from this suggested a felling date of 1338-9 – ten years before the Black Death hit the village. It is likely that the timber felled that winter was not put into a nave roof for some years. This supposition is based partly on the assumption that the agricultural depression, followed by the plague, caused disruption to the building programme and partly on the fact that the west end of the timbers in the chancel roof shows at least twenty years of external weathering.

All this suggests that there were two building phases, one starting early in the fourteenth century and finishing when the chancel was roofed in 1330 and the second finishing some time in the 1350s. The Lady Chapel (now the vestry), the roof of which leans against the chancel wall, must have been built at the same time as the chancel because the high arch in the north wall, now filled by the organ, was originally open to the chapel. The low arch, now walled up on the vestry side, was also accessible from both sides. It is likely to have been intended as the place for the tomb of the builder, Roger de Halberdyne. Indeed, there may well have been a tomb there before the Reformation destroyed virtually all the medieval internal features of the church.

The sandstone for most of the nave windows may have been cut at the same time as that for the chancel windows and not used for some years. This would explain why the technique and design of the windows in the two building phases is virtually identical, the only exceptions being the west window, which was originaly hidden behind the structure which supported the bell turret, and the Lady Chapel, where the windows have anyway been so greatly altered over the years that it is impossible to date them accurately.

The idea of two building phases fits well with the known history of the village. When Roger de Halberdyne decided to build a church, soon after Walter de Hopton had built himself a "tower house", the Clun valley was experiencing an agricultural boom and Pope Nicholas' Taxation of 1291 had shown Clungunford to be one of the richest local villages. However, that upward trend was reversed during the first building phase and by 1341 the village was so poor that its tax liability was reduced by almost two thirds. In 1346 the de Halberdyne family appear not to have been able to pay their tax at all. It may have become extremely difficult to complete phase one but it was impossible to start phase two until after the Black Death was over and there was a new owner of the advowson, namely the Earl of Arundel. He was rich enough to stand the cost of phase two even in a time of recession and, no doubt, did not like having an unfinished church on his home farm, with an old fashioned and deteriorating nave attached.

When even the chancel alone was roofed, the space in the building must have seemed awesomely vast to people who lived in tiny, single storey houses. It is amazing to us today that, at a time of exceptional poverty (described in the chapter on the fourteenth century), any church at all should have been built in the village, let alone a fine, spacious one. It is true that it was probably started in the prosperous early years of the century, but whereas we today might call a halt to building work during a crisis, seen from a fourteenth century perspective there was all the more reason to create an expression of faith because it was such a calamitous time.

The carting of the stone in slow ox-drawn carts and the building of the edifice must have taken years and been a huge expense for the patron before it was ready to be roofed in 1330. Even before the Black Death the reduction of the population and the malnutrition of the rest, resulting from the agricultural disasters described in Chapter 4, must have exacerbated the difficulty of the operation and, on top of this, professional craftsmen from elsewhere had to be employed. It is small wonder that the de Halberdyne family could not pay their tax bill in 1346 and had to hand back their "fief" to their overlord, the Earl of Arundel.

The fact that the Victorians included some fragments of medieval glass in the east window, suggests that there was stained glass in the windows at some stage in the Middle Ages, but we know nothing of it, except that the fragments are later than the construction of the church and may derive from a later medieval refurbishment – possibly that ordered in 1405. Apart from the glass fragments and, perhaps, the lamb and flag carving (of indeterminate date), the only thing surviving from medieval times inside the church is one of the oak parish chests. This chest has several features which suggest that it was made in the early fourteenth century – the single planks of wood from which the front, the top and the back are each formed, the slight curve inwards, the design which creates the legs out of the same piece of wood as the end panels of the front, and the jointing of the corners. These are classic characteristics for a chest of that date and suggest that it was made in the lifetime of Roger de Halberdyne. Of course the front has been altered to allow for the increased number of locks, which Thomas Cromwell ordered that all parish chests should have in the 1530s. The keen eye of a furniture restorer has found traces of where the original central metal band, holding the fourteenth century lock, passed right round the chest. This is the only surviving example of the original furnishings of Roger de Halberdyne's church. The jointing of the other oak chest, of primitive workmanship, suggests a later date.

It was also under the Earl's patronage that the oldest existing bell, now the Fifth, was cast, late in the fourteenth century, probably in Gloucester. It bears the inscription **+ MISSI : DE : CELIS : HABEO : NOMEN : GABRIELIS** (*My name is Gabriel, sent from heaven*). Was it given in thanks for surviving the Black Death? The Earl of Arundel is far more likely to have been able to pay for the bronze and the casting than the villagers and his bailiff would certainly have liked it because it not only rang the Angelus but was also a day bell to summon the peasants to work.

Refurbishments were already necessary in the medieval period. Bishop Mascall's register shows that in 1405 the chancel and the rectory were considered in need of repair. One might expect that this was due to Owen Glendower's depradations, but the fact that the original 1330 roof remains intact and not touched by fire, suggests that nothing serious had happened – just neglect. The Rector was required to restore the rectory. He immediately applied for a year of absence for study.

Soon after this, in the early fifteenth century, another new bell, the Tenor, the largest of the three mediaeval bells, was cast in Worcester. Its inscription reads **+ CUTHBERTI PRECE DULCE SONET ETAMENE** (*May it sound sweetly and pleasantly by the prayer of Cuthbert*). In each interval between the words is a small head of the king or the queen. Could it really have been the absentee landlord, William Ryman, who was responsible for this bell?

Many medieval people patronised the church as a penance to ensure their ultimate arrival in heaven. He is the only man recorded in the village at that date who would have had the money to commission a bell and he also had the advowson.

The smallest of the three mediaeval bells, whose successor is now the Fourth, bore the inscription **AETERNIS ANNIS RESONET CAMPANA IOANNIS** (*May John's bell ring for ever*). It was recast in 1703 by Isaac Hadley in Leominster, as recorded in the accounts of the Churchwardens, who took it there and paid £2.16.0 for the new casting. Hadley reproduced the original inscription and added **+ HADLEY + FECIT + 1703.** Bells cast by him are rare, so it is unfortunate that when the three old bells were taken down in 1895 in preparation for hanging them in the new tower, this bell was taken to Taylor's bellfoundry in Loughborough and replaced by a stock bell. This also meant that the mediaeval inscription was lost, because the new bell was inscribed only **RECAST 1895 * J : TAYLOR & Co. FOUNDERS LOUGHBOROUGH *.**

A further roofing project occurred some time around 1517 when the north chapel was re-roofed. One timber has been dendro dated between 1513 and 1517 and the rest are believed to be of the same date. In 1513 Bishop Mayew's register records that Clungunford should not have to pay its tithes because it was so impoverished due to floods and fires. One of the fires must have been in the chapel roof, so causing an early fourteenth century chapel to be re-roofed in the early sixteenth century.

The next reference to the church, specifically, comes in the Valor Ecclesiasticus of 1535, when Henry VIII commanded a survey of all parish churches in the country in order to discover how much they were worth. St Cuthbert's was valued at sixteen pounds as was the church at Hopesay, that being the value of the tithes from the land in the parish, whereas the tithes of Bedstone and Hopton Castle churches were each worth about four pounds only. This imbalance occurs because Clungunford parish included so much land that belonged to the lords of those neighbouring manors.

The difficulties experienced by the parishioners during the change over from Roman Catholicism to Protestantism are discussed in Chapter 6. We do not know the exact moment when the Catholic images and decoration were removed from Clungunford church, but in 1548 all images were officially banned and in that year all those in Ludlow church were taken down and sold privately. In 1551 the stone altar there was dismantled and set into the church floor. Earlier on, the Vicar of Stanton Lacy had just stuck pieces of paper over the Pope's name, saying "They are but fools who destroy their books for this world will not ever last". He was quite right because on 3rd Sepember 1553 the clergy of Shropshire began to celebrate mass again "by the excellent authority of our Queen Mary". We do not know how the Rectors, Thomas Haywarde and Sir William Shingler, dealt with the situation in Clungunford, but we do know from William Morris' Will that it was confusing for their parishioners.

For nearly six hundred years, the outside appearance of the church changed hardly at all. It must have had a bell turret from the time the nave was built, because the nave roof and its oldest bell both date from about 1350. Until 1895, the timber framed bell turret was close to the west gable of the church, but separated from it by a shoulder. Both bell turret and bell frame were constantly in need of repair, as is recorded in the Churchwardens' Accounts. In 1665, for instance, the turret had to be reconstructed, the bells rehung and the clock repaired and reinstalled. Large quantities of timber had to be bought and transported, wheels for the bells had to be made at Wootton, near Onibury and 204 lbs of iron and 42 lbs of brass had to be cast at Bringewood Forge, which was then operated by the Walker family of Ferney. The Churchwardens had to travel to Wootton and Bringewood Forge six times to make the arrangements and to see that the work was proceeding satisfactorily.

The bell turret and the bells were an expensive, but essential, feature of the church. Almost every year, money had to be spent on mending the clock, on repairs to the bell mechanism and on "bell tongues" and bell ropes. The accounts also record, every year, that the bell ringers had to be paid extra for the celebrations for the failure of the Gunpowder Plot on Guy Fawkes' Day, for royal anniversaries and the news of military victories. In 1727, Thomas Davies was paid 14/- for the combined duties of ringing the church bell and keeping dogs out of the church. Watercolours from 1802 onwards and a photograph of about 1890 record the appearance of the old timber framed bell turret. It had two openings to the sky on each side, a pyramid roof and, on the south side, the diamond shaped face of the clock that caused the parish so much trouble and expense. Such bell turrets still remain on several local churches and one with an ogee roof survives on the church beside Croft Castle. The structure supporting the turret on the roof of Clungunford church was concealed internally by a wooden partition, which cut across the middle of the westernmost windows on each side of the nave, while the window in the west wall lit only the bell chamber. This structure, which was described in 1894 as being "in a very dangerous condition, and bells, frames, etc.,in a most neglected state" was swept away when the new bell tower was added to the church in 1895.

The Churchwardens were elected annually at the Easter Vestry meeting. Each year, they levied a tax (known as a "lewne") on the property owners of the parish to raise enough money for the likely expenses of performing their many and varied duties. Quite apart from maintaining the church and its furnishings, the Churchwardens were responsible for the state of the roads and bridges. They paid for the construction of the bridge near the church at Clungunford in 1657 and Broadward Bridge in 1796, both of them wooden bridges with stone approach causeways, enabling the first dry river crossing in those places for vehicles. Through their officers, the Overseers of the Poor, the Churchwardens were also responsible for the social welfare of parishioners in need and even of itinerant poor. They made provision for the Schoolmaster and the parish school, which, in the years before 1857, used the north chapel beside the chancel of the church, with a door replacing the lower half of the easternmost side window and a fireplace and chimney installed beside it. The Churchwardens' more surprising duties included paying a bounty of 1/- for each dead fox and 2d for each dead "urchin".

At the church itself, money was spent, year after year, on repairing the churchyard walls and gate, on buying books concerning such events as the alleged Popish Plot of 1677, while in 1687, 1/- was spent on a book "to pray for the Queen" – perhaps in the vain hope that Mary of Modena would renounce Roman Catholicism. In 1700 there was an unusual payment of 1/- "for brushing down the cobwebs in the church" while there were frequent payments for the mending of church windows. In 1665, despite the heavy expenses for the bell tower, 8 Ells of

Holland were bought for £2.2.8. and surplices were made from it. Washing and repairs for the surplices and the other church linen feature as a regular expense in the Churchwarden's accounts during three centuries. In 1726, the pulpit cushion was recovered. The material cost 14/6, the tassels 6/6 and the labour 1/-. At that price, it was no doubt a splendid velvet cushion.

For over 200 years, all building work for the Churchwardens was undertaken by the Jukes family. In 1659, Jeremy Jukes was paid for constructing the causeway to "the great bridge" and in 1760, another Jeremy Jukes cleaned the inside and plastered the outside of the church. In 1846, the Rector was employing J. Jukes for building work and from 1867 for over 20 years Richard Jukes was paid £7.7.0 every year by the Churchwardens, initially as clerk and later as sexton. It was in 1905 that James Jukes, Mason, last featured among the commercial residents of Clungunford.

Throughout all these centuries, the record is one of careful maintenance of the ancient structure and observance of hallowed customs. Very few changes were made, although, in the early nineteenth century were installed high panelled box pews of very thin construction, which, in 1894, were removed because they were "inconvenient for kneeling in". A description of the church in 1881 reported that it was in a condition which was scarcely compatible with that age when so much had been done "whether rightly or wrongly in so called church restoration". St Cuthbert's church did not have to wait much longer for its restorers.

The application, in 1894, for a Faculty for massive changes and repairs was certainly comprehensive. The architect, Edward Turner of Leicester, submitted plans and drawings with his proposals. The most ambitious was a new bell tower to be constructed of stone, quarried near Onibury. The entrance from the church to the new bell tower was to be achieved by re-opening the old north door of the church, in the nave opposite to the south door. The north door had no doubt been the most used when the main route through the village lay close to the north side of the church. It was shown on Archdeacon Owen's watercolour of 1802, but by July 1825, when the famous Shropshire antiquary, artist and schoolmaster David Parkes visited Clungunford and drew both sides of the church, the north door had been blocked. He described the church as "a respectable building, lately repaired, new pewed and the floor flagged". The new box pews were fitted against both sides of the nave and the north door was filled in accordingly, as shown on the detailed plan of the old church, prepared in 1894, just before the major programme of alterations.

The new belltower was to contain a ringing chamber, a vestry below it and a heating chamber in the basement to heat the church by either hot water or hot air. A new church clock would be displayed on the south face of the new tower. The intention was to transfer the three existing bells to this tower and to add five new bells to make a ring of eight – an ambition still not fully achieved. The old timber framed bell turret was to be removed from the roof and the west end of the nave continued upwards to a proper gable, while the full length of the nave would then be opened to view and its roof extended to the gable end. The plaster ceilings, derided in 1881 as obscuring the view of the roof timbers, would be replaced by oak boarding with moulded ribs, so continuing to hide the beams. A bell turret, containing a small bell, above the junction of the nave and chancel roofs, was intended, but was not built. The porch would be rebuilt in stone and enlarged. Throughout the church, the perished stonework would be replaced and the windows would be reglazed. The roofs were to be stripped and retiled and provided with eaves, gutters and downpipes. The nave would be refloored with wood blocks and the chancel and north chapel with a combination of wood blocks and tiles. Finally, the doorway that had been made below the middle of a window in the north chapel when it was used as a school was to be removed and the window reinstated. The school fireplace and chimney had already gone.

There were also to be many new fittings and decorations. Instead of the high panelled pews, which were converted into wainscotting in the nave, chairs were to be provided for the nave and the north chapel, which it was proposed should be equipped for weekday services. New altars, altar rails, prayer desk, choir seats, lecterns and Litany desks of oak were to be installed. The pulpit was to be moved from its position on the north end of the chancel steps into the north east corner of the nave. New doors were to be provided throughout the church and the walls replastered where necessary.

The font of Wenlock marble, which had been installed in about 1835, just to the east of the framework which supported the old belfry, would be moved closer to the west door and supplied with a carved oak lid, attached by a pulley to the ceiling. Oil lamps would be hung from the ceiling at intervals throughout the church. Among the fittings and ornaments provided by various members of the Rocke family and by other parishioners was the carved wooden statue of St Cuthbert, which Miss Alice Rocke gave to stand in a niche over the new south porch to welcome people to his church. (see **Fig. 26**). Only three years later, Augustus Hare, in his guidebook to Shropshire, describes this statue with two swans "probably from a confusion with the swan of St Columba, instead of the two otters, which licked the frozen feet of St Cuthbert and dried them with their fur".

Three features were proposed for the central vista of the interior. There was to be a reredos in the form of a painted oak triptych on a stone base. The chancel arch was to be equipped with a low carved screen with gates. On the wall surrounding and above the opening of the arch it was intended to install an intricately carved oak Rood beam, with a carved crucifixion scene above and figures of angels at the ends of the beam and saints on either side below. Undoubtedly the most notable of the new fittings that was planned for the church was a two manual organ, built by James Binns of Leeds, using his patent pneumatic action. It is a magnificent instrument often visited by organists from many countries and, following a further Faculty in 1982, carefully restored to its former excellence. It was placed on the north side of the chancel, instead of the small organ that had been kept until then on the south side.

The parishioners of Clungunford, at a Vestry Meeting on 10 May 1894, unanimously approved that an application be made for a Faculty for all this work to be carried out. The Architect, Edward Turner of Leicester, prepared drawings and plans and estimated that the cost of the works "exclusive of the fittings and decorations" would be £2,530. When the Faculty was applied for, it was stated that the Patron of the living, John Charles Leveson Rocke of Clungunford House, had already provided this amount for the work and that Lt. Col. Richard Rocke, who had been brought up at Clungunford and was uncle to both the Patron and the Rector, had given a further £500.

On the advice of its expert, Dr Tristram, certain elements of the proposed programme of work were not allowed by the Deputy Registrar to the Diocese when the Faculty was granted on 20 June 1894. The removal of inscribed memorial stones bearing legible names from the floor of the chancel into the churchyard was not permitted and the new flooring was placed round them. The most serious refusal, however, concerned the proposed Rood beam and statues. The Rood beam was permitted, but was only to have a plain cross above it and no statues. It seems clear that Dr Tristram was influenced by recent decisions in other Dioceses and feared redolence of Roman Catholicism.

The Rood beam, the low screen below the chancel arch and some less prominent elements of the scheme were abandoned, but the rest of the permitted work was carried out during 1895. In the following June, a list was printed, showing who had contributed to the cost and who had provided certain specified items. There were many cash subscribers and members of the Rocke family and others provided altar frontals, brass candlesticks and all the other equipment needed for a completely restored church. The Patron of the living paid most of the expenses, which eventually amounted to over £4,000, and also £758 for the splendid organ which he dedicated to the memory of his sister, Constance Ida Thomas.

Just as the church was hardly altered for several hundred years before 1895, so there have been few alterations since. Electric lighting was installed in 1949, following over two years' negotiations between the Rector, Rev E Ingham Hoult and the diocesan authorities from whom a Faculty was required. The Parochial Church Council obtained an estimate of £150 for the work and proposed to raise the bulk of this cost by selling the 1758 silver flagon, which was no longer used and had been valued at £100. The Registrar of the Diocese refused to permit the sale of the flagon, but, eventually the proposed electrification was authorized. Lights were to be provided for chancel, nave, pulpit and the organ console as well as for the belfry and the choir vestry, which was still in the lowest room in the tower. In the correspondence and the Faculty, no mention was made of an electric blower for the organ, but this was installed at the same time and the young man who had been pumping the organ by hand for years was discharged and rewarded with a Bible.

A Faculty granted in January 1965 authorized the levelling of unkempt grave mounds and the removal of all broken and indecipherable tombstones, none of which was thought to have been in the churchyard for less than fifty years. They were to be broken up and removed in the cause of greater tidiness. Several nineteenth century watercolour drawings and a photograph of about 1890 show a clutter of box tombs and standing headstones near the south wall of the chancel. Sadly, the clearance from the churchyard of so many memorials to past village worthies has not only diminished the aura of historical continuity but has also opened the way for new gravestones of polished granite and other exotic materials, from India, South Africa and other foreign lands, that are not in sympathy with the colour and texture of the church fabric or the tradition of tranquility so appropriate to a country churchyard.

Surviving the 1895 changes in the church are a number of inscriptions to past parishioners. On the floors of the chancel and what was formerly the north chapel and is now the vestry are memorial slabs to several members of the Bayley family, who lived so long at Broadward Hall.

The earliest is to Francis Bayly (sic) "Doctor of Physick, son of Richard Bayly Gent", who died in February 1728/9, aged 70, and his wife, Ursula who died in February 1749/50 aged 75. Others are to their son, Dr Charles Bayley (died 1763) and his wife Mary (died 1789 aged 81), to their son, Francis Bayley (died 1761, aged 25) and Charles' sister, Ursula Bayley (died 1788, aged 92). There is also a large black marble memorial slab to Richard Prynce of Abcott Manor (died March 1683/4) and his sister, Mrs Mary Tayler, who died in 1741, aged 86. By the entrance to the vestry is a memorial slab to Mrs Hannah Morris, who died in 1747, aged 90.

On the walls of the chancel are other memorials. On the south wall there is a framed square of copper inscribed to the memory of William Freeman, who died in 1671, aged 32. He was the third son of Coningsby Freeman of Neen Sollers and his wife Beatrice, who inherited Coston Manor from her mother, the last owner with the Coston family surname. His epitaph is a lesson in eulogy. He was one of the numerous people of the past who are recorded as being paragons of virtue. Until some unknown date between 1785 and the 1895 reflooring of the chancel, an engraved slab under the west side of the communion rail recorded the burial below of his mother. On the south wall of the chancel is a stone tablet inscribed to the memory of John Edwards, Rector of Clungunford, who died in 1724/5. There was formerly an inscribed slab within the communion rails above the body of his wife, Eleanor, who died in 1741, aged 96. There was also a slab on the step on the west side of the communion rails recording the burial there of "Mary the wife of Samuel Barkley Gent who dyed the 19 day of July Anno Dni 1682". This is the only record of a memorial ever in the church to the Barkley family, who were Lords of the Manor of Clungunford for 150 years and provided its rectors for over a century

On the north wall is a frame with three squares of brass inscribed in memory of Thomas Evans, Rector of Clungunford from 1724/5 to 1762, his wife, Olivia, his elder sister, Mrs Blanch Pryce, and his younger sister, Susannah Evans. Nearby is a memorial to William Charles Rocke, the last of the four members of the Rocke family to be successive Rectors of Clungunford. He supervised the transformation of the church in 1895 and was still the incumbent fifty years later.

On the same wall is a grand marble monument to the last Walker owner of Ferney Hall, Francis Walker, who died in 1776. It commemorates, also, his parents, his wife, Rebecca, and their four children, who all died in their infancy. The Reverend Edward Williams, who recorded in 1785 many memorials now lost, copied a painted panel, proudly displaying the full arms of that Francis Walker, with crest , motto and no less than twelve quarterings, which was fixed on the north wall of the chancel, close beside the marble monument. The great great grandfather of this Francis Walker was an earlier Francis Walker who purchased Ferney Hall in 1656 and whose cast iron memorial slab of January1663/4, made in his family's forge at Bringewood, now lies in the churchyard, immediately outside the east window, having lain for two centuries on the chancel floor, within the communion rails.

In the ringing chamber of the tower are two armorial hatchments to parishioners who died in early Victorian times, when such records of death were still customary. These diamond shaped depictions of the Arms of the deceased and their spouses would, after the funerals, have been displayed over the door of the house during the period of mourning and subsequently hung inside the church. One Clungunford hatchment records the death in 1846 of General Sir Evan Lloyd, the long term tenant of Ferney Hall, survived by his wife, born Alicia Eustace. The other bears the Arms of Rev John Rocke, Squire and Rector of Clungunford, who died on 14 June 1849, survived by his wife, Anne, the daughter of Thomas Beale of Heath House.

Over the door to the tower is a memorial to James Green, who was master of the free school in Clungunford for twenty four years and died in 1820. Nearby, there are memorials to the twelve men of Clungunford Parish who died in the 1914-1918 war, to the two parishioners who died in the 1939-1945 war and to Lieutenant David Tinker R.N., who died in the 1982 Falklands campaign.

There are two stained glass windows in the church. In 1891, at a cost of £228.18.6, the east window was fitted with new glass depicting the Saints who were particularly relevant to Constance Ida Rocke, who in December 1882 had married Lt. Col. E.A.Thomas of the 7th Dragoon Guards. While he was serving in India in 1884, she had died, aged only thirty, four days after the birth of their only child, Evan, who, on inheriting the Clungunford estate from her brother in 1906, changed his surname to Rocke. Among the tracery at the top of the east window are fragments of mediaeval glass, the only survivors of what was described in Bagshaw's 1851 survey as "some fine specimens of stained glass" then remaining in the church. The other stained glass window is beside the pulpit and was erected in 1970 in memory of Margaret Ellen Vaughan, who died in 1949, having lived for many years at Abcott Manor. The window, designed by Francis Skeat at a cost of £680, portrays a charming scene, including Abcott Manor, the church and the river, somewhat rearranged, and also a flock of Clun Forest sheep. Apart from these two windows, all the others in the church were fitted in 1895 with the little squares of green and pink and other coloured glass, so beloved of Victorian church restorers, who seemed averse to letting in the light.

Although the 1895 ambition to achieve a ring of eight bells in the new bell tower has still not been fulfilled, two further bells, dating from 1870 and 1889, were obtained secondhand, tuned by Taylors of Loughborough to match the three bells already in the tower and hung in a new steel framework in 1996. Finally, a ring of six bells was completed by the addition of a new Treble bell, which was cast at Loughborough in 1997.

A further enhancement of the church at the end of the second millenium has been the designing and embroidery of splendid hassock covers by some of the parishioners, including the Rector's wife, Amaryllis Bell, who has portrayed St. Cuthbert and his eider duck.

Maintenance of the structure of the church has been a continuing concern for the Parochial Church Council and substantial repairs have been undertaken in recent years. Under the expert supervision of Wheatley & Lines, the Architects, most of the maintenance and repair of the church is now entrusted to the family building firm of L. & M. Grimes of Beambridge, near Aston-on-Clun, who have taken on the responsibility borne by the Jukes family in the seventeenth, eighteenth and nineteenth centuries. In raising the large sums required for this seemingly endless expense, the yearly fund raising achievements of the parishioners have been generously augmented by English Heritage, The Historic Churches Preservation Trust and The Shropshire Historic Churches Trust.

8

The Rectors of Clungunford

Until 1587, the names of the Clungunford clergy can only be discovered from references in the Bishop of Hereford's Registers and other documentary sources. The status of each individual is not always clear. Some were obviously Rectors while others were Curates and some are described as Chaplains. One was called an Acolyte, was not ordained and was married. In mediaeval times, a clergyman who was not a graduate of a university was given the honorific title of "Sir", as though he had been knighted. Those clergy of Clungunford who are recorded before 1557 and the dates when they feature in documents are as follows:-

c.1235 to 1245	*Radulpho – witness to a document at Haughmond Abbey.*
1277	*Stephen de Clun*
1302 & 1327	*Roger de Halberdyne (Acolyte)*
1349	*John Vincent*
1351	*Sir Roger Pyard*
1377	*Sir William Osmondson*
1387	*John Gamell*
1387	*Sir John Wyke – exchanged, after 3 weeks, with*
1388	*Sir Alan Thorpe*
1388	*John Allen (Chaplain)*
1406 & 1419	*Phillip ap David*
1418	*Henry (Chaplain)*
1432	*Walter Harold and Thomas Wyth (Two Rectors)*
1433 & 1439	*Walter Harold*
1445	*Sir William Hopkins (Chaplain)*
1449 & 1483	*Hugh Newton*
1519	*Sir Thomas Harris*
1536	*Thomas Haywarde*
1549	*Sir William Shingler (Confessor to William Morris of Abcott)*

When William Barkeley of Cressage bought the Manor and Advowson of Clungunford in 1558 and 1559, the Rector was Francis Baldwin, who had been appointed in 1557. It was in 1559 that the Parish Registers of Clungunford were started, but, even so, the retirement or burial of Francis Baldwin is not recorded. The Elizabethan silver chalice and paten, bearing no hallmarks but with the date 1571 scratched roughly on the foot of the paten and a band of interlacing engraved around the chalice, was perhaps given to the church during his incumbency. Thomas Escopp, Rector, was buried on 22 June 1583 and there is also record of John Bragger, Rector from 1582 to 1587. No doubt Thomas Escopp had retired.

In 1587, another William Barkeley, the squire's only son by his second marriage, signed the Clungunford Parish Registers as Rector, stating that it was the first year of his incumbency and the twenty sixth of his age. He had taken his B.A. Degree the previous year at Brasenose College, Oxford and received an M.A. the following year. In January 1599/1600, he recorded the burial of "William Barkeley Gent. Lord of the Manor of Clungunford." At about the same time, he married Frances Detton, from Detton, near Neen Sollers and they had sixteen children, many of whom died young. Indeed, in the month of August 1624, Jane, William and Mary were all buried over a period of three weeks. No doubt there was an epidemic. The Parish Registers record that on 26 May 1629, William Barkeley, the Rector, was buried at the age of sixty seven.

It is clear from his Will that he had considerable property and valuable chattels. After the customary bequest of his soul to Jesus Christ and his body to the earth in expectation of a joyful resurrection, he gave and bequeathed his wife and children unto the gracious protection of Almighty God. He gave to the poor of the parish of Clungunford £20 and £10 each to the parishes of Leintwardine, Clunbury and Hopton "to remayne unto the stock of the poore of the said parishes forever". He left to his eldest son, Samuel, "my great silver salt and a trencher salt and my two great silver boles after my wives decease to remain as heire-loomes to him and his heirs forever". He left the benefit of certain rents to his two younger sons, George and Edward, and all the books in his study to George, who took his M.A. from Brasenose College the following month. The bulk of his estate he left to his widow, whose name he spelt Frauncis, "for her maintenance and the education of my children", with power to raise marriage portions for his daughters. An annual rent of £20 was received from a farm then and still known as Gwernaffel, at Pilleth near Knighton, which the Testator had leased to three members of the White family. There was also a farm at Farrington, near Knighton.

Soon after the burial of Rector William Barkeley, there is recorded at The Public Record Office, in the Certificates of the Induction of Incumbents in the Diocese of Hereford, the name of a new Rector, Thomas Swift M.A., who was admitted on 3 June 1629. It is further recorded that the Patron of the benefice was then Sir Henry Wallop, the owner of the Hopton Castle Estate, which included the Broadward, Shelderton and Ferney parts of the parish. This appears to be the only instance when the owner of those outlying parts of the parish acted as Patron of the Living and the indecent haste whereby Thomas Swift's induction took place a mere eight days after the previous Rector's burial does cast doubt on the accuracy of the record. Thomas Swift does not feature again. From 13 May 1630, Samuel Barkeley, the eldest son of Rector William Barkeley was Rector of Clungunford and the Patron of the Living was stated to be Francis Barkeley.

Samuel Barkeley had been baptised at Clungunford in September 1600 and, like his father, he attended Brasenose College,Oxford, where he obtained his B.A., but he was at New College when he received his M.A. in 1626. From May 1630 until his death in March 1672/3 he remained as the incumbent of Clungunford, first Rector, later Minister and Registrar and finally Rector again, acccording to the dictates of the successive Parliaments of the period. He discontinued, in 1636, the ancient custom in Clungunford whereby the Rector provided every Easter Day, originally in the church but latterly in the rectory, a feast of bread, cheese and ale for the poor and needy. An appeal by some of the parishioners to Archbishop Laud obtained his support, provided that the feast was held in the rectory and not in the church.

Samuel Barkeley must have been nimble footed to retain his living throughout the liturgical convulsions of the reign of Charles I and the Commonwealth. Under the Arminianism of Laud he will have had to conform to the new uniformity and install a communion table, with stout altar rails on three sides. It may have been for reluctance to comply with such requirements that he was imprisoned for a while in July 1643, following information from some of his parishioners, on the orders of the King's representative, Lord Capel. However, in that very month, the Westminster Assembly, established by Parliament and of which the clerical members comprised 121 English Puritan Ministers and 5 Scots Presbyterian Ministers, started its deliberations.

The Westminster Assembly drew up the Solemn League and Covenant, which, in September 1643, the Members of the House of Commons solemnly swore to observe. They ordered that every person in England aged over eighteen must sign it by the following February. The Episcopacy was abolished, a Presbyterian Ministry was established and the Prayer Book and its services were forbidden. All altars and tables of stone were to be demolished before November 1643, communion tables were to be removed from the east end into the body of the church, all rails around them were to be taken away and chancels were to be lowered to the same level as the naves.

In August 1645, The Directory for the Public Worship of God, issued by the Westminster Assembly, was made the only legal service book and the use of the Book of Common Prayer was forbidden, under penalty of £5 for the first offence, £10 for the second offence and a year's imprisonment for the third. The new service provided for baptism by the Minister in church, but the only valid form of marriage was to be before a Justice of the Peace. Some clergy circumvented this requirement by marrying a couple in the presence of a J.P., who said nothing until the time came for him to declare the marrriage valid. The stern instructions for burial required that the body "be decently attended from the house to the place appointed for public burial and there immediately interred without any ceremony."

With the abolition of Bishops, Rectors and Vicars, each parish had to appoint one of their number as Registrar or Register. On 21 December 1653 a certain Charles Langford recorded that "the inhabitants of the Parish of Clungunford" had certified their desire "that Mr Samuel Barkely, Minister of the said parish should be their Register" and that Mr Barkely had given an oath to perform that trust according to the Act of Parliament. For the next eight years, Samuel Barkeley signed the parish registers as "Register", but in March 1661/2, following the restoration of Charles II and the re-establishment of the Church of England, he resumed the title of Rector. During all the years of his incumbency, under various jurisdictions, he recorded in the Parish Registers baptisms, marriages and burials. Unlike the clergy of some of the neighbouring parishes, he was prepared to compromise. He managed, like the Vicar of Bray, to retain his parish through all the changes of Church and State.

This was no mean achievement when religion and partisanship in the Civil War were so entwined and the horrors of war were so close. Although the Clungunford area did not witness any of the major battles between the Royalists and the adherents of Parliament, both sides had fervent supporters locally. Robert Wallop, who owned the Hopton Castle Estate, which included a swathe of Clungunford parish from Broadward to Shelderton and Ferney, was one of the Judges who tried Charles I. Other keen Parliamentarians included the Harleys at Brampton Bryan, the Salways at Richards Castle and the Mores at Linley, one of whom commanded the defenders of Hopton Castle. Ludlow was a Royalist stronghold and held out until May 1646. Hopton Castle and Brampton Bryan Castle were both lost to the Royalists following famous sieges in 1643/4 and 1644, while Stokesay Castle fell to Parliamentary forces in 1645. The massacre at Hopton Castle was notoriously barbaric and no doubt there was widespread violence for many years, with frequent looting and forced recruitment. It must have been as difficult to remain aloof from the political fracas as it was for a cleric to adapt to the related doctrinal upheavals of which clergy in nearby Clun, Hopesay and Bishops Castle were in opposing factions.

In June 1646, Presbyteries or Classes were established all over England to govern Ecclesiastical affairs under the general supervision of Parliament. A Classis was a voluntary association, or Board of Presbyterian clergy and laity, formed in each of the districts into which the country was divided, as a unit of church government and source of spiritual authority. Candidates for ordination submitted their qualifications for the ministry to the judgment of a Classis and derived their subsequent status from its call. The Fifth Classis for Shropshire included Clungunford and Samuel Barkeley. In August 1654, Parliament passed an Ordinance for the purpose of ejecting "scandalous, ignorant and insufficient or negligent ministers and schoolmasters". In every county, Committees were appointed with power to summon incumbents before them and inquire as to their learning and general fitness. The full title of these Committees was "Commissioners for the Approbation of Public Preachers" and Samuel Barkeley of Clungunford was one of the twenty Shropshire ministers assigned to the task. Such of the clergy who had shown support for King Charles and still retained their livings and others who were reported to be still using the Book of Common Prayer were now in danger of ejection, bringing the number of dispossessed clergy in England to over nine thousand.

In May 1660, the restoration of Charles II brought an entire reversal of ecclesiastical affairs. Although the Convention Parliament was composed mainly of Presbyterians, it hastened to pass an Act for Confirming and Restoring of Ministers of the Church of England, which ruled that every Minister (apart from Anabaptists and certain Independents) who had been turned out of his living should be restored to it by 25 December and his supplanter removed. In 1662, a new Act of Uniformity decreed that every Minister within the Church of England must, on or before St Bartholomew's Day (24 August) 1662 declare his assent and consent to all and everything contained and prescribed in the new Book of Common Prayer, abjure the Solemn League and Covenant and sign a declaration that it was not lawful, upon any pretence whatsoever, to take Arms against the King. Those failing to do so would have to depart from their livings.

The declared purpose of the alterations made to the Liturgy and administration of the established church after the restoration of King Charles II was to return to the situation that applied before "the late unhappy confusions", as the Preface to the new Book of Common

Prayer described recent events. It was accepted that there would be strong opposition to the reinstatement of the previous regime. "Those men who under the late usurped powers had made it a great part of their Business to render the people disaffected thereunto saw themselves in point of Reputation and Interest concerned (unless they would freely acknowledge themselves to have erred, which such men are very hardly brought to do) with their utmost endeavours to hinder the restitution thereof". The aim of those who compiled the new Book of Common Prayer was "not to gratifie this or that Party in any their unreasonable demands: but to do that which . . . might most tend to the preservation of peace and unity in the Church: the procuring of Reverence, and exciting of Piety and Devotion in the publick Worship of God: and the cutting off occasion of them that seek occasion of cavil or quarrel against the Liturgy of the Church". They did not "expect that men of factious, peevish and perverse spirits should be satisfied with anything that can be done in this kind by any other than themselves" yet they had good hope that the Prayer Book that they had compiled would be "well accepted and approved by all sober, peaceable and truly conscientious Sons of the Church of England".

The new Prayer Book confirmed the restoration of the Episcopacy by providing forms of service for making, ordaining and consecrating Deacons, Priests, Bishops and Archbishops. A service was also reinstated, for use on 5 November each year, giving thanks "for the happy Deliverance of King James I and the Three Estates of England from the most Traiterous and bloody intended Massacre by Gunpowder". Even more politically controversial were new forms of service to implore God's forgiveness, on every 30 January, for the barbarous murder of the blessed King Charles I by "violent and bloodthirsty men" and to give thanks to God, on every 29 May, for the Restoration of King Charles II and "the wonderful deliverance of these Kingdoms from the Great Rebellion, and all the Miseries and Oppressions consequent thereupon, under which they had so long groaned".

Many of the clergy were not prepared to make the various public declarations required to be made by them before St Bartholomew's Day 1662 in their respective churches before Morning and Evening Prayer. Large numbers left their parishes. Samuel Barkeley felt able to conform and remained as Rector of Clungunford. When he signed his last Will on 20 September 1672, he spelt his surname Barkley, with only one "e", and described himself as "Clerk", perhaps deliberately avoiding the word "Rector", which his father had used in his Will. Samuel Barkley stated that he was sick in body but of sound and perfect memory. Indeed, his signature is very shaky, although, beside it, he impressed on black wax his signet ring bearing the full shield of the Berkeleys of Berkeley Castle, of which family, despite differences in spelling, the squires and rectors of Clungunford in the seventeenth century were considered members. From 1320 until today their arms, as impressed on Samuel Barkley's Will, are "Gules, a chevron between ten crosses pattee argent".

By his Will, he left his body "to the earth from which it came, to be orderly and decently buried" and his soul he bequeathed "to him that gave it, hoping through the merits of my saviour Jesus Christ to have eternal life". He left £5 to the poor of the parish of Clungunford, £100 to his daughter, Mary and all his personal Chattels and Estate to his dear and loving wife, Martha, "for and towards the maintenance and breeding up of my younger children by her, to be disposed of according to her discretion to and for her and their best benefit and advantage".

Martha was his second wife and the mother of his eight youngest children. His first wife had borne him seven children, but they do not feature in his Will. The Parish Registers record the burial on 7 March 1672/3 of "Samuel Barkley, Rector of the Church of Clungunford". The Inventory of his belongings makes interesting reading. The books in his study were worth £40 and he had a good supply of household equipment – twelve beds with eight bolsters, blankets and coverlets, brass pots and pans, much pewter, chests, coffers and hanging presses. His silver was worth only £12 and perhaps he no longer had the fine silver heirlooms that his father had left him. It is, however, clear that he farmed his glebe, which his father does not appear to have done. He left ten cows and a bull, four oxen, eight swine and eleven pigs, eight horses and colts, corn in the barn worth £5, carts and implements of husbandry (which he mentioned specifically in his bequests to his wife) and £35 worth of wheat, rye, barley, peas and oats (which were no doubt growing in the glebe fields in March and for which payment would be expected from the next Rector).

It seems that there was no member of the Barkley family ready to be appointed Rector in March 1672/3, when Samuel Barkley was buried. The Hereford Diocesan Records show that John Wilcox was Rector from 29 July 1673 until he resigned in September 1675, to make way for Samuel Barkley's twenty four year old son James, who had followed the family custom by taking an Oxford Degree, having left St Alban Hall in March 1671/2. James Barkley was Rector of Clungunford for nearly seventeen years. He was buried there on 5 March 1689/90, when he was succeeded as Rector by his younger brother, Benjamin, who had been at Pembroke College and All Souls College, Oxford. He had already been Rector of Shelve, near Bishops Castle, and then Vicar of Hanley Castle, Worcestershire, but when the living at Clungunford became vacant, he moved again. He remained for only three years before transferring to a parish in Wiltshire, so ending over a century of almost uninterrupted tenure of the Rectory by his family.

By 1693, John Edwards was signing the Parish Registers as Rector and he continued until February 1724/5, when they record his burial. On the south side of the chancel in Clungunford church is a stone wall monument to "John Edwards, D.D., Rector of this Church", stating that he married Eleanor, daughter of Sir John Winford of Astley in the County of Worcester. The style and execution of the memorial is somewhat primitive, unlike the Winford family monuments in Astley church, near Great Witley.

It was while John Edwards was Rector that the Churchwardens and Sidesmen of each parish had to answer in writing nearly forty searching questions concerning the parish church and its equipment, the incumbent's performance of his duties, tne parish officers and the behaviour of the parishioners. In 1716 and again in 1719 this questionnaire had to be answered and the answers for the two years are virtually identical. The replies give interesting details about the parish, the Rector and the other parishioners in those years, even though the information given was no doubt modified to satisfy the diocesan inquisitors. In 1716, it was recorded that the roof was well covered. The windows were well glazed and the floor paved and kept plain and even and the inside walls were white and clean. There was a "convenient Reading Desk and Pulpit". The Communion Table was covered in time of Divine Service with a decent purple carpet of woollen cloth and with a fair linen cloth at the time of the Administration of the Holy

1. *The two entries for Clungunford in Domesday Book. In both, Clungunford is described as "Clone" (Clun) – that part of Clone which had belonged to Gunward. The "P" in the first entry stands for Picot de Say, who had replaced Gunward in part of the parish. In the second entry, Rainald has replaced Gunward in the other part. Rainald was the Sheriff of Shropshire in 1086, when Domesday Book was compiled. There is a translation of both entries on page 6.*

2. *The view over Clungunford from Clunbury Hill.*

3. *Water colour of the south side of St Cuthbert's Church in 1802 by Archdeacon Owen, who was a relation of the Rockes.*

Clungunford Church 1802. 40. ns.

4. *Water colour of the north side of St Cuthbert's Church and a former Rectory in 1802 by Archdeacon Owen, whose portrait hung in Clungunford House until the sale in 1990.*

5. *The Rev Barney Bell in front of St Cuthbert's in 2002.*

6. *The interior of the church during Lent in 2001, showing the low arch on the left, which was probably intended to hold a tomb.*

7. *Sheep being milked and inspected for disease.*

These four paintings, showing medieval farming methods, come from the Luttrell Psalter. The Psalter was made in the mid-fourteenth century and was acquired by the Earl of Arundel soon after it was completed. They do, of course, show how things were done on a large farm.

8. *Ploughing with oxen.*

9. *A watermill with fish traps.*

Life on a peasant's holding was somewhat rougher. At the same date, the Earl became Lord of the Manor of Clungunford and joined this Manor into his large home farm in the Clun valley. Thus these depictions of medieval farming methods can be said to show how things were done in Clungunford in the Middle Ages.

10. *Reaping.*

11. *South view of Abcott Manor.*

12. *Chimneys at Abcott Manor.*

13. *Half timbered east gable of Abcott Manor.*

14. *View of Clungunford. Watercolour by W. Pearson. August 1802.*

15. *Glebe Cottage, formerly Rectory Cottage.*

16. *Clungunford Farm with Bowes Rocke and family.*

17. *Rowton Grange.*

18. *Church Farm.*

19. *Beckjay Mill. Oil painting by William Curtis. 1855*

20. *Beckjay Farm with Jim Bason.*

21. *Broadward Hall.*

22. *The Bird on the Rock, formerly The Rocke Arms.*

23. *Ferney Hall 2001.*

24. *Heath House.*

25. *Clungunford House on Silver Jubilee Day. 1977.*

26. *Fred, Bert and Jim Bason farming. 2002.*

27. *John Rocke as High Sheriff. 1971.*

Sacrament. There was a silver Chalice, two pewter plates and a pewter flagon. There was "a decent Font of Stone for the Administration of Baptism", a "comely Surplice for the Minister wash'd and repair'd att the charges of the Parish", a large Bible of the last Translation and a book of Common Prayer, whole and entire. There was a "Register book in Parchment" to record all Christenings, Marriages and Burials. During the seven years from 1709 there had been a total of six marriages, forty nine christenings and forty two burials.

The replies then deal with the Minister. "The Minister hath a Parsonage House. It is in good Repair. He resides Personally upon his Cure". There was no chapel within the Parish. There were Prayers twice every Sunday and one Sermon . The services were between 9 a.m. and noon and between 2 p.m. and 4 p.m. and the Minister always read the entire service as prescribed in the Book of Common Prayer, without any omission or alteration. The Minister began to catechize in the church on the first Sunday in Lent yearly and continued to do so until the comers thereto were perfect in their catechism. "The Parishioners duly send their children and servants to be instructed by him". The Minister baptized publicly in the church, except for private baptism in cases of necessity, when, if the child, recovered, he received it publicly into the church, as the Law required. The Sacrament of the Lord's Supper was administered in the church six times in the year and the Minister did carefully visit the sick to prepare them for the Holy Communion or for their departure into the other world.

Answers to the next batch of questions described the facilities available in the parish. There was no Hospital or Alms-House, but there was a Free-School, founded by the parishioners and with a revenue of £8.6.6. The School was kept by a clergyman, who was a curate in a neighbouring parish. The churchwardens were appointed yearly and kept careful accounts. "The Parish Clerk diligently performs his office, keeps the church clean from dust & cobwebs and other annoyances".

The final questions enquired about misdeeds of parishioners or church officials. The answers given follow closely the wording of the questions. "There is not any Person in our Parish who lieth under a common fame of Adultery, Fornication or Incest, or that is a common Swearer, Drunkard or Blasphemer of God's holy Name or Word". "There are not any who on the Lord's Day follow their Callings and worldly Employments that wee know of". There were no Dissenters or Meetings of Dissenters and nobody had refused to pay the Church Rates. No Ecclesiastical Officer had extracted excessive legal fees or accepted bribes and no public Penances had been performed in the church or commuted for money. All very commendable.

By 1716 the Clungunford estate and the Advowson had become the property of Richard Rocke, who chose the next Rector, Thomas Evans, who came from Llandrinio, north of Welshpool, close to the Rocke family's original Montgomeryshire estates. He was inducted on 9 March 1724/5 and remained Rector for thirty seven years, being buried at Clungunford in March 1762, aged 64. Among the Clungunford Church Silver are a tall lidded wine flagon and a salver, both inscribed with the words "The Gift of the Revd. Mr. Thos Evans Rector of this Church" and the date 1758. These two handsome silver pieces are both in a style more common in the previous century. The flagon bears the hall-marks of the London assay office for 1758 and the maker's mark of A. Cox while the salver was assayed in London in 1730 and made by Paul Crespin. On the north wall of the chancel at Clungunford are framed three sheets of brass inscribed in memory of Thomas Evans and his wife, Olivia, who had predeceased him by six months, his elder sister, Mrs Pryce, the widow of the Rector of Llanginew, and his younger sister, Susannah, who lived with him. Under his Will, New Hall, a late seventeenth century red brick farmhouse beside the church at Llandrinio, and its farm, together with the residue of his Estate, passed first to Susannah Evans and, after her death in 1767 to his great nephew, Richard Rocke. His Will also provided legacies for his maidservant, his manservant and for the poor of the parishes of Clungunford and Llandrinio, to whom clothing was to be given on St Thomas' Day each year. He wished to be buried in as private a manner as decency would admit in the church at Clungunford and that he should be carried by eight poor labourers or workmen of the parish of Clungunford to each of whom he bequeathed half a guinea.

Thomas Evans had another sister, Mary, who married Owen Vaughan and it was their daughter, Mary Vaughan, who, in 1749 became the first wife of John Rocke, who by then was the owner of the Clungunford estate. Sadly, she died soon after their son, Richard Rocke was born, in 1751. The fact that John Rocke was described in his father's Will as his "natural son, commonly called John Evans" and that he had been born in 1727, two years after Thomas Evans came as Rector to Clungunford may indicate that he was already related to the Rector's family before he married the Rector's niece.

John Rocke did not inherit from his father the Advowson of Clungunford on the vacancy after the death of Thomas Evans. In the Will of his father, Richard Rocke, dated 14 October 1745, the Advowson of the Rectory of Clungunford was devised to his five executors, upon whom he said he relied, after the death of Thomas Evans, to "dispose of the next presentation of the said Advowson" to his nephew Richard Morgan, the eldest son of his sister, Mary Morgan, the wife of Henry Morgan of Shrewsbury. The executors duly carried out his instructions and Richard Morgan was inducted on 31 July 1762, but within four years he had died. The executors' right of presentation having ended, John Rocke chose the next Rector.

In July 1766, there was no member of John Rocke's family qualified to be Rector of Clungunford. His elder son, Richard, was only fifteen and his younger son, John was eleven. Both were to become prominent men of business and Mayors of Shrewsbury, but John was also prepared for the Church. Evan Humphreys was appointed Rector until such time as a member of the Rocke family was ready to fill the family benefice. It was in 1767, soon after he became Rector, that Evan Humphreys had to reply to the inquisition directed by the Bishop of Hereford to every parish in his Diocese. The Rector wrote "My Lord, I have the Pleasure of acquainting your Lordship that there is no Papist, Methodist, or any Person of a different Religion from our own in my Parish. I am my Lord, your Lordship's most obedient and most dutiful humble servant ." This short letter shows the concern of the established Church at the immense success of John and Charles Wesley and other dissenting preachers as well as the survival of Catholicism, but it also highlights the deference required from the parish priest to the prelate.

In 1779, the patron's younger son, John Rocke, was twenty four and in Holy Orders. He had taken his B.A. at St. John's College, Cambridge in 1778. He was appointed Rector of Clungunford, while Evan Humphreys resigned to become Curate, in which capacity he continued for a year to care for the parish and to sign the parish registers, which show that for many years the new Rector took no part in the work of the parish of Clungunford. Evan Humphreys moved to Montgomery, but he and his family retained friends in Clungunford parish. A wall monument in the south transept of Ludlow Church records that Thomas Mathews "of Ludlow and Shelderton" who died in 1816, aged 79, had devoted his entire fortune to the comfort and advancement of the widow and numerous family of his beloved Pastor, Evan Humphreys M.A., Rector of Clungunford and Montgomery. The monument was erected by three members of Evan Humphreys' family.

John Rocke stayed in Shrewsbury where he had so many business interests and it may be that he carried out some of the work appropriate to his other parish, for he was also Vicar of Wellington from 1782 to 1792, in which year he became Mayor of Shrewsbury. In Clungunford, there was a succession of Curates, who did all the work of the parish for a small fraction of the income that the absentee Rector received: a practice all too frequent in the Church of England at that time. Some of the Curates in Clungunford were Evan Humphreys in 1779, John Jones from 1780 to 1803, George Braithwaite in 1805 and 1806, and the Rector's own son, John Rocke junior, at various times between 1808 and his appointment as Rector in May 1814, on the resignation of his father. The parish registers show that throughout this period the services were, almost without exception, taken by the Curates and it was they who signed the registers at the end of each year.

John Rocke junior was the first member of the Rocke family to consider Clungunford to be his home. Like his father, he had taken his Degree at St. John's College, Cambridge. After thirty five years when his father was Rector in absentia, it must have been a cause for local rejoicing when he was inducted. Ten years later, on his father's death, he also became the first resident Squire of Clungunford for more than a century. After building his new mansion at Clungunford House, he naturally wanted to live in it. During the Nineteenth Century, many incumbents had no wish to live in their rectories, which were often small and primitive, as at Clungunford. Often they were themselves the Patrons of the living, or members of the Patrons' families and they had comfortable houses of their own. Others held their livings in plurality. Under such circumstances, they had to obtain the Bishop's Licence for non residence in the rectory.

John Rocke junior wrote to the Bishop of Hereford for such Licence on many occasions. They were often given for only one year. When he applied in 1845 for leave to live in his own mansion house in the parish, six hundred and four yards from the church, the Rector made it clear that he intended to perform the duties of the benefice, assisted by his Curate, Other Philpott, who would reside in the glebe house or rectory. The Rector's income from the living was £519.1.2, from which he would pay his Curate £80 and maintain the rectory. What the Rector did not tell the Bishop was that after November 1832 almost all the funerals had been conducted by Other Philpott. This situation continued with the new Curate, John Daniel Lewis, who was appointed in 1846. It was in April 1845 that the Rector had bought for £11 "a Bath chair", which may well have been for his own use, although he was only sixty two years old. However, when he applied in April 1848 for a similar Licence for the calendar year 1849, his writing was very shaky and he said that he did not intend to perform the duties of the benefice, but had employed John Daniel Lewis as his Curate to do so. The new Curate would have a stipend of £100 a year and reside in the glebe house. John Rocke, the Squire and Rector died on 14 June 1849. In his dual capacity, he had had unprecedented influence in Clungunford. His two eldest sons were at Trinity College, Cambridge, where they obtained their B.A. Degrees. His oldest son, John, succeeded him as Squire at Clungunford House. His second son, Thomas Owen Rocke, aged twenty seven, became the Rector and for him a substantial new rectory was needed.

When John Rocke junior was seeking leave from the Bishop to live in Clungunford House instead of in the rectory, he had to say that the rectory, occupied by his curate, was a fit building. In 1847, for instance, his request was supported by a certificate from the Vicar of Bromfield and the Rector of Hopton Castle, who said that they had "inspected the Glebe House of Clungunford and the buildings belonging thereto and found the same to be in good and sufficient repair and condition". However, only eleven years later, the new Rector's Architect, when seeking to justify the need for a replacement, described the old rectory as totally inadequate. It was "of timber filled in with lath and plaster, of very small dimensions, built originally for a village Public House". Downstairs it had only one room with a boarded floor and three small rooms with stone floors. There were five bedrooms, including attics and one cellar. The stable, barn and cowhouse were "all in the last stage of dilapidation" and the house itself was "exceedingly cold and comfortless and altogether unfit for the habitation of a gentleman".

This old half-timbered rectory is clearly shown to the east of the chancel in the 1802 watercolour of the north side of the church by Archdeacon Owen. It was L shaped and at the south end it had a picturesque black and white gable, facing the church. It is possible that the watercolour showed it rather closer to the church than it was and that the Victorian rectory was built on its site and incorporated its cellar, while the old lane which served it and continued to the cottages to the north, then known as Tradesmen's Row, was closed and became exclusively the Rector's drive. The old rectory having been described so disparagingly, the Faculty for the spacious Victorian rectory was soon forthcoming and the Rector borrowed, on mortgage of the Glebe, the Tithes and his stipend, the £1,267.3.0 contract price for its construction, after making allowance for the use of some of the materials from the old buildings. The Architect was Abraham Edward Perkins of Worcester.

During his forty three years as Rector, Thomas Owen Rocke was assisted by a series of Curates and after 1883, while retaining the position and stipend of Rector of Clungunford, he lived in Royal Crescent, Cheltenham until his death in 1892. His Curate in Charge at Clungunford, Rev Frederick Cooke, who took his funeral, had been living in the large brick rectory for nine years and his modest curate's stipend had clearly proved inadequate for the costs of upkeep. On the Rector's death, a Dilapidations Order was served on his Executors, under The Ecclesiastical Dilapidations Act 1871, requiring them to pay the large sum of £420.15.0 for much needed repairs to the Rectory, its outbuildings and glebe fields and to the chancel of the church, for the upkeep of which the Rector, as the recipient of the tithes, was personally responsible. Almost every room in the spacious Rectory needed repairs, as did the fences and hedges in the fields, but the most alarming part of the Schedule must have been the work required to the church chancel, including the complete stripping, relathing and retiling of the north side of the roof.

Perhaps the comprehensive restoration of the whole church, mainly at the expense of the Squire, only three years later, saved the Executors of his uncle, the late Rector from the full cost of complying with the Dilapidations Order.

His second son, William Charles Rocke, aged twenty five, graduate from Emmanuel College, Cambridge, was then appointed Rector. The first few years of his incumbency coincided with the enlargement of the church in the 1890s and at the end of his tenure of fifty three years at the Rectory, he was able to celebrate the victory in the war against Germany and Japan. When he died in November 1945, he and his father had together completed ninety six years as Rector. For one hundred and sixty six years the living had been held successively by his great grandfather, his grandfather, his father and himself, all Cambridge graduates and each of them either Squire of Clungunford or a close relation of the Squire.

After the four Rectors of the Rocke family from 1779 to 1945, the change of incumbents became more frequent. Edward Ingham-Hoult had been Vicar of Bettws-y-Crwyn with Newcastle–on-Clun for four years before being appointed Rector of Clungunford in 1946. He stayed until 1953, when he left to become Vicar of a parish in New Zealand. It was in 1949, during his incumbency, that electricity was installed in the church, even though the parish was forbidden to sell the flagon that had been given in 1758 by the then Rector, Thomas Evans. Robert Lee succeeded as Rector from 1953 to 1957 and after his death a silver Lavabo Dish and Jug, both bearing London hall-marks of 1975, were given to Clungunford church in his memory. Doughty Shemilt was Rector from 1957 to 1962 and was the last Rector to live with his family in the spacious Rectory that had been built in 1858. During his incumbency, a silver plated Wafer Box was provided for Clungunford Church. It bears on top the inscription "St. Cuthbert's Parish Church Clungunford Shropshire" and on the side "Easter 1960 Hereford Diocese".

After 1962, Clungunford had no Rector for sixteen years. In 1963, it was joined to a group of parishes under the charge of Prebendary Riou Benson, the Vicar of Clun, assisted by at least one Curate. The parishes in the Clun group included Chapel Lawn, Bettws-y-Crwyn, Newcastle-on-Clun, Clungunford, Bedstone, Hopton Castle and sometimes Clunbury and Clunton. Several of the Curates were resident in Clungunford. In 1964, David Porter lived as Curate for a year at Garden Cottage while the new Rectory was being built and he was its first occupant from 1965. Dennis Samways succeeded him from 1967 to 1968, when Stephen Thomas took over as Curate living in the Rectory. In 1973, Richard Basten moved in as Curate and in 1977 he was appointed Priest in Charge of Clungunford, while retaining responsibility for several of the other parishes. From 1978 to 1988, he was Rector of Clungunford with Clunbury, Clunton, Bedstone and Hopton Castle. On 5 December 1988, the benefice of Rector of Clungunford was suspended and for the next thirteen years the group of parishes was in the care of Priests in Charge. Paul Welch held this position from 1989 to 1993, followed by Simon Barnaby (Barney) Bell until 3 December 2001, when he was instituted and inducted as Rector in the church at Clungunford by Bishop John Saxbee of Ludlow, newly appointed as Bishop of Lincoln.

9

Communications around Clungunford during two thousand years

There were no roads in Shropshire until, in about A.D.60, the Romans reached Wroxeter (Viriconium), which became the Romanised capital of the British tribe of the Cornovii. Between 125 and 250 the city became the fourth largest town in Britain. The Romans constructed the famous Watling Street (represented by the A 5) to link Viriconium with London and a branch, also now called Watling Street, leading south from Viriconium to the much smaller Roman settlement at Leintwardine (Bravinium) and on to Kenchester, near Hereford. The Romans' purpose was to promote trade and also to enable their legions to maintain control.

Until the end of mediaeval times, that lesser Watling Street, ever more decayed, was the only proper road between Shrewsbury and Hereford, the Saxon successors of Viriconium and Kenchester. For fifteen centuries, it was the spine of communications to which were attached a network of ancient drovers' routes and tracks of varying passability, including the important drovers' route from beyond Kerry to the Midlands, which passed beside the church at Clungunford. Some monasteries and market towns took care to maintain the roads and tracks in their neighbourhood, but the general standard of upkeep was primitive and was not helped by the dissolution of the monasteries under Henry VIII. By Statutes of 1555 and 1563, the task of maintaining the highways was imposed upon the parishes through which they ran. Fragmentation and lack of incentive to ease the passage of outsiders resulted in poor upkeep. With further Statutes establishing Turnpike roads in South Shropshire, in the eighteenth century, the users could be charged a toll, and this enabled such roads to become reasonably fit for travellers.

Fig. 28. *Part of Christopher Saxton's Map of Shropshire. 1579.*

The maps of the counties of England before 1695 make no attempt to show any roads, although towns and villages and castles were recorded, surprisingly often in the correct positions. Such were the maps made by Saxton (1579) and Speed (1612). Like them, Robert Morden (1695), refers to Clungunford as "Clungonas" but he indicates roads (often inaccurately) by lines between some of the villages. Morden includes mention on his map of three large houses in the neighbourhood built when Robert Wallop had split up and sold the Hopton Castle estate in about 1656. Heath House, Ferney Hall and Broadward Hall (then called "Brodart") are all shown, more or less correctly placed.

The maps made by John Rocque in 1752 and by Robert Baugh in 1808 both attempt to record the exact routes of roads. It is interesting to compare the situation today. The present road between Clungunford and Leintwardine was not constructed until after the building, in 1796, of the first Broadward Bridge that was capable of taking vehicles. The 1752 map shows the road in its present position from Long Meadow End as far as Clungonas, but progress further south would have meant going via Cross Horn to Shelderton and then along the old Watling Street

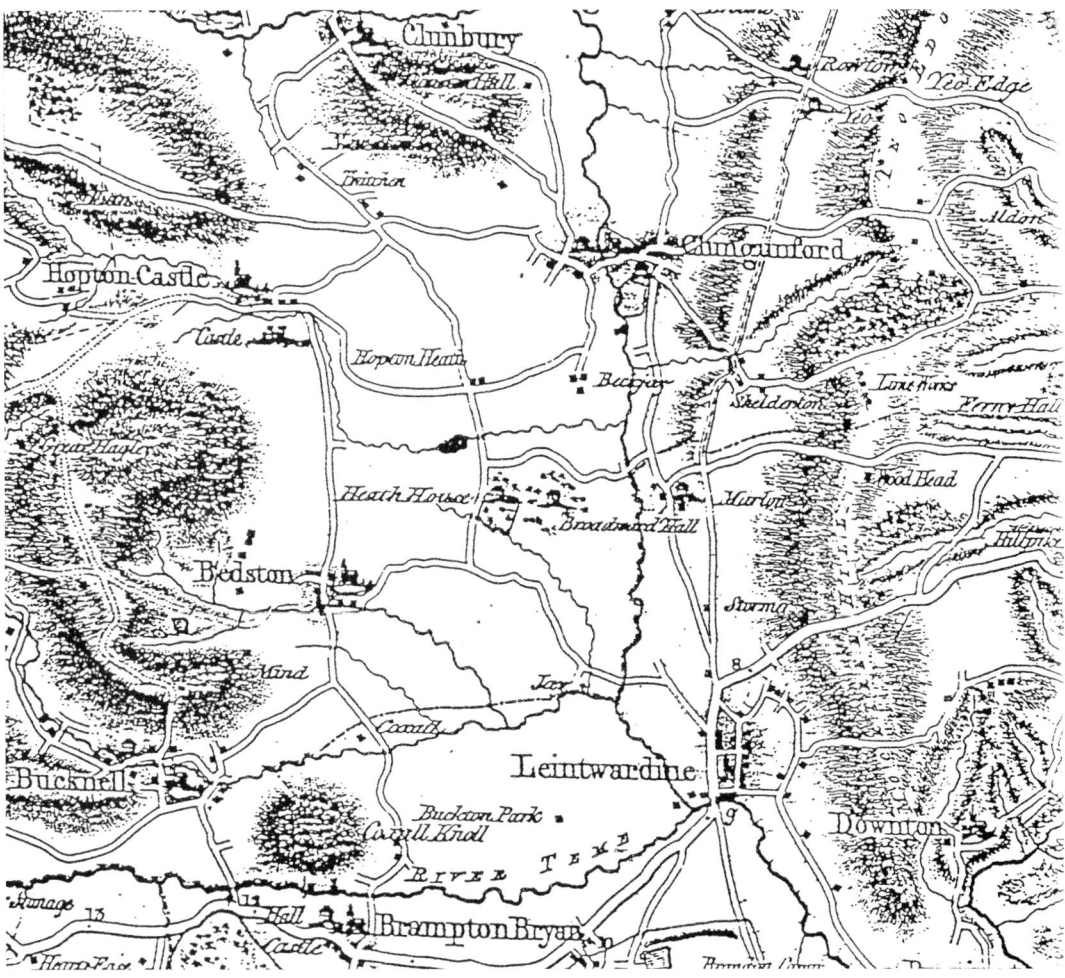

Fig. 29. *Part of Robert Baugh's Map of Shropshire. 1808.*

behind Marlow and past Stormer Hall to Leintwardine. Most of the Shelderton to Leintwardine section of Watling Street became redundant at the end of the Eighteenth Century, although Robert Baugh's map of 1808 shows the 1796 Broadward Bridge, the new road running close to it and also the nearly parallel stretch of old Watling Street, by then seldom used.

The 1808 map shows several roads that now exist in only rudimentary form It shows School Lane meeting Watling Street at the Crossways, as at present, but also continuing onwards up May Hill to Aldon, so justifying the use of the name of the Crossways, which now seems so inappropriate. Another track shown in 1808 leads from Marlow over Shelderton Hill towards Woodhead, Far Barn and Wetmore. Today this track is incomplete. These two routes eastwards over the hill from Watling Street do not appear on the 1752 map, nor does the track over Clunbury Hill, which is shown in 1808, leading off the lane to the north of Abcott Manor, going up Hope Dingle and then descending to the crossroads in Clunbury, so explaining the metal arm, bearing the cut out inscription "Cn.GUNFORD", but pointing towards Clunbury, on the 1800 signpost at Little Brampton. The steeper sections of that track can then, as now, only have been fit for packhorses and pedestrians.

Both the 1752 map and the 1808 map show the road which climbs Shelderton Hill and, at the top, branches across what was then Shelderton Common, left to Brand Hill and right to Ferney Hall. The 1808 map shows Lime Kilns by the right side of the road, half way up Shelderton Hill. The earlier map is somewhat sketchy as to the direction.taken by these roads, which can only have been the roughest of tracks across the Common until 1828. An Award was then made under the 1818 Enclosure Act which divided the Shelderton Common lands between Francis Hurt Sitwell (of Ferney Hall), Charles Bayley Unett (of Broadward Hall), Rev. Henry Cowdell (of Shelderton House) and Thomas Andrew Knight (of Downton Castle, in his capacity as the owner of much of Brand Hill).

The 1828 Award stipulated that parts of the Common should be reserved for five public carriageways, two private carriageways and a footway. Two roods of land (half an acre) on the south side of the road near the top of Shelderton Hill were allotted to "the Surveyors of the Highways of the township of Shelderton for digging and getting stone and gravel for repairs to Public and Private roads therein". A Public Carriage Way, thirty feet wide, was required where the present road runs past the lodges of Ferney Hall. Another, surprisingly, Public Carriage Way, twenty four feet wide, was required from that road to Ferney Hall itself. Other Public Carriage Ways, also twenty four feet wide, were required from the parish boundary on Green Lane to the present junction at the top of Green Lane and then right to the parish boundary and left to the top of Shelderton Hill. A further twenty four feet wide Public Carriage Way, which is now a mere track, was also required leading south from the top of Shelderton Hill towards Marlow. A Private Carriage Way twelve feet wide was to be created down Brand Hill Gutter and a four feet wide Footway was to be made from the bottom of Brand Hill Gutter to join Green Lane on the parish boundary. Finally, to enable the new owners (F.H.Sitwell and C.B. Unett) of the former common arable strip field to the south of Upper Shelderton House to reach their portions of that field, a Private Carriage Way, eighteen feet wide, was to be created off the Shelderton to Marlow stretch of Watling Street "which said road is for the sole use of the Owners or Occupiers of the said Allotments".

Fig. 30. *The wooden bridge built near the Church at Clungunford in 1657.*

The original bridge, where the present bridge is near the church at Clungunford, was built in 1657. It was only a wooden bridge, with three ten foot spans resting on stone piers and with railings either side of the carriageway. It was approached at each end by a stone causeway. (see also ***Colour Plate 14***) The churchwardens' accounts record many loads of stone from Broadward and elsewhere and timber from Hopton Castle. Three of the leading parishioners, Mr Barkley, Mr Prynce and Mr Bore were each paid 2/6 for providing transport for the materials. The owners of the timber had to be paid as did the carpenters, who made the planks and rails required. Other workmen constructed the causeways, for which gravel had to be brought. "Ale for the workmen" was a recurring item in the expenses, but even so, the total cost of "the great bridge" was only £6.9.0.

Before 1657, there had been a ford, upstream, where the old drovers' route, coming from Watling Street, via the present School Lane and Chapel Lane and passing between the Church and the so-called Motte, continued on its way towards Abcott. Almost all the old houses in the village were on that track. It was the main east-west route through Clungunford before the building of the bridge, and was also the Clungunford section of the pre-Roman drovers' route from Kerry, via the Anchor and Twitchen to the Crossways and on to Onibury and the Midlands. When the ford had to be negotiated by all vehicles crossing the river, there were frequent occasions when such crossing became impossible and there are tales of teams of horses being swept away. Because it was the inhabitants of the parish who had built the 1657 bridge, disputes arose about the liability for maintenance, which proved to be a constant drain on the parish funds. In a report to the County authorities in April 1828, Francis Marston, the grandly titled High Constable of the Stow Division of the Hundred of Purslow, said that there was at Clungunford a Carriage Bridge of ancient structure, gone into decay and become dangerous. He described the maintenance arrangements that then applied. "The Township of Clungunford mend the road to the centre of the Bridge on one side and Abcott mend the road on the other side and when any of the timber work or planks have wanted repair it has been paid for out of the poors' rates by the Overseers and sometimes when a hole was broke in the Bridge the person who next wanted to go over it would mend the planking and put in some gravel. There was never anything done to the Bridge by the Surveyors of the roads of either of the Townships of Clungunford or Abcott except hauling gravel on it". The County authorities refused to pay for the repairs that were so urgently required and, in October 1828, the Clerk of the Peace for the County reported to the Quarter Sessions that "there is evidence that the Inhabitants of the Townships in which the Bridge is situate are immemorially and by prescription liable to repair it and not the Inhabitants of the County at large". So the rickety old bridge continued to be patched until in 1935 the County Council provided the stone bridge and causeways which stood up so well to the pressures of the flooding in January 2001, when the river at Clungunford swelled to a width of nearly a quarter of a mile.

The other roadbridge in the parish was constructed at Broadward to replace another ford. A contract was made in September 1796 between the Churchwardens of Clungunford and Thomas Smith of Ludlow, Joiner, who, for the sum of £100, agreed not only to "build a substantial bridge" forthwith but also to maintain it in good repair for seven years. The Contract exempts Thomas Smith from the task of "gravelling the external surface of the said bridge forming the roadway over the same and such occasional repairs as may be requisite from the passing and repassing of Horses and Carriages over the same road way". Although expressly designed for horse drawn vehicles, this bridge was to be made of wood. The Churchwardens' accounts record several earlier bridges at Broadward, but they were all wooden footbridges and they had to be repaired frequently by local craftsmen. Expenditure on such a footbridge at Broadward is recorded in 1716 and 1724 and, again in 1740, when planks and posts for it cost six shillings. The 1796 vehicle bridge, commisioned from the Ludlow joiner for the considerable sum of £100 would be far more useful but its life was short.

By October 1817, Thomas Beale of Heath House, an influential Magistrate who lived close to the bridge, was writing to Joseph Loxdale, the Clerk of the Peace for the County and, as such, the local official ultimately responsible for the County bridges, complaining about the state of the road through Clungunford. He wrote again in January 1818, asking that the County Surveyor should inspect Broadward Bridge as a matter of urgency, adding "It appears that £20 at least will be necessary to prevent immediate danger and more for a thorough repair". Surprisingly, in the case of Broadward Bridge, the County authorities made no attempt to deny liability for the cost of maintenance and, in August 1818, the County Surveyor's Department wrote confirming instructions to Evans of Clunbury, a carpenter, to extend the timber framing of the bridge at the Marlow end. However the repairs proved to be more expensive than expected. Loxdale reported a week later that "Upon Evans taking the bridge to pieces, he found the trusses in a very bad state, owing to their not being properly supported in the bed of the river". Repairs continued for a further nine years until, in October 1827, Thomas Beale was able to confirm to Loxdale that Broadward Bridge had been fully repaired by Evans.

The continual expense and worry caused by the timber bridge at Broadward obliged the County authorities to propose a stone replacement. In April 1831, Thomas Stanton, on behalf of Thomas Telford, the Surveyor of Bridges for the County, wrote to Loxdale that the old timber bridge was very dilapidated and insecure and "in every respect unworthy of further repairs, which would only be a waste of money". He submitted a colour washed design for a sophisticated new stone bridge of two segmental arches of dressed stone with two long and almost flat embankments leading to it for 100 yards at each end.. The arches were each to be 27' 6" wide and the road width between the parapets was to be 18'. The limestone was to be obtained from the quarry at Shelderton. The estimated total cost was £710.

By June 1831, four builders had tendered for the work and Richard Jones of Bucknell was awarded the contract at £650, following argument about who would have the materials from the old wooden bridge. The 1831 bridge was some yards further downstream than the 1796 bridge, which had crossed the river obliquely. The course of the river was straightened under the new bridge and Mrs Rebecca Unett, the owner of the ground where the new channel was cut and the old circuitous channel left empty, was awarded £18.3.6 compensation. The bridge still gives good service, but it seems unlikely that the long embankments at either end were ever properly constructed.

While Clungunford had, since Roman times, been able to benefit from the proximity of the increasingly derelict Watling Street, it was the rise of Craven Arms as a centre of communications in the Eighteenth and Nineteenth Centuries that greatly improved its connections with other parts of the country. During the Seventeenth Century, the Craven family had bought a string of villages from Stanton Lacy to Wistanstow. With the construction of the road on the west side of the Onny between Onibury and Bromfield and the increase in coach traffic, the New Inn, at Newington (beside the junction with the hilly road via Edgton to Bishops Castle) which features on the maps from 1695 to 1808, and the Red Lion, a primitive hostelry at Newton (near the present Stokesay Castle Hotel) proved increasingly inadequate to cater for the needs of travellers and their changes of horses. The 1808 map shows the Craven Arms Hotel, which had been built five years earlier with its large stable block. The obelisk, built outside the Hotel at the same time, records the distances to thirty six likely destinations, from Plymouth, 205 miles to the southwest, to the curiously spelt Edingburgh, 295 miles to the north.

The situation of the township, which was soon called after the Hotel, was superb. It was at the junction of valleys to the four points of the compass, through which ran roads maintained for over thirty years by the 1756 Second Ludlow Turnpike Trust (joining Craven Arms to Ludlow, Church Stretton and Corvedale) and the 1768 Bishops Castle Turnpike Trust (joining Craven Arms to Clun, Knighton, Bishops Castle and onwards to Montgomery and Welshpool). All these roads were frequented by mail coaches and goods waggons, which provided connections with distant towns. They were maintained in passable order with the proceeds of the tolls levied on all who used them. After Telford's appointment in 1788 as Surveyor to the County, many of its roads were improved and new and elegant cast iron bridges were thrown over the intervening rivers, such as the graceful 1823 Stokesay bridge over the Onny, sadly replaced in 1964 by one more suited to juggernauts. Shropshire was indeed fortunate to have for the last forty six years of his life the services of one of the greatest engineers of the time, called by Southey and others of his contemporaries "the Colossus of Roads".

In 1824, Clungunford became better connected with this network of roads when an Act of Parliament provided for mending and widening the roads coming "through Aymestry, Wigmore, Leintwardine and Marlow in the County of Hereford and Clungunford and Broom to a place called The Cross Moor or Long Meadow End" at which point it reached the turnpike road leading from Craven Arms to Clun and so connected with all the other turnpike roads described above. There had been an unsatisfactory turnpike road along much of this route before and the new Trustees were given power to continue or remove all or any of the Toll Gates erected previously and to "set up any other Toll Gate or Gates, Bar or Bars, Chain or Chains in or upon or across any part or parts of the said roads and upon the sides therof". Toll houses were built, including probably the stone cottage at the northern entrance to Clungunford, but none so decorative as the round toll house on the Craven Arms to Clun turnpike road at Aston on Clun.

Fig. 31. *Hopton Heath Station in the late twentieth century.*

A scale of charges was established by Statute and displayed at the toll houses. Cows were charged 1/8 a score, sheep 10d a score and oxcarts 3d. All wheeled vehicles drawn by horses or mules were charged according to the number of animals so harnessed and in the four winter months, from November to February, the charge was half as much again as in the other eight months, no doubt because of the greater damage likely then to be done by wheeled traffic to the road surface.

The hub of communication at Craven Arms was only four miles from Clungunford. In 1852 it became even more effective. The railway from Shrewsbury to Ludlow was constructed, with the main intermediate station at Craven Arms. Within forty years a web of other lines reached out to Much Wenlock and Wellington, to Bishops Castle and, via Knighton, to Swansea, passing through Abcott on its way and with a station at Hopton Heath on the very edge of Clungunford parish.

Although this last, the Central Wales Line is now the only remaining branch at Craven Arms from the railway between Shrewsbury and Hereford, the road network grows ever busier, radiating from Craven Arms since long before the railway age, and freed from turnpike tolls before 1880. With cattle and sheep now transported by lorries, the old drovers' routes are now used only by local farmers, but until half way through the Twentieth Century, on market days at Knighton, Ludlow or Craven Arms the roads around Clungunford, and in particular the nearby stretch of Roman Watling Street, would often be blocked by large numbers of animals on their way to or from market, being driven onwards by farmers and their dogs.

10

Clungunford Parish Management

In medieval times the responsibility for maintaining the roads and bridges of the parish rested upon the Lord of the Manor, as did that of relieving the poor, although, if he failed to comply with his obligations, these fell, in practice, upon the church. Until the abolition of the monasteries by Henry VIII after 1536, people living near flourishing religious Houses could often receive in rudimentary form many of the benefits now expected from the welfare state, including medical care, education and sustenance in case of need. However, long before the Reformation, the problems of vagrancy and begging resulted in the passing of Acts of Parliament imposing penalties of increasingly severe mutilation and eventually hanging for "sturdy vagabonds", while greater compassion was shown to those unable to work, who were eventually licensed by the magistrates to beg within strictly defined limits, until an Act of 1536 imposed upon the clergy and churchwardens of their parishes the duty of providing for them by collecting voluntary alms from the parishioners. By an Act of 1572 the office of Overseer of the Poor was established for each parish.

In 1601, close to the end of Queen Elizabeth's reign, a comprehensive Poor Law system was established, which continued with occasional amendments until the Poor Law Act of 1834. Overseers of the Poor were to be nominated from among the substantial householders in each parish and they had the task of maintaining and finding employment for the poor, while local taxation was imposed to cover their expenses. As the Seventeenth Century progressed, the mechanism of the Poor Law was strengthened. The parish constables were to apprehend vagrants, whom the magistrates would commit to houses of correction. "Lewd women who have bastards" and parents who could not provide for their children were to be sent there also. Strangers arriving in a parish had to provide a certificate from their own parishes, agreeing to take them back if they proved to be a charge on the community and parish constables spent much time removing paupers to other parishes in which they had last had a legal settlement. Parish officers were required to establish workhouses or contract with another parish that had a workhouse, so that the poor who were a charge on the parish could be sent there.

During the Eighteenth Century, further regulations were introduced dealing with financial indemnities to be obtained by the parish from fathers of illegitimate children, the whipping of vagrants and amended rules for the apprenticeship of children of poor families. Until 1834, each parish was responsible for the administration of the Poor Law and its dependant regulations, but from that year groups of parishes were compulsorily joined together for the purpose into Unions, each with its own Board of Guardians, until the County Councils took over the responsibility in 1929.

Clungunford is fortunate to have, in the possession of its Parochial Church Council, various documents and Accounts recording the administration of the Poor Laws in the parish between 1659 and 1821 and many other parish expenses relating to the Church, the construction and maintainance of bridges and various other subjects. Many of these documents were found in the Clun Museum, of which one of the founders, in 1932, was Herbert Jones, who was then Headmaster at Clungunford School.

The organization of parish business was dependant on the election of the parish officers, which took place at a meeting of rateable householders, held annually in the Church, just after Easter. Two Churchwardens, two sidesmen, two Overseers of the Poor and a Petty Constable were elected and, under the chairmanship of the Parish Priest, they would constitute the local authority for the parish until Civil Parishes were established in 1894, when the Parish Councils took over that role. Each year, a parish rate (or lewne) was levied to provide funds for the Churchwarden's expenses and a separate lewne or Poor Rate was levied to fund the expenses of the Overseers of the Poor, whose duties included providing help in cash or kind to parishioners in need. It was the duty of the Petty Constable to issue arrest warrants and enforce the parish laws. The Overseers of the Poor and the Petty Constables all required the approval of the Magistrates before they could take up their appointments and they received no pay, but could charge expenses. In a farming community such as Clungunford, the time required to perform their duties as such parish officers must have been a serious sacrifice, and the task of so doing was rotated among a small section of the community.

The records of expenditure show many payments to impoverished parishioners and to vagrants for whom the Poor Laws discouraged such charity. In 1687, the Churchwardens themselves made five separate payments to "soldiers" of 6d or 1/-. In 1691, they paid money to various beggars, including "a woman who was robbed by the French" and "two widows out of Lancashire". By 1694, their generosity to strangers had expanded to such an extent that they made payments of 1/- or 1/6 each to a man from Wolverhampton, a man from Lancashire, a petitioner out of Flintshire, a woman with a letter of request, another woman with a petition, a distressed Minister, a woman out of Ireland, a man with a letter of request, a man with a petition, another man with a request, a man out of Oxfordshire, three poor women and two more men with requests. It seems likely that the Churchwardens of Clungunford had developed a reputation for kindness to strangers when the total available to them from the annual lewne was seldom more than £12 to cover all their varied commitments. The sums involved in each payment to the indigent poor were usually the equivalent of at least one day's pay for an agricultural worker. The policy of the Churchwardens was to show generosity to needy strangers, provided that they were not a long term charge on the parish. In 1714, they paid two men 3/- "for carrying away lame cripples", while in the two following years they made payments to men who claimed to be shipwrecked mariners.

The expenses of caring for ill parishioners were usually borne by the Churchwardens until the middle of the Eighteenth Century, after which the Overseers expected to pay. In 1719, several Clungunford children contracted smallpox and one died. Smallpox struck again in 1725 and 1742. Each time, the Churchwardens paid the costs of nursing or funerals. In 1778, the Overseers paid £1.15.0 for Richard James to innoculate against smallpox forty two people who were in receipt of Poor Relief, but, as it was nearly twenty years before Jenner made his great discovery, it seems unlikely that such innoculation was effective. Some years earlier, nearly £2.3.0 was paid when Ann Mullard was sick of the smallpox. This payment covered bread, cheese, butter, firewood, wheat, milk, ale, candles,sugar and the salary of a nurse.

As well as making provision for the sick, the Overseers made payments to those too old to work and to widows. When it became necessary to send a parishioner to a workhouse, they sent him to Cleobury Mortimer and a fee had to be paid to cover his maintenance. However, whenever the Overseers could persuade unemployed parishioners to work locally they would do so. In 1740 and 1741, having supplied the necessary looms and wool to enable cloth to be made by old people in the village, the Overseers took the cloth to sell at Ludlow Fair, Wigmore Fair and Knighton.

Often the Overseers had to journey to the Magistrates Court at the Hundred House at Purslow to obtain Removal Orders (for sending paupers back to the parish which had the legal obligation to maintain them), Filiation Orders, Bastardy Bonds, Apprenticeship Indentures or any of the other processes for which the approval of the Magistrates was required. The Magistrates were invariably local landowners, such as the owners of Ferney Hall and Heath House. If a dispute arose, whether with another parish or with an individual, the case could be sent to Quarter Sessions at Shrewsbury or even Hereford and the Overseers would be engaged for several days. Their outgoings, including the fees of Attorneys, they could recover, but their time they had to give freely.

When people moved from one village or town to another on more than a temporary basis, they were wise to obtain from their previous community a written confirmation that they would be accepted back there if their financial circumstances made them a charge on the public. Without such a document, they might be rejected by the community to which they sought to move and this was particularly so if there were numerous dependant children Such a document would avoid dispute between two parishes in the event of Poor Relief being needed. Without it and if the impoverished person had not established a legal settlement in his new parish, a Removal Order would be applied for from the Magistrates so that he could be escorted back to his old parish and handed over to its Churchwardens and Overseers, who might well apply to the Quarter Sessions to revoke the Order.

The Overseers were also concerned to secure the maintenance of illegitimate children born within the parish. When it was suspected that a local woman was so pregnant, she could be summoned before a Magistrate, who, after questionning her, would be able to make a Filiation Order, requiring the alleged father to pay to the Overseers a monthly sum during such time as the mother and her child remained a charge on the parish. Such an Order could be devastating to the father. In 1767, Thomas Jones was ordered to pay 4/- each month, although his total annual pay as an agricultural worker was only £5.10.0. If the mother did not agree to appear before the Magistrate before the birth of her child in order that a Filiation Order could be made, she was obliged to undergo a Post Natal Examination for that purpose. The father could avoid the continuing obligation to make regular payments by giving a Bastardy Bond, in favour of the Churchwardens and Overseers, for payment to them of a capital sum within a short specified time. Such Bonds given in Clungunford were for sums between £40 and £100. If his financial substance appeared inadequate, one or more of his friends or relations would be required to join as parties to the Bond.

Another duty which fell on the Overseers was to ensure that all boys and girls from pauper families were trained to achieve independence from parish welfare. Under the auspices of the parish officers and local Magistrates, Apprenticeship Indentures were entered into with respectable people of the parish, who agreed to take named children, sometimes as young as seven, into their households for a specified number of years, often until they attained twenty one, and train them in the Art of Husbandry (for boys) and the Art of Housewifery (for girls), meanwhile providing the Apprentice with "sufficient Meat, Drink, Apparel, Lodging, Washing and other Things necessary and fit for an Apprentice" while the Apprentice was required to serve his or her Master or Mistress "in all lawful Businesses according to (his or her) Power, Wit and Ability". Such Apprenticeships seldom referred to any particular trade or skill but were intended to provide the boy or girl with the experience of growing up in a secure household, which he or she could aspire to emulate. Money hardly ever passed on such Apprenticeships, but the Magistrates and parish officers were able to monitor future developments. In the surviving Clungunford documents there are Apprenticeship Indentures dating from 1659 to 1821. The system flourished until the end. On 1 November 1821, nine Apprenticeship Indentures were entered into in Clungunford, seven for boys and two for girls.

Throughout the centuries when it was the duty of the parish officers, through the Petty Constable, to maintain Law and Order in the parish, there is no evidence of any cell or lock-up in Clungunford. There is a tradition of a set of stocks in the churchyard "where the old road came near the iron gate out of the Rectory gardens". This description is hard to interpret, but one of the old watercolours of the church and churchyard made in about 1850 appears to show stocks, close to the base surviving from the mediaeval preaching cross. The same tradition also refers to another set of stocks "at Beckjay, on the left hand side of the road, just below the turning opposite Mr Davies' farm, under some wych-elm trees". This Beckjay position, away from the centre of the village, seems an unlikely site for stocks, one purpose of which was to subject the unfortunate occupant to the ridicule of passers-by and acquaint them with his appearance.

11

Clungunford Schools and Charities

From the mid sixteenth century there are records of gifts and legacies to benefit the poor and educate the children of Clungunford. Some of the money received for such purposes was no doubt spent within a short time, but other sums were invested to provide for future generations. In 1629, the Rector of Clungunford, William Barkeley, left the then considerable sum of £20 "to be added to the stock of the poor for ever". When his son, Samuel, who was Rector from 1630, died in 1672/73, he left £5 to the poor of the parish of Clungunford, as did Francis Walker of Ferney Hall, who died in 1663/64. Francis Walker also left a very generous bequest of £50 to four of the leading people in Clungunford parish "towards the maintaining of the free schools in Clungunford", from which wording it seems clear that there was already such a school. No doubt there were many other gifts and bequests from people in Clungunford and further afield.

Before the founding of the Bank of England, the usual form of investment was the purchase of land. The earliest Indenture recording the investment of money by the Trustees of the parish funds is dated 30 April 1658, when the Rector, Samuel Barkley, and Wrottesley Prynce and Lane Harris of Abcott and Thomas Corne of Rowton spent £104 in the purchase of a dwelling and twenty eight acres of meadow and arable land in several small pieces, all at Abcott and formerly part of the Hopton Castle estate. The Indenture stipulates that the four purchasers were to hold the land "to and for the benefitt of a scholemaster in the said parish of Clongunford for teaching the children of every inhabitant within the same parish". These words suggest that the school began then, although the parish Registers for 1599 record the baptism of "Nathaniel, the son of Lewys Morries Schoolmaster".

The four Trustees had unfortunately overlooked the fact that some of the £104, with which they had bought the land, was money that had been given for the benefit of the poor of Clungunford and should not have been used to support education in the parish. In September and October 1658, two endorsements were added to the Indenture, stating that a total of £15.10.0 of the £104 had come from bequests for the poor and that the appropriate part of the income was to be spent each year for the benefit of the poor, as the Rector and the Overseers of the Poor for the parish should decide, and not for education. So began the mixing of the two charity funds and the ownership by Trustees of the parish Charities of farmland at Abcott to which were added other investments as the centuries passed.

By 1708, Lane Harris was the only survivor of the four Trustees who had bought the Abcott land in 1658. He executed a Deed, which stated this fact, said he was very aged and recounted that he had made several exchanges to improve the school lands by reducing the said lands into enclosures. By the Deed he appointed five new Trustees, to whom he transferred the trust property. In 1718, Thomas Dunne of Broadway, Montgomeryshire, father of Bowen Dunne of Broome, gave £50 to the Trustees so that the children of the part of the township of Broome that was within the parish of Hopesay should thereafter be taught by the schoolmaster of Clungunford School and this arrangement continued until the School closed more than 240 years later. Later in 1718, the Trustees used £85 that had accumulated from gifts and legacies to buy from the Corne family a three acre meadow in the parish of Clunbury, known as Coston Meadow.

By 1749 there was again only one Trustee alive. Thomas Corne of Rowton, grandson of one of the 1658 Trustees, was now Warden of Clun Hospital and was the only survivor of the Trustees appointed in 1708. By Deed he recited this fact and that he had, in 1748, bought from James Lucas of Edgton, with £81.10.0 of trust money, a six acre meadow at Abcott known as Longwell Gate. He then transferred all the trust assets to eight new Trustees. Of these eight, only the Squire, John Rocke, described as "late of Trefnanny in the County of Montgomery but now of Shrewsbury" and Thomas Harley "late of Beckjay but now of Hopton" were still alive in 1782, when they handed over to eight new Trustees. In 1811, the three survivors of those eight Trustees appointed six younger men to join them. By these Deeds, made at intervals of thirty, forty or fifty years, the assets of the parish charities were entrusted to reliable local men.

The Trustees who looked after the property held for the School and the Poor of Clungunford, as set out in all these early Deeds and the subsequent ones of 1847, 1894, 1907 and until today were among the most influential inhabitants of the parish and, sometimes, people who lived elsewhere but owned property in the parish. The names of most of the Trustees appear in the lists of Churchwardens and Overseers of the Poor. The same surnames recur many times, Harris of Abcott, Corne of Rowton, Harley of Beckjay, Bridgwater of Bentley House and Wolley of half the farmhouses in the parish, as well as the Barkleys, Rockes, Walkers, Sitwells, Knights and Bayleys who owned most of the land. Until 1914, the Deeds and even the Minutes of Meetings of the Trustees distinguish carefully between those called Esquire, those called Gentleman and those described as Yeoman, Farmer or Mr., but from the outset of the Great War the Minutes make no such distinction. The trust property always included land at Abcott, let to neighbouring farmers, and usually Government Stock. The nucleus of the land held today originated in the 1658 purchase and a similar 28 acres of meadow, pasture and arable fields are very carefully described in a Deed of 1847. In late Victorian times, the part of the Trustees' income from land and investments that was available to support the School was about £62 a year.

There is little reliable information concerning the whereabouts of the School, the number of scholars or the identity of the teachers until the late Eighteenth Century. However, the Churchwardens paid the schoolmaster £3 in 1706 and £3.5.0 in 1707, in each case probably additional to what he had been paid by the School Trustees. In 1712, Mr Whittle, the schoolmaster left and the Churchwardens paid him 15/-. They also paid 5/- to Mr Keys, his successor, who may have been a disciplinarian because, in the following year, the school table was mended at a cost of 2/- and a whip and bell were bought for 6d. There are references in the

Churchwardens' accounts between 1728 and 1734 to the gradual improvement of a school building. Every other year work was paid for. 700 laths and 1000 tiles in 1728. pavement, fireplace and repairs to the windows in 1730, the roof and floor mended in 1732 and the school window sloped down in 1734. However, there is no indication of where the building was.

In 1757, the balance of a 21 year Lease of "Esqr's House" at Clungunford granted by the absentee Squire, John Rocke of Trefnanny, was assigned by the Lessee to the same John Rocke and his seven fellow Trustees of the Free School at Clungunford, in return for a payment of £21 and an undertaking by the Trustees that the Lessee's children would receive free education at the School during the remaining 15 years of the Lease. Whether "Esqr's House" was the manor house near the Church is not revealed, nor is it certain that the School was moved into that house.

In Clungunford Church, over the door to the tower, is an elegant marble memorial tablet to James Green, Gent, who died near Oswestry in 1820, aged 76. For twenty four years he had been Master of the Free School in Clungunford, but his dates as Master are not recorded. However, it is certain that he was Master between 1780 and 1787, when he paid rent each year to Richard Rocke, who for his part gave a subscription of five guineas to the School. James Green paid £2 for a building, which was probably his home as well as the School, 5/- for "part of school yard" and 1/4d for "schools land". From the position of the entries in the Rent Roll, it seems possible that during the 1780s the School was on the Abcott side of the river.

The Rules for the School, printed in March 1819 and bearing the names of a majority of the Trustees, emphasize the link between the School and the Church, in whose north chapel it was then located. On every schoolday the Master was to read prayers before the children were dismissed and every Sunday morning, Christmas Day and Good Friday the children would have to come especially to the School to be inspected by the Master before attending Divine Service, which he would also attend to enforce proper observance. The School day was long From 7 am to 5 pm between Lady Day and Michaelmas and from 8 am to 4 pm during the rest of the year, with always a break for lunch from 11 am to 1 pm, so that the children could walk home for a meal. On Thursdays, lessons ended at 3 pm and Saturdays were half holidays, but on those two days each week the children were to be catechized.

The parents of the scholars had to ensure that their children complied with the Rules and freely submit them to be chastised for their faults. The children were to be sent to Church and School cleaned, washed and combed and they had to be supplied with the necessary books and a Prayer Book when they were capable of using it. Every morning and afternoon of schooldays, the Master would record the names and times of all scholars present and frequent absentees could be expelled from the School by the Trustees. Despite its description as a Free School, fees had to be paid, based on the means of the parents, for all children except those from the poorest families. Apart from the entrance fees, which varied between 2/6 and 10/- for each child, there were annual payments, ranging from 5/- to 10/- per child towards the cost of heating the classroom. These payments, known as School Pence, formed an important part of the revenues of the School, together with the annual Government Grant, the income from the land and investments and subscriptions from the Trustees.

By about the end of the Eighteenth Century, the School was accommodated in the north chapel off the chancel of Clungunford Church, the furthest east of its north windows was replaced by a door for direct access from the churchyard and a fireplace and chimney were installed beside the door. This arrangement was unsatisfactory for both the School and the Church. In 1853, the School Trustees decided that a new building should be erected, incorporating classrooms and a house for the Master. A Committee of the Trustees published their reasons in a printed statement. They recorded that land provided by past benefactors for the support of a schoolmaster produced annual rent of nearly £50, but that it was impossible to employ an efficient teacher because there was no proper schoolroom and no residence for the Master, whose small salary did not enable him to rent one. As for the accommodation in the Church, it was too small, gloomy, dirty and unhealthy and the lack of a playground caused injury and desecration of the Church and churchyard by the children.

As a site for the new School, John Rocke of Clungunford House gave half an acre of the field known as Braziers Close, a subscription list was opened and application for Grants was made by his brother, the Rector, as Chairman of the School Trustees, to the Committee of Council on Education, to the Hereford Diocesan Board of Education and to the National Society for Promoting the Education of the Poor in the Principles of the Established Church (known as the National Society). The need for a new School was obvious. The population of the parish was 601 and there were currently 80 boys and girls from Clungunford parish and Broome at school, so that the new School should accommodate up to 90 children. The Master's house should have at least three bedrooms. With the assistance of the National Society, plans for such buildings were prepared and estimates obtained. £279.9.6. was collected locally and various tenant farmers agreed to lug the stone, timber and other materials. The schoolrooms were calculated to cost £243.18.1. to construct and the Teacher's house £257.1.7. With necessary fittings, the total estimate was £533.19.8., so a considerable shortfall was anticipated. Nevertheless, in 1855 the Trustees signed a Contract with Messrs Price to construct the buildings.

In August 1857 the Rector was able to report to the National Society that the work had been completed. The Committee of Council paid £287, Hereford Diocese paid £5 and the National Society £35, but, even so, there was a deficit, because the actual cost had soared to over £726 and the Trustees had to raise further sums locally during the following years. The children and Master moved into the new premises, which they must have considered spacious. The style was Victorian Gothic and the walls were brick inside and local limestone on the outside. The lofty schoolroom was over 36' long and the smaller room over 17 ', while the Master had a three bedroom house and garden. The future of the School appeared assured, but, at the next meeting of the Trustees, in June 1858, William Holland, the Master had to be reprimanded "for inebriety" and, in 1863 it was reported that on several occasions he had sent children for "intoxicating liquors" during school hours. To pre-empt inevitable dismissal, he tendered his resignation. The Trustees' continual problem was to find suitable Masters for the School as well as Assistant Teachers and Articled Pupil Teachers. Three Masters came and left during the next ten years while, in 1875, Mr Randle, the Master, was required by the Trustees "to make a written apology to Mrs Rocke for the use of the word 'bother' hoping that Mrs Rocke will overlook the offence".

It was during the 1860s and 1870s that the discipline and morale of the staff and students were at a particularly low ebb. The Logbooks for the School, now in the Shropshire Records and Research Centre at Shrewsbury, reveal the fluctuating attendance, the reasons for absence and the behaviour of the children, with details of punishment when inflicted. A recurring problem was the custom and often necessity for the children to help their parents during the busy times of the farming year. Every July, nearly half the children would be absent, gathering whinberries, helping in the hay harvest or turnip singling and, in acceptance of this situation, the start of the summer holidays would sometimes be announced when the whinberry picking season began. Corn harvest in September and potato and apple picking in October and other farming activities caused further absenteeism.

Poor attendance and setback to educational progress could also be attributed to outbreaks of whooping cough, measles and mumps and to atrocious weather conditions. When all the children had to walk to school, often leaving home before dawn, and when there were very few maintained roads in the parish, heavy falls of snow would result in only a handful of scholars attending and the headmaster would understand. Many years in the winter months there were days when the Abcott and Beckjay children were unable to get to School because of floods and the same situation continued as late as 1933. The new bridge, built over the Clun in 1935, seems to have solved that problem.

Even when the children could reach the School, education was sometimes impossible. One day, the entire floor was under an inch of water, while on other days it was intolerably cold, not helped by occasional broken windows on the playground side. Fires were seldom lit in the School before the end of October and an entry in the Logbook for 29 January 1912 records that there had been a fire in the stove since 2 pm the previous day and yet, at 9 am, the thermometer stood at only 26 degrees Fahrenheit. On such days, the children would be sent home at lunchtime, but this would cause a problem for the headmaster, who had to be able to report that there had been 400 sessions of teaching during each year (with morning and afternoon counted separately) and also to record the average number of pupils each week. Every effort was made to achieve success with both returns and when the fairs were at Craven Arms, Leintwardine or Knighton, the children were expected to come to School for at least one lesson. In April 1883, the otter hounds met at the bridge at Clungunford, so the teachers, fearing a very poor attendance of their pupils, proclaimed that lessons would begin that day at 7.45 am and end at 10.15.

The Logbooks and, during the last years of the School, a special Punishment Book, record lapses in the behaviour of the scholars and the retribution meted out to them. The cane was always available but seldom used. More frequent were such punishments as "a month's imprisonment in School during playtime", which was imposed in 1867 on two boys and three girls, caught by a farmer stealing his turnips on their way home from School. Another regular punishment was being kept in for an extra hour. Punished offences were of great variety. Laughing when addressed by a teacher, unpunctuality and refusing to stand up when told to do so were frequent. Fighting in the playground, climbing over the railings, throwing ink and even pushing a dead mole into the face of a girl pupil were more unusual. All were recorded carefully.

During the nineteenth century, the interest taken in the School by the Rector and his wife and by the Squire and his wife was most impressive. Scarcely a week would pass without a visit from one of them, who would sometimes test the children's progress and at other times read to them or assume the role of teacher. Occasionally, prizes would be distributed, such as caps, scarves, pinafores, gloves, Hymn Books and Story Books. Attendance at church was required and the children would be reprimanded if they failed. However, there were other outside activities. Tea parties at the Rectory, musical events and trips to Ludlow fair feature in the Logbooks. The curriculum was extensive and gradually expanded, but no foreign languages are mentioned. English literature, history, arithmetic and scripture were regularly taught. Poetry was learnt and recited and there were frequent singing lessons. There were lessons in bookbinding, basketry, gardening, dairy work, woodwork for the boys and for the girls needlework. The Inspector of Schools came regularly to assess the quality of all the teaching and the progress of the pupils.

Towards the end of the nineteenth century, the number of scholars was increasing and the Government Grant grew accordingly, so the Trustees decided to pay higher salaries to the Schoolmaster and the Articled Pupil Teacher, but even by 1878 the Master's salary was only £113, out of which he had to pay £10 rent for his house and another £10 to a sewing teacher for the girls. The turnover of staff continued to trouble the Trustees, although the teaching of such subjects as Religious Knowledge and Drawing sometimes won high praise from the Inspectors. In 1903, the Trustees of the Clungunford Charities chose some of their number to be Managers of the School in future, while continuing as Trustees of what was described as the School and Poor's Land Charity. An Order of the Charity Commissioners, dated 2 May 1905, instructed them to expend four fifths of their net income for educational purposes and the other one fifth to help the poor in the parish.

Not until 1909 was a Master appointed who was prepared to devote his career to Clungunford. Mr Herbert Jones came at a salary of £105, but in a few years he was receiving the same as his predecessor thirty years earlier and in 1917 his wife was appointed as Supplementary Teacher. In 1922, he went to Clun School as Head Master, but in 1926 he returned to Clungunford, where he continued as Master until he died in May 1940. It was recorded in September 1931 that the Managers had received a letter from the Local Education Authority, asking them, owing to the serious financial condition of the country, to notify their teachers of a 15% reduction in salaries as from 1 October 1931, subject to the Finance Bill becoming law. The Managers complied with this request, but there is no record of this cut in salary taking effect.

In the years following Herbert Jones' original appointment in 1909, there were considerable changes at the School. The inadequacy of heating in the two schoolrooms was a frequent problem, which the Managers, sought to solve by a succession of Tortoise Stoves in the larger room and new grates in the smaller. In 1914 it was found that the timbers of the bell turret on the centre of the roof were badly decayed, so it was removed. The bell was not rehung and in 1940, being no longer used for school purposes, was handed over for conversion into war munitions. The water supply to the School was always uncertain, despite the connection made in 1903 to the reservoir for Clungunford House at such a level that Clungunford House, its kitchen garden and the village spout would retain priority. Often the Master had to fill tanks with water at Broome. In 1922, during Mr Jones absence at Clun School, a Motor House was built between the School House and School Lane and in 1923 the Master was allowed to erect "a wireless apparatus" on the School House. In 1938, Herbert .Jones asked the Managers whether they would allow electric light to be installed. Estimates were received in May 1939, which were accepted by the Managers for the Master's house but not for the School.

Herbert Jones was joint founder, with Tom Hamar, of the Clun Museum in 1932. He was a keen local historian and donated to the Museum his own collection of locally found flints. His enthusiasm must have inspired the children in Clungunford School in its last years before its decline began. It was the drop in the number of local children that sealed its fate. On the outbreak of war, in September 1939, an influx of refugee children from Liverpool provided a temporary respite. The school buildings could not hold everyone at once. Teaching had to be in two shifts, with the visiting children in the afternoon. They were from the Roman Catholic school of St. Francis de Sales and they had brought their own teacher. Inquiries were made about building an extra classroom, but soon the refugees began to drift back to Liverpool. On the death of Herbert Jones in 1940, the Local Education Authority decided that the number of children in the School did not justify his replacement by a man as Head Teacher, despite the Managers pointing out that there were more children in the School than when he had returned from Clun in 1926. They also said that "owing to inferior housing conditions the type of children was rougher and less intelligent than in some neighbouring parishes" and that this required a man in charge. The L.E.A. was not persuaded and a succession of Head Mistresses was appointed. First, in 1940, Miss Wilkins, followed by Mrs Hughes in 1945. The Managers in 1946 applied to be allowed to appoint an additional Teacher, because Mrs Hughes had to teach a top class of 44 children, aged between 7 and 14 years and complaints had been received from several parents, who said that their children were not receiving proper attention. This request was refused, but the following year the older children were transferred to Stokesay County School, at Craven Arms, leaving only the Juniors and Infants at Clungunford.

Miss Evans succeeded as Head Teacher in 1947, when all the children over 11 years old were taken by bus to Craven Arms. Some of them had never been in a bus before and were very excited at the prospect. Although all the last few Head Teachers seem to have been popular with their pupils, Miss Evans acquired a special reputation as a tomboy, because she wore hobnail boots and shorts and sometimes slept in the garden. The Ministry of Education Reports in 1950 and 1956 both criticize the effectiveness of the teaching in the Infant Class, but say that the Teacher was giving of her best and that one problem was that all the equipment normally associated with modern Infant teaching was missing. By 1956 the School had two classes of 20 Juniors and 15 Infants and it was obviously heading for closure. The last Head Teacher, Miss Player was at Clungunford for only two years from January 1959 until December 1960, when the Juniors were transferred with her to Hopesay School, leaving the Infants, being taught by Mrs Holder. The final closure of Clungunford School was marked by a service at the Church on 26 July 1961, attended by Mrs Holder and her pupils.

The site for the School having been provided by John Rocke, the Squire of Clungunford in 1857, under the provisions of the School Sites Act 1841, when the School closed the property reverted to his descendant of the same name, who arranged for his retired gardener, Richard

Wilkes and his wife Gertrude Wilkes to move into the Master's house. The empty schoolrooms were used for grain storage and various other temporary purposes until they were sold in 1973 to Alick and Fiona Barratt for conversion into a private house.

Fig 32. *The School and Master's House after conversion to private houses.*

The closure of Clungunford School in 1961 did not end the support from parish Charities for the education of the children of the parish. In January 1950 and March 1976, Orders made by the Charity Commissioners made changes to the constitution of the Clungunford Charities, dividing them into two, but with the same five Trustees for each, of whom two are appointed by the Parish Council, two are co-opted and the fifth is the Rector, ex officio, whenever there is a Rector of Clungunford. The Trustees meet six times each year to administer their property and consider applications. The Educational Foundation promotes the social, physical and artistic education of people under 25 years old normally resident in the parish by helping with the cost of equipment, travel, accommodation and other expenses for which neither the Local Education Authority nor the District Council is liable. The other Charity, for relief of poverty, also continues its good work. It assists parishioners who have modest income by helping in times of bereavement, sickness or other distress and with the costs of travel to hospital and other necessary journeys, provision of clothing and furniture and assistance with the cost of heating in the winter as well as in many other ways. A delivery of coal to elderly parishioners in recent bleak weather continues to fulfil the generous intentions of four centuries of benefactors

12

The Squires of Clungunford after 1558

The ownership of land in Clungunford during the last four and a half centuries has never observed Parish boundaries. The Lordship of the Manor (with its rights and duties derived from feudal times) and the advowson of the parish church belonged to the owners of the central section of the Parish, roughly between the Roman Road, called Watling Street, and the river Clun. Most of the Parish east of Watling Street and also the farmland at Shelderton, Broadward, Hopton Heath and even part of Abcott belonged, until the seventeenth century, to the Hopton Castle Estate.

As described in an earlier chapter, that Estate had been given to the de Hopton family shortly after the Norman Conquest. They retained it until the death in 1499 of Elizabeth de Hopton, who had inherited the Hopton Estates on the death without children of her brother Sir Walter de Hopton. Elizabeth's first husband was Sir Roger Corbet of Moreton Corbet, north of Shrewsbury, and their grandson, Sir Robert Corbet, inherited from her. The ownership of the Hopton Castle Estate remained with the Corbet owners of Moreton Corbet through four more generations. They were powerful people with many other estates in Shropshire and beyond, most of them were knighted and were High Sheriffs of Shropshire. They were allied by marriage to equally prominent families and the tombs in the church at Moreton Corbet of Sir Robert Corbet and one of his sons show them in full armour and a panoply of heraldry with their ladies beside them in the latest finery. For them, Hopton Castle was a minor possession, but they were careful to retain it. In 1578, Sir Andrew Corbet died. His eldest son, Robert, was a diplomat, sent by Queen Elizabeth on a series of missions abroad, particularly to the Habsburg Emperor and to William the Silent to counter the influence of Spain in the Netherlands. Robert Corbet stayed with his uncle in London in 1583 and there he died of the plague. He left two daughters, but no sons. The inventory of his assets, taken in Shrewsbury on 3 August 1583, listed a large number of properties and included lands in "Hopton, Hugley, Sholderton, Broward, Abcote, Clangonyas, Sybden, Swiftanstowe, Whittingstowe, Nynton, Burwarden Co. Salop".

Just as landed estates were accumulated by strategic marriages, so the lack of a son could cause disintegration of property. Robert Corbet's elder daughter, Elizabeth, married Sir Henry Wallop, whose family had for centuries owned in Hampshire the Estates of Middle Wallop and Farleigh Wallop, which is still the home of his descendant, the Earl of Portsmouth. On her father's death, she took over the Hopton Castle Estate while her sister, Lady Carey, obtained other parts of the Corbet inheritance. Litigation ensued from 1601 to 1606 between them and Sir Richard Corbet, Robert Corbet's next brother at Moreton Corbet, to obtain the judgement of the Court. A compromise was eventually reached. Hopton Castle remained with the Wallop family and Sir Henry, by now a Shropshire landowner, was High Sheriff of Shropshire in 1606. Once more, the owners of Hopton Castle did not live there. When they were not in Hampshire, they lived at Peynton, in the parish of High Ercall, close to Moreton Corbet.

Sir Henry Wallop died in 1642, having recently completed a programme of modernization and improvements to Hopton Castle, by then over 300 years old. His son, Robert Wallop, succeeded as the owner of the entire Hopton Castle Estate, including Shelderton, Broadward, Corbet's Wood (where Ferney now is) and land stretching westward from Abcott. The Civil War was just beginning and Charles I had established his headquarters at Oxford. With a few exceptions, the people of Shropshire supported the King, but Robert Wallop was one of the fiercest of the opposite faction and had instructed his retainers at Hopton Castle accordingly. When it was besieged in February 1644, a few men were sent to its aid by the Harleys from Brampton Bryan Castle, which was also being besieged by a Royalist force. After a fortnight's continuous siege, Hopton Castle was forced to surrender. On the pretext that they had been unreasonable to try to defend the indefensible, the twenty nine remaining defenders were barbarously massacred in a muddy pit beside the Castle, while their commander, Samuel More of Linley, was taken prisoner to Ludlow Castle, of which a few years later he became Governor for Cromwell. When news of the fate of the defenders of Hopton Castle reached Brampton Bryan Castle, they prudently decided not to continue their defence and surrendered on honourable terms.

Robert Wallop sat in the House of Commons, representing parts of Hampshire, almost continuously from 1621, when he was aged only twenty, until the restoration of the monarchy in 1660. He represented Andover and the County and, finally, Whitchurch. It was during the short period between 1653 and 1658, when he was not in Parliament, that he split and sold the Hopton Castle Estate. The Corbet's Wood section was sold to Francis Walker, who moved into Ferney Hall, where his family were still living a hundred years later. Broadward became the property of Richard Bayly, whose descendants lived there for almost two centuries. Heath House and the major part of the estate, including the ruined Castle, were sold to Bartholomew Beale of Windsor, whose descendants retained them for two hundred years before selling them to the Ripley family. The farms at Shelderton were divided between various purchasers as was the Abcott portion of the Estate and when the Trustees of the School at Clungunford made their original purchase of twenty eight acres of land at Abcott in 1658 it was stated that those acres had formerly been part of the Hopton Castle Estate.

Robert Wallop's interests lay in national politics. He was one of the Judges in the trial of Charles I at Westminster Hall in 1649, but he managed to avoid adding his signature to the warrant for the King's execution. Under the Commonwealth, he was appointed a Member of the various Councils of State between 1649 and 1653 and he was again a Councillor of State under the Rump Parliament in 1659 and 1660. After the restoration of the Monarchy, Parliament passed a resolution, disbarring him from the enjoyment of his Estate, degrading him from his gentility and imprisoning him for life. The resolution also sentenced him, on each succeeding anniversary of Charles I's execution to be drawn upon a sledge to and under the gallows of Tyburn with a halter round his neck. He died in the Tower of London in November 1667.

In 1558, when Philip and Mary were on the throne of England, the largest part of the parish, as described above, formed part of the Hopton Castle Estate, then owned by the Corbet family. The Morris family owned the house now called Abcott Manor, the Knight family owned Beckjay and the Corne family owned Rowton Grange, all with many acres of land. Church Farm, the Glebe land and other smaller areas were also excluded from the Lord of the Manor's estate. The farmland that belonged to the Lord of the Manor of Clungunford, amounting to less than 600 acres, was divided between two owners. John Littleton sold his half of it to William Barkeley of Cressage and in the following year, when Elizabeth had become Queen, William Barkeley bought the other moiety and the advowson from Thomas Stringfellow, with the concurrence of the Earl of Oxford, who had the right to buy it himself. In 1587, another William Barkeley was appointed Rector. He was aged twenty six, the only child of the second marriage of the Lord of the Manor to Elizabeth, the daughter and heiress of Richard Day of Halton. He looked after the parish until his death in 1629, and his son, Samuel, and two of Samuel's sons held the living successively from 1630 until 1693, except for two years. In the parish register for January 1599/1600 the Rector recorded the burial of his father with the words "William Barkeley Gent. Lord of the Manor of Clungunford".

The Visitation of 1623, which recorded the genealogy of the Shropshire gentry, shows that the Barkeleys of Cressage and Clungunford were descended from the second son of a Fourteenth Century Lord Berkeley and so were a branch of the family which, since Norman times, has owned Berkeley Castle, where Edward II was so foully murdered. Indeed, Samuel Barkeley, the Rector of Clungunford from 1630 to March 1672/3, had on his seal the Arms of the Berkeleys. Spelling of surnames was haphazard in those days. The Clungunford branch of the family spelt their name Barkeley until the second half of the Seventeenth Century, after which many of them omitted the first "e".

Just as the descendants of the second marriage of the original Barkeley purchaser became Rectors of Clungunford for over a century, so the descendants of his first marriage continued to own the Estate as Lords of the Manor until 1709. By his first marriage, to Katherine Chambers, William Barkeley had two sons and two daughters. His sons, Thomas and Edmund, married Jane and Mary, the two daughters and co-heiresses of William Felton of Ewdness, in the parish of Worfield, near Bridgnorth. While the younger brother, Edmund, and Mary settled in Shrewsbury with their family, Thomas and Jane moved with their children into Ewdness Manor, a red sandstone house with gabled wings. Even after inheriting the Clungunford Estate, Thomas preferred to live on his wife's property and, after they had both died, their son, Francis Barkeley continued to live at Ewdness When he died in 1639 he was buried at Worfield. His Will gave £5 to the poor of Clungunford and also referred to an Entailing Indenture which he had made in 1608, when he had conveyed his estates to Trustees to hold for himself and his wife, Elizabeth, and thereafter for various of his Barkeley cousins in Shrewsbury in tail male successively, so that Clungunford and Ewdness should continue to belong to the Barkeleys.

Francis and Elizabeth Barkeley had no children. After they had both died, Clungunford and Ewdness and the ancestral property at Cressage all passed by the terms of the Entailing Indenture to Thomas Barkeley, a grandson of Francis' uncle Edmund. Thomas had married

Margaret, daughter of Sir Andrew Corbet of Moreton Corbet, where all their children were baptized. Margaret was descended from many generations of de Hopton and Corbet owners of the Hopton Castle Estate. The Clungunford and other entailed Barkeley estates all passed to their eldest son, William, who continued to live in Shrewsbury and was spelling his name Barkley. He had a son and three daughters, Frances, Hannah and Martha. In May 1698, the son, another William, sold Ewdness Manor and Ewdness Farm and all the associated land to Sir William Whitmore of neighbouring Apley. There were tenants in both houses. It seems that it was the William Barkley who sold Ewdness who built the old Manor House, which is shown in the 1802 watercolour by W. Pearson. It was a house of some presence, simple in appearance but seven bays wide and having large sash windows on two floors. It is almost impossible that a house with such sash windows would have been built in this part of Shropshire before 1700 and their proportions make it improbable that the windows were converted from mullions and transoms. There is no record of either William Barkley, father or son, in the latter half of the seventeenth century, ever living in Clungunford, but in the Lease and Release by which he sold Ewdness in May 1698, the younger William Barkley was described as of Clungunford, so he may, indeed, have been living there by then and could soon have begun to build the old Manor House while he lived in Clungunford Farm. By April 1708, the Indenture appointing William Barkley and others as Trustees of the Clungunford Charities describes him as of the town of Montgomery and within another two years he had died unmarried.

William Barkeley's Will, made on 14 March 1709 caused swift application to the Court of Chancery. It read "I give and devise to my loving brother-in-law, Edward Morris of Montgomery Gent. and his heirs all my Manor or Lordship of Clungunford alias Clungunnas alias Clungunwas ...... and the advowson of the Rectory...". Edward Morris was an Attorney in Montgomery, who had married the Testator's youngest sister, Martha and had lent him money on mortgage. In the Chancery action, entitled Prince v Morris, there were allegations of undue influence. One of Martha's sisters, Frances, had married Michael Middleton in 1695 and the other, Hannah, never married. Michael Middleton represented both Frances and Hannah, claiming for them shares in the Estate and certain people in Clungunford, who had exchanged land in a Trustee capacity with the Testator, joined in the action to validate their transactions. The Court's decision confirmed the Will and the validity of the exchanges of land but obliged Edward Morris to purchase annuities for his wife's sisters, Frances and Hannah. Thus Clungunford passed to Edward and Martha Morris. Their daughter, who was also called Martha Morris, married Richard Rocke of Trefnanney, Montgomeryshire, on 17 June 1715, but died eight months later, when Richard Rocke inherited from her the Clungunford Estate.

The final link between Clungunford and the Barkley owners of the estate is to be found in the Will of Hannah Barkley of Montgomery, Spinster, who died shortly after her niece, Martha Rocke. She made her Will on 17 April 1716 and it must have been worded by someone accustomed to Welsh place names. Before giving the residue of her estate to her sister, Frances Middleton, she gave to the poor of the parish of Montgomery and the poor of the parish of "Llangunnas in the County of Salop" the sum of £40 for each parish, to be paid into the hands of the Parsons and Churchwardens for the time being of each parish and to be spent on "such security as they shall approve or in the purchase of land" so that the income should be distributed half yearly amongst the poor. Within two years, the Trustees of the Clungunford Charities had used this bequest and money from other sources to buy three acres of land called Coston Meadow.

The Rocke family, who owned the Clungunford Estate for nearly two hundred and eighty years from 1715, had, for several centuries, featured prominently in Shrewsbury and later also in Montgomery. Some of them were glovers and many of them were Burgesses of Shrewsbury. They married into similar Shrewsbury families. In March 1603, a Patent of Arms was granted to Richard Rocke, who had been born in 1564. The Arms granted were "Or three chess rooks and a chief embattled sable" while the crest was "On a rock proper a martlet or" : ingenious canting Arms with both the shield and the crest alluding to the surname, Rocke. With his status thus advanced, he was appointed Sheriff of Montgomeryshire in 1620. His grandson, another Richard Rocke, married Margaret Rogers, a widow who was the daughter of John Matthews of Trefnanney Hall, Montgomeryshire, and it was their son, yet another Richard Rocke (1688-1746), who inherited Trefnanney from his mother, Margaret, nee Matthews, and then, in 1716, inherited the Clungunford Estate from his first wife, Martha, nee Morris, after his brief marriage to her. The Clungunford and Trefnanney Estates were kept in the same ownership for over ninety years and during that long period successive Rocke family owners lived almost always at Trefnanney, in the parish of Meifod ten miles north west of Welshpool, or in Shrewsbury. Richard Rocke married three times in all, but had no children by any of his wives.

His Will, made on 14 October 1745, refers to the fact that his natural daughter, Jane Wynne and his "natural son John Rocke, commonly called John Evans", then aged eighteen having been born between his second and third marriages, were both living with him at Trefnanney. The Will, which took effect when Richard Rocke died in 1746, aged fifty eight, provided annuities for his widow and sisters and a legacy for Jane Wynne, but only on her marriage with the approval of his Executors. The Trefnanney and Clungunford estates and his other property he left to his young natural son, John Rocke, alias John Evans.

The only mention prior to 1811 of the surname Rocke in the Clungunford Parish Registers of those being baptised, married or buried there is on 30 March 1753, recording the marriage between "Mrs Jane Rocke" of Clungunford and Mr Thomas Littlehales of Leintwardine Parish. The Littlehales family were farmers at Marlow for many generations. In the Eighteenth Century, it was normal to describe mature unmarried women as "Mrs", just as until recently all women employed as cooks in private houses have been so called, whether married or not. It seems that Jane's first marriage did not meet with the approval of her father's Executors, because it was only when Mrs Jane Littlehales, widow, was married again in November 1778 to Rev. Pryce Woosnam, the Vicar of Leintwardine, that her father's legacy was released to be included in her Marriage Settlement. Jane Woosnam remained in close touch with her Rocke relations, although they lived in Shrewsbury, and when she died, in 1792, she left her property to her nephews, Richard Rocke and Rev John Rocke.

John Rocke, who had ceased to be called John Evans, lived mostly in Shrewsbury, where he was admitted a Burgess in 1758 and was Mayor in 1760. An Indenture of 1771 describes all the land that he owned, including Trefnanney and 85 acres at Cressage, producing annual rent of £45, clearly inherited from William Barkeley, who had bought the Clungunford estate over two centuries earlier. John Rocke's land at Clungunford was only about 550 acres, let to various farmers, but he also owned twelve cottages, of which three were let at rents of £1.10.0 a year but most at rents of 5/-,!/- or a mere sixpence. No house for his own occupation is listed. He married twice. His first wife was Mary Vaughan, from Glascoed in Montgomeryshire, whose mother was a sister of Rev. Thomas Evans, who had been Rector of Clungunford since 1725. He married her in October 1749, but she died when their only child, Richard, was born in July 1750. His second wife, Mary Wingfield from Preston Brockhurst, he married in 1753. By that marriage there was also one son, John, born in 1755, and a daughter, Mary, a year younger, who when only sixteen was to marry Thomas Eyton of Eyton, near Wellington. John Rocke, the father, died in May 1782 and was buried in Shrewsbury Abbey.

At the age of twenty nine, Richard Rocke inherited his father's Estates, following family litigation in the Court of Chancery and a Deed, described as "Agreement for ending Differences", made on 28 January 1780. The Rent Roll Book covering the decade from 1780 to 1789 shows that until Richard's father died in 1782 he was paid an annuity out of the rents by half yearly instalments of £315 every Michaelmas and Lady Day. Additionally, Richard paid interest at 5% per annum on £2,000 which he owed his father and on £1,000 which he owed his brother, John. There were other annuities to be paid out of the rents from Trefnanney and Clungunford so that until his father died Richard had little benefit from them. The gross annual rents from Trefnanney were about £1,400 and from Clungunford only £330, but, as Landlord, he had to pay for many repairs to buildings and also make contributions to the Poor Rate and the School in each parish. Fortunately, Richard was in business in Shrewsbury, where he was admitted a Burgess in 1771 and was Mayor in 1786, in which year he was also the High Sheriff of Montgomeryshire. He never lived in Clungunford.

In 1777, Richard Rocke married Elizabeth Kinchant, but they had no children. He died in 1807 at his house in the Crescent, Shrewsbury and is buried at St.Chads. His assets included 22 dozen bottles of port. Elizabeth, his widow, died in London in 1817. He was succeeded by his half brother, John, who had entered the Church. From 1779, John was Rector of Clungunford (of which his brother was patron) and for ten years from 1782 he was concurrently Vicar of Wellington with Eyton (of which his brother-in-law, Thomas Eyton, was patron). He was also a Burgess of Shrewsbury in 1777 and Mayor in 1792. On inheriting the Estates of Trefnanney (which he sold in 1812 to Rev. Richard Mytton of Garth) and also Clungunford, Rev John Rocke became Squire of Clungunford as well as being its Rector.

He had a fine house in Quarry Place at Shrewsbury and it is unlikely that he ever lived at Clungunford. He was proud of his pedigree and, in 1820, installed in the south aisle of Shrewsbury Abbey Church a heraldic window recording the marriages of earlier Rockes with twelve other armigerous families. In 1782, he married Harriet, daughter of Rev. Pryce Owen of Shrewsbury. She was painted in a Gainsborough style hat. She was the link between the Rocke and Owen families. They had a daughter and four sons, the eldest of whom, John, born in 1783 and educated at Shrewsbury School and St John's College, Cambridge, also took Holy Orders and was Curate of Clungunford from 1808. In May 1814, the father resigned the living of Clungunford and his son succeeded him as Rector. When his father died in 1824 at his house in Shrewsbury, the Rector also became Squire of Clungunford. His three brothers had all died, one in infancy and the other two, aged eighteen and seventeen in the wars against Napoleon.

The younger Rev. John Rocke had married, at Leintwardine in 1812, Anne Beale from nearby Heath House. They had five sons and four daughters. They and their children were the first members of the Rocke family to live regularly in Clungunford. Until their marriage, it is possible that, as Curate of the parish, he lived in the primitive Rectory, but later he may have occupied the old Manor House, which features so prominently with its smoking chimneys in the water colour drawing made by W. Pearson in August 1802. (see **Colour Plate 14**) However, it may not have been in a habitable state, because in a Deed dated 25 March 1812 the Reverend John Rocke the younger was stated to be of "Fearny Hall".

Because it was over a hundred years since any member of the Squire's family had lived in Clungunford, the Manor House will have been in serious need of modernization, although it was far more spacious than the ancient Rectory. The assessment of Land Tax and Window Tax in 1784 appears to ignore the Manor House altogether. According to the official list of the amounts of Land Tax and Window Tax paid by everyone in the parish, Richard Rocke, who then owned the Estate, was charged a mere 11/6 Land Tax and no Window Tax whatsoever, so it is clear that he had no house for his own occupation. We know from his own Ledger of rents and expenses that, after putting the Old Mill into working condition in 1784, he paid Land Tax of 11/6 for it in that year and the drawings of it show no windows. The 1802 view of the Manor House shows that it had many windows and yet in 1784 no person in Clungunford was charged Window Tax for so many and one must conclude that the house was then empty and exempt. The only documentary clue to possible occupation of the Manor House during the Eighteenth Century is the reference to "Esqrs House" in the Lease for 21 years granted in October 1751 by John Rocke of Trefnanney to Richard Powis of Clungunford, wheelright, requiring an annual rent of only 12/6 but an obligation to put the property into good and sufficient repair. The Lease was later transferred to the School Trustees.

When, at last, a member of the Rocke family was living in Clungunford as Curate, the link between the Estate and the family which owned it became closer. In October 1811, the Squire's only daughter, Mary Anne Rocke was married in Clungunford Church to John Wingfield of Shrewsbury, fifty eight years after the only previous mention of the Rocke family in the parish Registers, except as Rector or Curate. Described in the Register as "of the parish of Clungunford", she was no doubt staying with her brother, the Curate, at the time of her wedding. A charming oil portrait of her in a white Empire-style dress was kept at the new Clungunford House, which her brother commissioned to replace the old Manor House, soon after inheriting the Estate on the death of their father in 1824. As the first head of his family to make Clungunford his home, the younger Rev John Rocke needed a comfortable and fashionable house and, in letters to his Solicitor, he explained that his family had decided to sell off the remainder of their Montgomeryshire property and to buy such land as became available to enlarge their Clungunford Estate. Indeed, his own 1812 Marriage Settlement recorded that his father had purchased from the Earl of Tankerville Abcott Manor and its land, while he was to buy land at Twitchen in 1837 from his brother-in-law, Thomas Beale of Heath House.

John Haycock, the leading Shrewsbury Architect was then sixty five, but his son, Edward, aged thirty five, a pupil of Jeffry Wyatville who had just begun his transformation of Windsor Castle, had already designed or altered a few Shropshire houses and was soon to establish a far bigger and more prestigeous practice than his father. Clungunford House, which was built to Edward Haycock's design between 1825 and 1828 on slightly higher ground to the southeast of its predecessor, is a severe brick house, until recently stuccoed, two storeys high with an attic invisible from outside. Its entrance front faces west and is of four bays, with the first and fourth in projecting gabled wings and, between them, a low porch of Doric columns. (see **Colour Plate 25**) The south front of five windows, with a wide bay of two storeys at its centre, faced a formal garden and the park beyond. The austere appearance of the house belies the elegant Grecian detail to be found in the interior and, in particular, in the central staircase hall. Close by are a stable block and a now roofless octagonal dovecote with its serried rows of over 350 nesting holes. It was built of bricks on a rat resistant base within and appears to be of the early Nineteenth Century, when Lords of the Manor could still expect the surrounding farmland to nourish their flocks of pigeons, providing them with tasty squabs for the table and guano for the garden. The construction of the embankment and sluice to create Clungunford Pool, fed by a spring uphill to the east, must have been undertaken at about the same time to provide fishing recreation. It is shown on the 1848 map, with a boat house at its north west corner. Surrounded by its fertile Estate, the new Clungunford House with its elegant interior filled with fine late Georgian furniture and silver, much of it brought from the Rockes' Shrewsbury house, made a clear statement that the head of the family would in future live at Clungunford the agreeable life of both country gentleman and parson.

Receiving as he did the rents from his Estate and also the tithes from the entire parish, he had an income that allowed his family a comfortable life. At the end of each year, he was paid over £200 in tithes. Every April, Rev. Henry Cowdell, who lived and farmed at Shelderton House, paid him £35 tithe and other parishioners paid even later in the year. John Langslow, the tenant farmer at Abcott Manor, paid him over £1,000 in rent and tithe annually and he received smaller sums from other tenants. His only investment dividend was from the Worcester and Birmingham Canal Company, which paid him over £240 each year, while his farming business enabled him to sell cows and calves and sheepskins from time to time. His total income in the 1840s was always between £1,750 and £2,000.

The details of his expenditure provide an insight into the lifestyle of a typical Shropshire squire of modest estate in the second quarter of the Nineteenth Century. The overwhelming impression is of a caring husband and father and a close knit family. Each of his nine children was educated carefully and given allowances every quarter, which increased in amount as they grew older. His two eldest sons were both sent to Cambridge, following family custom. John, who was born in 1817, was at school at Harrow and went on to Trinity College in 1835, while Owen, born in 1822, was at Bridgnorth School before following his brother to Trinity in 1841. The cost of Owen's time at University is recorded by his father, showing that out of Owen's annual allowance of £250 there was little left after his Cambridge expenses had been paid. However his Degree enabled Owen to succeed his father, five years later, as Rector of Clungunford and to retain the benefits of the living for the remaining forty three years of his life, even when he had retired to Cheltenham.

The third and fourth sons, Richard and Herbert, went into the Army and their father had to purchase their commissions for £250, while continuing to pay them allowances of £32.10.0 each quarter. The girls were taught by a series of governesses, several of them French, who were paid £20 every six months, and some of the children learned to play musical instruments. Emily had an Erard harp and Alfred had a flute. All the children were encouraged to travel in the neighbouring counties and their father paid for their coach fares. Whenever any of the girls went on a journey, perhaps to Cheltenham or Leamington, John or Owen would accompany them on the coach. John went to Scotland and Ireland and, in May 1841, his father paid £100 for him to go fishing in Norway with his friend Solley and £25 for the tackle. The trip was a great success. John caught 98 salmon weighing from 4 lbs to 35 lbs. Solley caught 76 salmon, the largest of which weighed 47 lbs and, while he played it for two and a half hours, took him nearly 17 miles down the river with 80 yards of line. In 1845, John set off for the north of Scotland and with another friend, Campbell, was at Langwell, on the river Oikel in Ross-shire, from 30 August to 8 October. Whether they caught any fish is not recorded, but they shot 647 grouse, 11 hares, 9 snipe, I golden plover and 30 black game.

The parents seldom travelled far from their Estate and parish, although they made regular excursions to see their friends in the neighbourhood or to shop in Ludlow, Leominster or Shrewsbury. Turnpike charges are carefully recorded. A return journey to Ludlow cost 3/-, Wistanstow or Walcot 2/-, Bishops Castle 4/- and Shrewsbury £1.15.0. They subscribed to Archery Societies at Shobdon and elsewhere and they went to Balls in Ludlow and Shrewsbury, sometimes after dancing lessons for unspecified members of the family. The accounts make no mention of guns or cartridges, but at least John, the eldest son, will have made full use of the sporting possibilities of the Clungunford Estate in view of his later renown at field sports. His father bought flies from a Ludlow supplier and no doubt fished the Clun. The accounts mention no expenditure connected with the church or the Rectory, which was usually occupied by his Curate, although it may well be that some of the work for which payment was made to J. Jukes, the builder, was for their repair. Each year he paid Poor Rates towards the fund maintained by the Overseers of the Poor for the parish and an annual subscription of £1.2.0. to Clungunford School. He also paid the Bishop's visitation fee during the years of such visitations.

The household menu included frequent purchases of fish and game. Salmon was 1/- a lb, whether fresh, dried or salted. Partridges, pheasants and venison feature often in the accounts and grouse arrived by the box at Craven Arms, where carriage had to be paid for long before the arrival there of the railway. Other regular purchases for the table were salt butter, Stilton cheeses at 15/4 each, large quantities of honey at 1/- a lb and sometimes a box of Carrs biscuits at 5/6. All vegetables were supplied from the large walled garden and meat and milk from the farm. There is an occasional mention of the purchase of apples or other fruit, but no doubt the garden produced most of the fruit required. Grocers' bills were paid from time to time and every two or three weeks, Anne Rocke was given £5 by her husband to pay for "sundries" required for the house as well as frequent sums for her own use. Other items for the house that feature regularly in the accounts are coal, candles and malt and, of course, wages for the servants. Purchase of wine is seldom recorded, but, with postage costing a penny a letter, 5/- was spent on stamps every few weeks.

The Squire of Clungunford had his hair cut professionally in Ludlow for 1/-, but his accounts contain no record of any of his family going to the hairdresser. Perhaps they paid out of their allowances. Tailors' and dressmakers' bills were paid for all the family at various times. Two hats in London cost £2.6.0, military gloves £1.10.0 and silk handkerchiefs 16/6, while 15/- was paid for a pair of trousers for Herbert, £2.19.6 for bonnets for Mary Anne and Emily and £5 for a show saddle and habit for their mother, Anne.

The garden, farm and stables employed many people. Payment of their wages is recorded as well as the purchase of equipment and stock. Iron railings, lengths of various kinds of timber, a brown waggon mare for £22, a bay horse for £31.10.0 or 30 sheep from Clun at 13/9 each, with 7/3 to the man who drove them and 1/3 for the turnpike tolls. Oats cost 3/- a bushel, Barley 4/2 and Wheat 9/-, although the prices of each varied slightly from year to year. Payment of £1 was made to Mr Morris when two cows were sent to his bull and another cow was bought for £30.10.0. Mr Blakeway, who farmed at Upper Shelderton, had the lime kilns further up the hill. Every year, quantities of lime and straw were bought from him and he was sometimes employed as a carrier and when extra help was needed on the farm.

Life for the Rocke family at Clungunford in the early years of Queen Victoria's reign must have been very pleasant, if provincial. The hectic pace of the City did not worry them. While the two eldest boys were to spend most of their lives in Clungunford and the youngest, Alfred, was to marry the daughter of the Rector of Hopesay, the third and fourth sons, Richard and Herbert, as professional soldiers were to see more of the world. The two eldest daughters also remained close to home, marrying the Rectors of Bitterley and Wistanstow. As their father's health declined after 1845 he gradually transferred his parish duties to his Curate and led a more sedentary life. In June 1849, he died at Clungunford, where a hatchment of his Arms impaling those of his widow hangs in the tower of the church. When she died in 1856, she was described as living in Ludlow.

Their eldest son, John, was thirty two when he inherited the Clungunford Estate, while his next brother, Owen, aged twenty seven was appointed Rector of the parish. John was a member of the banking firm of Rocke, Eyton & Co, formerly known as The Shrewsbury Old Bank. It head office was in Shrewsbury but it had a branch at 18 Broad Street in Ludlow, where the smaller door had been added for the Bank's customers, while the Manager lived upstairs. The Rocke family's connection with that Bank had begun before 1821 and still continued in 1894, when the Bank Manager, Thomas Atherden, subscribed five guineas to the enlargement of Clungunford Church. John Rocke also took a prominent part in the affairs of the County. He was a magistrate and in 1869 was High Sheriff of Shropshire. For many years he was a Deputy Lieutenant of the County.

Within a year after inheriting the Clungunford Estate, he was gazetted a Lieutenant in the South Salopian Yeomanry, army reservists whose officers were all drawn from the Shropshire gentry and whose commanding officer was the Lord Lieutenant, the Earl of Powis, whose main residence in the County was at Walcot Hall, close to Clungunford. In May each year, the Yeomanry was summoned to a week's camp and manoeuvres. Although John Rocke took part every year for the first ten years after his enlistment, his enthusiasm waned and after 1866 his excuses show great originality. By then, of course, there was little enough risk of England being invaded. In 1859, John Rocke asked Lord Powis to excuse him from attending "the campaign" because he did not want to leave his wife alone. In 1861, he would be a few days late because his children had scarlatina. In 1864, Mrs Rocke told Lord Powis that her husband was weak and languid and much pulled down by illness, so she would send her son, aged nine, as a substitute to see the Review. In 1866 and 1867 he was not well enough to attend and suggested resigning his commission in favour of some more aspiring soldier, while in 1868 his charger was unwell. It had put its foot on a rolling stone on the Broome road, come down and hurt both knees. John Rocke had no horse left that was steady enough to lead a troop. Lord Powis offered to lend him a horse, but the charger recovered so speedily that the loan was refused. The next year, young Johnny had measles and by 1870 John Rocke said that he could not stand the number of hours that they would have to spend on horseback. In 1871, John Rocke retired as Lieutenant. Clearly he was not a natural soldier.

In 1853, he had married Constance Anne, daughter of Sir Charles Cuyler, the second Baronet. They had a daughter and two sons, the younger of whom died in his infancy. They lived at Clungunford, where he formed an exceptional collection of stuffed British birds, for which he added a large room to the house. He wrote a learned article on the Birds of Shropshire in "The Zoologist" for 1864 and his observations informed the section of the Victoria County History for Shropshire concerning the birds seen in the County in mid Victorian times. It was he who reported that a pair of honey buzzards was trapped at Ferney Hall in June 1865 and that three more birds of the same species were seen in the Ferney district in August 1881. Not only was he "an ardent and indefatigable naturalist", as described in his obituary, but he was also a keen sportsman "always at home whether in the hunting fields or among the turnips and stubbles, both of which pastimes he followed with a relish". His Game Register, in which from 1837 to 1880 he recorded meticulously not only the dates of shooting at Clungunford, details of the bag and the names of the guns but sometimes an assessment of the weather and its effect on the prey, shows that this was an absorbing interest, which only declined during the last four years of his life, when perhaps he was less fit.

As a landed proprietor he was prudent and "whilst caring for the welfare of his tenants, he at the same time considerably improved and extended his estates". It was during his time that the Beckjay land was added to Clungunford Estate. On his death, in April 1881, his only surviving son, John Charles Leveson Rocke, born in 1855, succeeded to the Estate. His widow contemplated taking a Lease for 14 years of Bentley House, close to the drive gate of Clungunford House. Although a draft Lease was prepared, it was never implemented. She died in 1908.

John Charles Leveson Rocke was only twenty five when he inherited the Clungunford Estate. He never married and his involvement in local affairs was much less than his father's had been, although he was a magistrate for some years. It was, however, during his time that the massive programme of work on the church was undertaken. He was the guiding force and he bore almost the entire cost. As a keen musician, he was particularly concerned with the provision of the organ and took immense care to ensure that it was the best that could be obtained for its purpose. When he died in 1906, the heir to the Estate, Evan Meredyth Thomas was only twenty two. He was the only child of the sister of John Charles Leveson Rocke, Constance Ida Rocke, and her husband, Lieut Col. Evan Aubrey Thomas. He had never known his mother, who had died four days after he was born. On inheriting the Rocke property, he assumed by Royal Licence the surname and Arms of Rocke. As is customary on such grants, the Arms given to him in 1907 were a variation on those used by his maternal Rocke ancestors. They were "Per chevron or and sable, three chess rooks counterchanged, on a chief embattled gules a leopard's face of the first". The crest remained a martlet on a rock, but between upright red ostrich feathers. After his change of surname, Evan Rocke's cousins at Clungunford Rectory were apt to refer to him and his family as the sham-Rockes.

So far as the available records show, the part of Clungunford parish that Evan Rocke inherited in 1906 was, in essence, the part that had been bought in 1558 and 1559 by William Barkeley and had descended to him through so many generations together with the Abcott property that been bought a hundred years earlier from the Earl of Tankerville and the Beckjay land that had been bought in 1863 from the Knight family. In September 1931, he attempted to sell most of the Estate by auction, but only one small lot reached the reserve price, so that the Estate remained intact under his ownership. Evan Rocke was educated at Radley and Pembroke College, Cambridge, where he was a keen oarsman. In his youth, he also shot pheasants and in 1910 he recorded with pride how he had killed two woodcock at once, no mean feat. His interest in shooting evidently waned after 1912, when the Clungunford shooting was let. In 1911, he married Charlotte Mary Williams and they had a son, John, born in 1915, and two daughters, Ida and Eva. Ida never married, but Eva married Richard Turner and, after his death, Tim Edye. Evan Rocke was a keen gardener and vied with his neighbour, Cyril Habershon of Hesterworth, in breeding daffodils. In 1954 he died, aged 69. His widow continued to live at Clungunford House, where she was joined in due course by her son and daughter-in-law and their two children. She died, aged 90, in 1971.

John Rocke was an engineer by training, having done his apprenticeship at Listers at Dursley and then worked for the Bristol Aircraft Company during the 1939-1945 War. Just before inheriting the Clungunford Estate, he had been Farm Manager at the Borstal Prison for young offenders at Usk. He had married Sarah Joan Burnet in 1938. They had a son, David, and a daughter, Susanna. Following family tradition, John Rocke was High Sheriff of Shropshire in 1971. (see *Colour Plate 27*) For many years he was Chairman of the Ludlow Bench. He was an enthusiastic shot and every summer he went to Scotland to fish for salmon.

The shooting on the Clungunford estate had been let since 1912, recently to a syndicate. John Rocke chose some of his friends to continue this arrangement, but, year after year, his Game Register shows what a struggle he had to maintain a sufficient stock of birds to shoot. During the rearing season it was usually too wet and occasionally too dry for the chicks to flourish. The partridges were often in danger of extinction and there were years when they were not to be shot. In late Victorian times the annual bag of partridges on the estate had sometimes been over 400 and in 1903 it was 551. Even in 1929 it was 492, but that was before the fundamental changes in farming methods, which caused their increasing decline, so that in the eight years after 1964 the average number of partridges shot was less than 20. Pheasants were reared to supplement the wild stock, but the return was dismal. In some years, kestrels, rats or foxes took a heavy toll. In 1968, 511 young birds were released, but the total shot by the syndicate was only 156. Despite every inducement to stay on the Clungunford estate, it seems that the young pheasants would set off for the attractions of Saddle Hill, safe from the guns of the syndicate. In 1969, the results were even worse, so John Rocke resolved to disband the syndicate, to endeavour to build up the stock of wild birds and to ask a few good guns to shoot on fewer days. This policy proved successful for the next few years and the bag of pheasants in the early 1970s was higher than in any recorded year since 1930.

Soon after he took over the Clungunford Estate John Rocke decided to farm the Home Farm, which had previously been managed for his father by the Makelins of Upper Shelderton. After his daughter, Susanna's, marriage to Anthony Daly, he transferred to her Abcott Manor and its farmland. Having sold most of the Beckjay land in 1972, the Clungunford Estate at his death, in December 1985, was very similar in extent to that bought by William Barkeley from whom it had descended to him through four centuries. His wife had predeceased him in 1978, after falling from a bedroom window at Clungunford House. John Rocke took a keen interest in all that happened in the district. In Clungunford itself, he was popularly referred to as "the Squire" and the end of his benevolent influence was a great sadness.

When he died, his son David was living in Canada. The Clungunford Estate was left to Susanna, who changed her surname to Rocke. In 1990, Clungunford House and its grounds and park were sold to Jonathan Roberts and Janet Thain. At the same time, its contents, including much superb furniture and silver acquired by the Rocke family in the reigns of George III and George IV, were dispersed by auction. Almost all the remainder of the Estate was split up and sold before the end of the century, although Susanna Rocke and her three children still retain Clungunford Farmhouse and several cottages.

13

Abcott Manor

One of the oldest and most fascinating houses in the parish of Clungunford is Abcott Manor. It was long the home of the Morris family (see Chapter 6), who established themselves as country gentlemen in Tudor times and whose descendants, through three changes of surname, retained until the first decade of the nineteenth century the ownership of the house and 250 acres of scattered farmland between Hopton Heath and the river Clun, strips in the common field stretching downstream from the west end of Clungunford Bridge and also a 20 acre farm and over 80 acres of parkland on Goat Hill. Abcott Manor was never an actual manor in the technical sense, although it has been called by that name for nearly a century.

The earliest parts of the external structure which we can see today have been refaced with brick, but date from the beginning of the Morris tenure in the 1540s. (see **Colour Plate 11**) The house clearly replaced an earlier building on that prime site. We know that in 1221, when the widow Alice from Abcott took a case to the High Court in London, there must have been a substantial house for her to live in. She would have been relatively rich – otherwise, before the days of legal aid, she would not have been able to take a case to Westminster. Her house may well have been a predecessor of the present Abcott Manor, built in the best position on that important road. We also know that the Lord of the Manor, Simon de Halberdyne, gave fifteen acres and a "messuage" at Abcott to Haughmond Abbey, near Shrewsbury, in the thirteenth century. This land was soon let to another widow, on condition that she took the Abbot's advice before remarrying. There is no clear proof that those fifteen acres contained the site of the present house, but later developments in the story of Abcott make this very likely.

The oral tradition states that there was a religious connection for Abcott Manor and is best recounted by the present owners, who came to live there in 1986 and were given the following account soon after their arrival. "Monks used to live in the house : everyone in the village knows that. There is a tunnel out of the house for monks to escape by when they were in danger. It leads to Coston." The owners say "We were also told categorically by an elderly lady, whose forebears had lived there for some considerable time, that the house was built by the Knights Templar, ergo before their disbandment early in the fourteenth century. It was then, so she had been taught to believe, handed over to the Knights of the Order of St. John of Jerusalem. During all this time, it had been used as a hostel for pilgrims making their way to the shrine of St. Winifred, Holywell. It was believed to have been run in conjunction with a similar establishment at Coston, where a stone cross on a barn was said to have existed, showing that it was once a recognised refuge."

There is little doubt that the the oral tradition is accurate when suggesting a monastic connection for Abcott in the early Middle Ages. To add to Haughmond Abbey's possession of land and a house, there is another record of a connection with Wigmore Abbey. After the Dissolution of the Monasteries, when a large number of small parcels of monastic property were sold off, not only does the Haughmond land appear in the list, but also another fifteen acres in Abcott, "which had belonged to Wigmore, in the tenure of William Morris". Unfortunately, Wigmore, unlike Haughmond, had no cartulary, so we cannot discover when that land came into the possession of the Abbey, but it was clearly at some point in the Middle Ages. No doubt the monks from both monasteries came to inspect their land and, when they did so, probably stayed in the house on the site of the present Abcott Manor.

The Templar connection, suggested by the oral tradition, is more problematic. It is undoubtedly true that the possessions of the Templars were handed over to the Knights of St. John (the Hospitallers), but there is no record, in the list of the Templars' Shropshire possessions, of any land at Abcott, although there are records of other land close by. You could say that the land at Abcott might have been too small an acreage to be recorded in such lists and it might have just been handed over to the Hospitallers without record. However, in that case it should have turned up in the more detailed lists of Hospitaller properties in the neighbourhood. Land at Coston is listed in the accounts of the Hospitaller foundation at Dinmore in 1505 and it was referred to in a court case in 1599, when several extremely ancient local men gave evidence that it had belonged to the Hospitallers in their youth. As yet, there is no documentary proof of the assertion by the oral tradition that Abcott itself was a Templar possession. Perhaps more evidence will come to light in the future. With the undoubted monastic connection, perhaps, over the years, "Haughmond" became confused with "Hospitaller" in the way that "Clungunward" became confused with "Clungunford". In both cases, there is a good reason for the confusion.

The house, itself, is of several different periods, but the evidence here provides yet another puzzle. Unfortunately, the two remarkable and huge beams at ground level between the hall range and the cross wing are impossible to date by dendrochronology, because they lack sapwood. Thus we cannot tell from which of the predecessors to the present house they came. Their size does, however, suggest that there was a medieval building of considerable status on that site. Perhaps it will be possible in future to discover a date for them.

The beams of the present hall range, when tested by dendrochronologists, produced a number of felling dates, ranging between spring 1541 and spring 1546. Thus we know for certain that William Morris' hall house was ready for roofing by 1546. Later, possibly quite soon after the hall was finished, a floor was inserted to make bedrooms above and a fine chimney was erected between the two northern bays, so separating the present dining room, with its rich Tudor panelling, from the cross-wing, which nowadays contains the kitchen and bedrooms above.

This cross-wing, always with two floors, was probably built soon after the hall was finished, since the felling dates of the roof timbers lie between 1543 and 1546. The junction of the two wings shows unusual alterations to the timbers of the roof space, implying that the cross-wing was not part of the original plan. The roof timbers close to that strange junction between the hall and the cross-wing are blackened by smoke damage and it is possible that, at some early stage, this end of the building was used as a "smoke bay" to channel smoke up from an open fire.

Until some date is found for the two huge beams at ground level, it is impossible to speculate accurately as to how an older building on the site of the cross-wing could have impacted on William Morris' plans for the hall.

The Morris family appear to have changed their minds soon after the hall was finished and decided to add, not only a two storey cross-wing, but also a bedroom floor and chimney to the open hall house. For some reason, at the end of the 1540s, the decision was taken to build a considerably grander house than had originally been envisaged. It is strange that they had the courage to build such a fine house on land which they did not yet own. They were still tenants of the crown in the 1540s and were only able to buy the land in 1553, when it was included in a long list, in the State Papers, of small parcels of former monastic land being sold off by the crown. Perhaps by the time William's son, Thomas, inherited in 1549, he was certain that he would be able to buy the land and the additions were made by him.

The original front door of the sixteenth century house was on the west front and is now covered by a later extension. The sixteenth century infilling of lath and plaster for the timber frame has been replaced with brick. Further clues to an earlier house may lie in the infilled cellar. The open stone cellar under the seventeenth century wing may be of earlier origin and the present windows seem to have been inserted after the structure was built. This is sometimes called "the undercroft", because of the oral tradition that it could have been used as a chapel. Unfortunately, there is, as yet, no firm evidence for this. At some stage between the completion of the cross-wing and the building of the seventeenth century wing, the need was felt for another large fireplace and a bread oven to be inserted on the east wall of the present kitchen, which they now grace. At one stage an outside staircase was added to this wall, possible descending onto the basement, but it was removed when the new wing was built. The remains can just be made out inside the later structure.

The foundations of the medieval kitchen building, separate from the house as a precaution against fire, lie between the north façade of the house and the perimeter wall, which ran along the edge of the road from the ford – the medieval village street. There is a well between the house and the medieval kitchen. The remains of the fish pools, which you would expect a medieval or Tudor house of substance to possess, are still just visible, although the stream which fed them has been diverted.

The distinguished east wing, with its half timbered gable (see *Colour Plate 13*) and tall brick chimneys, with ribbed patterning on the outer faces and zigzag open brickwork between the shafts (see *Colour Plate 12*) is likely to be of early Stuart period and the stout balusters on the staircase were probably installed soon after November 1643, when the Rector of Clungunford, an opponent of the ritual established by Archbishop Laud, will have been quick to remove the altar rails from the church. The cellar beneath the east wing was equipped at about the same time with a set of stone mullioned windows, using masons' mitre techniques. These windows were intended to be admired from outside the building, where the mullions have ovolo mouldings, while the interior has straight chamfers. There also survive remains of the garden terraces, perhaps also dating from the seventeenth century, which descend towards the river.

The fine plaster ceiling in the upper room of the east wing incorporates not only strapwork and heraldic beasts but also pomegranates, a feature originally associated with Catherine of Aragon.

There is a ceiling of a different design, but with the same heraldic beasts, clearly from the same pattern book, at Reaside Manor, near Cleobury Mortimer. The Abcott ceiling could date from 1620, but, with other improvements, could well have been added in the second half of the seventeenth century, when new owners with Shrewsbury tastes and money will have required changes. When Hearth Tax was collected in 1672, at the rate of a modest two pence for each hearth, Abcott Manor was the most highly taxed house in the parish, with nine hearths, while Mrs Beatrice Freeman, at Coston, listed with Clungunford although actually in Clunbury parish, paid for seven hearths, Broadward Hall had seven and Samuel Barkley paid for only six. By the Land Tax and Window Tax Return of 1784, the charge on Abcott Manor for both forms of tax was still among the highest in the parish. Its windows cost the tenant, Thomas Langslow, £1.4.6. tax. Only the owner of Broadward Hall paid more.

In 1644, the then owner, Francis Morris, died. His only son predeceased him and he was survived by two daughters, aged twenty two and eighteen. The elder, Judith, married John Owen of Stowe, near Knighton. In 1652, the younger daughter, Beatrice, married Wrottesley Prynce from a prosperous Shrewsbury family. His grandfather, Richard Prynce, is recorded to have been a very eminent lawyer. Blakeway, in his book on the Sheriffs of Shropshire, says that Richard Prynce was also "a very excellent man, the founder of his own fortune, for he had no pretentions to illustrious origin" and that he built in the Abbey Foregate at Shrewsbury, a handsome residence called Whitehall. The house still stands today, behind its gatehouse. It is three storeys high and square in plan, with three gables on each facade and mullions and transoms in its windows. It was surrounded by large formal gardens and there are still a stable range and a dovecote. It was built between 1578 and 1582 from the red sandstone masonry of the monastic buildings of the Abbey and is said to have been painted white, originally, to diminish the owner's embarrassment about the source of the building material. All sign of the white paint disappeared long ago. Richard Prynce's son, Sir Richard Prynce, was a prominent Royalist and, after the Restoration, was Mayor of Shrewsbury in 1662. Philip, his elder son, inherited Whitehall and the very valuable Shrewsbury property, while Wrottesley, the younger son, lived in his wife's house at Abcott Manor.

Beatrice and Wrottesley Prynce had ten children, who were all christened in Clungunford church between 1653 and 1669. Beatrice died in 1675 and her husband in 1677, when Abcott passed to four of their sons successively. Over the years, the Abcott Prynces bought from their cousins, the Owens of Stow, the parts of the Abcott farmland that had formed the portion of Judith Owen, so restoring the integrity of the Abcott property. Richard, the eldest of the four Prynce brothers who succeeded at Abcott, died in March 1683/4 as his black marble memorial in Clungunford church records. His memorial slab provided a blank space so that the subsequent death of his widow could be recorded, but her name does not feature. The space was used, instead, to refer to the death in 1741 of his eldest sister, Mary, who was, by then, aged eighty six and the widow of Nicholas Tayler. It also portrays the Prynce Arms, "Gules a saltire Or surmounted by a cross engrailed Ermine".

After Richard's death, Abcott belonged successively to his next surviving brothers until their deaths. None of them lived beyond the age of forty. Philip died in 1687, Francis in 1698 and William in 1703. In 1690, the Abcott branch of the Prynce family inherited from Wrottesley Prynce's brother Philip, who had left no son, the immensely valuable Shrewsbury property, including the mansion at Whitehall. With this increase in wealth and status, Francis Prynce was appointed High Sheriff of Shropshire in 1694. When his brother, William died, leaving no son, all the family property, including Abcott, passed to Francis' widow, Mary, who moved into Whitehall and lived there until her death in 1724.

Francis and Mary Prynce had a daughter, Mary, who married Sir John Astley of Patshull in Staffordshire, the second and last Baronet. On the death of Lady Astley's mother, Mary Prynce, the Astleys moved from Patshull into Whitehall and Sir John, benefitting from his wife's local importance, was M.P. for Shrewsbury from 1727 to 1734 and was one of the two M.P.s for the County of Shropshire from 1734 until his death, thirty eight years later.

The Astleys had nine children, but only Alicia, who was born in 1716, left any issue. In 1742, she married Charles Bennet, Lord Ossulston, who, on his father's death, in 1753, succeeded as third Earl of Tankerville, with his main home in Northumberland. Alicia's mother died in 1760 and her father in 1772. Meanwhile, her husband had died in 1767, when her twenty three year old son succeeded as the fourth Earl of Tankerville. In due course, he inherited Abcott and her other Shropshire property. He had many sisters, who were entitled to large payments from the family estates. In a Deed of 1804, which lists his Shropshire assets, it is explained that he found the income from rented property too uncertain and he intended to arrange his affairs to ensure a sufficient fixed income. Within five years, he had sold Whitehall to the Bishop of Litchfield, in whose Diocese it stood, while Abcott Manor and its neighbouring farmland became part of Rev. John Rocke's Clungunford House estate, as did Lord Tankerville's 106 acres of park and farmland on Goat Hill at the north east boundary of the parish. Abcott Manor and its farmland remained an integral part of the Rocke family's Clungunford estate for 170 years, but the Goat Hill land passed to Rev. Thomas Owen Rocke, the second son and Rector of Clungunford, before 1847 and was sold by his family on his death.

During the ownership of the Astley, Tankerville and Rocke families, Abcott Manor was let to a succession of farming tenants. For much of the eighteenth century, the tenants were members of the Langslow family, who played a prominent part in the parish as Churchwardens and Overseers of the Poor. When the assessment for Tithe redemption was made in 1848, it was recorded that Abcott Manor and 175 acres was let to John Blakeway by Rev. John Rocke. From 1909 Hugh Vaughan lived there and farmed 355 acres. His widow was the tenant in 1931, when most of the Clungunford Estate was offered unsuccessfully at auction. The description of Abcott Manor in the auction particulars emphasized the old panelling and the half-timbered eastern wing with its beautiful moulded plaster ceilings. The farm buildings, in two sections, for the large, mixed farm were particularly generous and included stabling for eleven carthorses. Near the pulpit in Clungunford church is a memorial window installed in 1970 by Gerald Vaughan in memory of his mother, who had died in1949. The window includes a delightful representation of their home from across the river Clun.

After the Vaughan tenancy ended, John Rocke, the owner of the Clungunford estate, gave Abcott Manor and its farm to his daughter, Susanna, who lived there with her husband, Anthony Daly, and their three children until she sold it all during the 1980s. Two of the barns have since been converted into houses and are separately owned, as is the bulk of the farmland. Abcott Manor, now the home of Patrick and Hope Ramsay, is no longer a farm, but retains a few acres of land.

14

Old Farmhouses and a Hostelry

For a century from about 1550, there was a "great rebuild", because of the prosperity of Tudor and Stuart England. In this area, the prosperity was based on farming. Houses were enlarged, wings were added, second floors were created, sometimes by dividing a tall room horizontally. New houses were built, often where earlier buildings had stood beside the old roads. In Clungunford parish, there are notable survivors from this period although some have prominent later additions.

ROWTON GRANGE

Just inside the northern boundary of the parish of Clungunford is Rowton Grange, a large farmhouse, dating from the sixteenth century or earlier. (see *Colour Plate 17*) The name "Grange" often denotes a link with a monastery or other religious house, but there is no evidence of any such connection with Rowton Grange, which may have been so called to distinguish it from nearby Rowton Manor, in the next parish.

The house now consists of a hall range with cross-wings at its east and west ends. The results of dendrochronological tests and evidence of weathering suggest that the hall range was built in the 1570s abutting a low building where the west cross-wing now stands, although with a smaller ground plan, as indicated by its small cellar. The weathering at the top of the west gable of the hall range shows that this part, now protected from the elements, was against a lower building for some twenty years before the present west cross-wing was built. There is similar weathering on what was the outside of the east gable of the hall range, but at a much lower level, showing that the east cross-wing, which now contains the sitting room/playroom and kitchen was not built until some years later. The hall was evidently never open to the roof timbers, because the great chimney stack and upper floor are original, but even the height of the upper room was found to be excessive and the strange coved ceiling was inserted later.

It is not always possible to be certain that timber in a building is original to it, but the results of dendrochronological testing do support this assessment. Recent tests of some of the timbers high in the hall range give felling dates of summer 1571 and winter 1571/2, indicating that construction took place in 1572 or 1573. Felling dates for timbers in the east cross-wing are the winter of 1596/7 and the summer of 1598, so it is probable that that part of the house was built during the last two years of the sixteenth century.

Rowton Grange has long been the home of prosperous farmers. John Rowton of Clonegunwas, whose Will was proved in 1445, probably lived where Rowton Grange now stands. Thomas Corne lived there until 1590. It is likely that he altered the hall range, by installing the coved ceiling in the upper floor, while his son subsequently built the cross-wing. The Corne family featured prominently in the affairs of Clungunford. Thomas Corne of Rowton was one of the four trustees who, in 1658, purchased as endowment for the parish school and charities a house and twenty eight acres of land at Abcott. His grandson, another Thomas Corne, was churchwarden in 1724, 1734 and 1740. In 1708 he had been appointed a trustee of the parish charities and by 1749, having retired from farming and become the Warden of Clun Hospital, he retired also as trustee of the charities. Francis Corne was still the owner of Rowton Grange in 1790.

In the nineteenth century, Rowton Grange belonged to Owen Edmund Hemming, but he lived elsewhere and it was rented with 153 acres for over thirty years from 1841 by Timothy Bishop. From 1916 until his death in 1950, it was tenanted by Morris Wolley, son of Tom Wolley, the tenant of Clungunford Farm. Thomas Wilks (known as Grenville Wilks) was there from 1951 to 1970, when Mike Reid of Rowton Manor, close by but in the parish of Stokesay, bought the freehold of Rowton Grange in order to add its land to his own farm, while he sold on the house to Mr and Mrs Botley. By 1989, Rowton Grange and its farmland had been rejoined and the freehold was bought by J.T. Morgan & Son. Frank and Linda Morgan live there now and farm over 280 acres.

CLUNGUNFORD FARM

In the centre of the village is a spacious H shaped farmhouse, which is now faced in brick on its east façade, overlooking the farmyard. On the garden side, it appears considerably older, with a large jettied half timbered gable at its northern end. (see **Colour Plate 16**) This cross-wing has been dated by dendrochronology to 1592 or within the next few years and at first floor level on the farmyard side there is a large room, bearing the ancient inscription "Cheese Room". The northern wing, close to where the old drovers' road still led down to the ford, was probably the first part of the house to be built. Similar investigation of the hall range indicates a date of 1629 or 1630. One of its timbers had grown for 356 years by the time the tree was felled, making it one of the longest lived timbers to have been so tested in Britain.

William Barkeley, who bought the central part of Clungunford in 1558 and 1559, came from Cressage, between Much Wenlock and Shrewsbury. Although he retained some property at Cressage and, indeed, 85 acres of land there were held with the Clungunford Estate until the late eighteenth century, Clungunford was his main estate and, when he died in January 1599/1600, he was buried there by his youngest son, the Rector. William Barkeley had bought the estate from people who owned many other estates and had no need for a house here. There is no record of a manor house at Clungunford before the house that appears in Pearson's 1802 watercolour, which could not have been built before the end of the seventeenth century, because of its original sash windows. It seems likely that Clungunford Farm was built by William Barkeley as his own residence.

After 1600, it is probable that other members of the Barkeley family lived in Clungunford Farm. The owners of the estate made their usual homes at Ewdness and elsewhere in Shropshire, but they could have retained Clungunford Farm as an occasional home. Both the Rectors between 1587 and 1673 were Barkeleys and had many children, who would have found the Rectory cramped. In 1672, when houses were assessed for Hearth Tax, the Rector was still Samuel Barkley, who had, by then, omitted the first "e" from his surname. Six hearths were paid for by a Samuell Bartly, who must surely have been the Rector, allowing for the customary erratic spelling. The Rector's Will, made in September 1672, lists a large amount of furniture, including twelve beds, indicating that he lived in a big house. The only other houses in Clungunford parish that were assessed at more than five hearths were Abcott Manor (where the Prynce family lived) and Broadward Hall (home of the Bayley family) so that Clungunford Farm seems likely to have been the home of the Rector, his wife and his many children. He kept a considerable stock of farm animals and equipment and may well have used some of its fields as well as the Glebe.

After the end of the Barkley ownership in 1709, Clungunford Farm and its fields must have been let for nearly three hundred years. Before the middle of the nineteenth century, the available records seldom name the properties being referred to. Details are given of the acreage, the rent and the name of the tenant. In 1771, for instance, when Richard Rocke, the Squire, was absentee, a farm of 200 acres was let to Thomas Boore for £80 a year, and three farms of just over half that size were let at appropriately lesser rent to George Wooley, William Howells and Robert Thomas. The tenants were still the same in 1781. Which of them was at Clungunford Farm is unclear. The Tithe assessment of 1848 shows that the tenant of Clungunford Farm and 225 acres was then John Howells, who is recorded as being simultaneously the owner and farmer of Church Farm, which then had 81 acres, so he seems to have farmed over 300 acres. Thomas John Wolley, known as Tom Wolley, member of a well known local farming family, qualified as a Surveyor and, from 1891 became the farmer at Clungunford Farm and also the Agent, managing the Rocke family's estate, both of which roles he continued to fill for forty years.

On 25 March 1932, Edwin Davies, his wife and their seven boys and three girls arrived as the new tenants at the farm from their previous farm at Rhewey, Franksbridge, near Builth Wells, 32 miles away. The Davies family have been in farming for as long as their records go back and in 1650 they had a farm near Llandrindod Wells. Father and mother and the three girls drove to Clungunford in their Wolseley car, but the seven boys, aged between 16 and 32, walked all the way, driving more than 500 sheep and 7 carthorses with waggons, laden with farm equipment and furniture. The migration, before the lambing season, took two days and a halt was made for the night at a farm about half way on the journey. More than 100 cattle had been left behind and this required a second expedition to collect them in May.

Donald Davies, almost the youngest of the boys who had driven all the farm animals so far, eventually succeeded his father as the tenant of Clungunford Farm. He has recorded his memories of the house and of the operation of the farm. The farmhouse, which the particulars of the abortive 1931 auction describe as "a comfortable, picturesque old building", had a large dining room and a rather smaller sitting room. There were two staircases and upstairs were five bedrooms, a bathroom (very rare in Clungunford in those days) and an attic. Clungunford Farm was the only other house in the village that was linked to the Clungunford House private water supply from the spring in the fields above the pool. Other people had to collect their water from Spout Bank, close to the turning to Shelderton, unless they had wells. There was a cold water tap at the sink in the back kitchen. There was also a front kitchen, with an old black range and grate, fuelled by coal and wood. Within three years the Davies family had replaced it by an Aga, fuelled with furnacite, which also heated the water and kept the kitchen warm. When Tom Wolley had rented the farm, he had installed a gas generator, which provided the light downstairs, but candles had to be used upstairs until electricity was installed about three years later, after which most of the house was lit by electricity, although there were no power plugs.

Outside, there was quite a large garden with two lawns and space for growing most of the family's vegetables, apart from potatoes and swedes, which were grown in the fields. There was no garage for the car, so one was built immediately and another later. There were extensive farm buildings for animals and implements, including a stable for five carthorses, a cowhouse for sixteen, with calf boxes and yards for bullocks, two Dutch Barns, pig pounds, loose boxes, a cart shed and a number of other buildings, around a yard close to the house.

The farm was 306 acres of very good land, but farming at that time was in deep recession right up to the outbreak of war in 1939. Although skilled cowmen, waggoners and shepherds could earn about 36/- a week, the ordinary farm labourer would be paid only 27/- and, if the farmer had provided him with a cottage, 3/9 could be deducted from that very modest wage. At that time, with seven sons to help their father on the farm, the only employee was a waggoner. Until the war began, most of the farm was used for grazing. 65 acres were ploughed for wheat, barley and oats and 20 acres more for sugar beet, mangolds and kale. The sugar beet was a cash crop, but the mangolds and kale were grown to feed the sheep, cattle and horses, as were 60 acres of hay. Five or six men were needed to run a farm of this size and with that mixture of pasture and arable.

When the war began, food production became paramount. Men sent by the War Agricultural Committee arrived at each farm and issued orders. Clungunford Farm had to plough more land and increase its grain harvest by 30%. The harvest was achieved with horse drawn machinery – reapers and binders, which cut the corn about 4 to 6 inches from the ground and bound it with twine into sheaves. Four men would then group the sheaves in stooks – six sheaves in a stook of wheat and four sheaves for oats or barley. The stooks were left in the field for three weeks, before being carted into barns to await the arrival of the threshing machine, which was taken around the farms by horses and powered by a coal fired engine.

The harvest routine in Clungunford changed in about 1955 with the arrival of the self propelled combine harvester, which required the corn to ripen further before cutting it, while separating the grain from the straw. With this miracle, all the old methods were abandonned and the labour force was reduced by half. In 1954, Edwin Davies died, aged 92, but his widow and four of his children continued to run the farm. The following year, Donald married Marian Marsh, whose father had owned the nearby farm at Broome. His mother, two of his sisters and one of his brothers left Clungunford and bought a farm at Madley, south of Hereford, while he began to take a more scientific interest in the soil, getting a comprehensive analysis to ascertain what was required to improve its yield, especially of arable crops. His main concern, however, was his flock of Kerry Hill sheep. Two ewes bred by him won at the Royal Show at Stoneleigh in 1967 and a champion ram in 1968. Markets had to be attended, usually at Craven Arms and Knighton, not only for sheep but also for store cattle. Clungunford Farm had a pedigree herd of Herefords and also some commercial beef cattle.

Fig. 33. *Donald Davies with champion Kerry Hill ram.*

During his last twenty five years at Clungunford Farm, Donald Davies employed only Reg. Mellings, John Barber and Norman Mills and with so small a workforce the production of the farm had never been greater. He retired in 1986, when he and Marian moved to Shelderton. After a lifetime spent in farming, he had no regrets and considered himself lucky to have seen some of the best years for agriculture in England. Perhaps he retired at exactly the right time, having for so long taken a central role in the life of the village as a leading employer, member of the Parish Council, stalwart of the village choir and friend to everyone.

Clungunford Farmhouse has since been shorn of almost all its farmland and become the home of Bowes Rocke, grandson of the former squire, John Rocke, who lives there with his wife Suzanne and their children.

CHURCH FARM CLUNGUNFORD

One of the oldest houses still surviving in Clungunford must be Church Farm (see ***Colour Plate 18***) which lies close to the bridge over the river Clun and opposite the south door of the church. The house is T shaped with the cross-wing parallel to the river. One of the V struts in a partition truss of the cross-wing and also one of the twin longtitudinal beams in the ground floor of the cross-wing, recently dated by dendrochronology as having been felled in the summer of 1598, indicate that the house was built during the last two years of the sixteenth century, although it does contain timbers from an earlier building, which could have been on the same site. The lobby entrance into the house is, for Shropshire, an early example of such an arrangement. It was necessitated by the position of the huge chimney which is incorporated in the structure at the junction with the cross wing.

Until the building of Clungunford bridge in 1657, the road through the village to the river had been the ancient drovers' road, on the other side of the church and leading to the ford close to Abcott Manor. Church Farm had then been reached from it by the track, still in use, beside the west end of the church.

Church Farm was the home of yeomen farmers. The Church did not own it. In the nineteenth century it belonged to the Howells family, who owned and farmed 81 acres, some distance from their house and farm buildings. John Howells lived there in 1841, with his wife and four children, but by 1879 he had been succeeded by his son Thomas. Apart from the fields beside the house, half of their land was on either side of the main road between Little Common and the lane leading to Beckjay Mill, while the other half was on the east side of the road between Clungunford and Broome. The Howells family are recorded in Clungunford as early as 1752, when William Howells was a Churchwarden. The following year, he was one of the Overseers of the Poor for the Parish. After 1850, the scale of their farming was reduced, so that in 1906, when the executors of Thomas Howells sold Church Farm to Samuel Hotchkiss, there were only about 30 acres of land left and Thomas Moseley was the tenant in occupation.

While the house was occupied by a series of tenants, the remaining acres were gradually sold off. Along the road in front of Church Farm, where there had long been a small pool, land was sold in 1926 to the Clun Rural District Council for the construction of three pairs of Council Houses and other land was sold in 1945 to Nellie Kathleen Hamar of Bentley House. The farmhouse, itself, and the adjacent farm buildings were sold to the Council to provide accommodation for Council tenants, which use continued until 1975, when the South Shropshire District Council sold them on to David and Eileen Chapman.

Since the Chapmans purchased the house, it has received much needed repairs and been made habitable by modern standards. From 1981, part of the ground floor was run as the Clungunford Post Office, with grocery and general stores being added in 1982, but that business was ended in 1985.

Church Farm features prominently in a watercolour painted in 1802 by W. Pearson. Earth banks and excavations still visible between Church Farm and the river could have been intended to enable another watermill to be constructed between the bridge and Beckjay Mill. The fall in the river does not seem adequate, although the 1848 Tithe Map does show subsidiary channels that could have been part of such a scheme.

BECKJAY FARM

The Harley family, from Harley in Shropshire, inherited the Brampton Bryan Estate in Herefordshire as a result of the marriage in the fourteenth century between Sir Robert Harley and Margaret, one of the two daughters and co-heiresses of Sir Bryan de Brampton. Six generations later, John Harley of Brampton Bryan, who fought against the Scots at Flodden Field in 1513, had four sons and four daughters. His eldest son, John, inherited Brampton Bryan Castle and the Estate in 1542. His second son, Thomas, became Rector of Brampton

Bryan in 1555, being appointed by King Philip and Queen Mary, the Patrons of the living. His third son, William, moved to Beckjay, where his descendants lived as farmers for two hundred years. Little is left of their original house, but a part remains to which the fine new brick addition was added in the early eighteenth century.

The heirs of John Harley flourished at Brampton Bryan and, in 1601, they added to their Estate the Castle and Estate of Wigmore, for so long in the Middle Ages the centre of the powerful Mortimer family. Robert Harley of Brampton Bryan was Lord High Treasurer to Queen Anne, who ennobled him as Earl of Oxford and Mortimer. The double Earldom was partly to show the Wigmore connection but also to differentiate from the De Vere Earls of Oxford, which title had died out only a few years earlier. Robert Harley survived impeachment and his son, the Second Earl, having married an heiress, accumulated a notable collection of manuscripts, documents and books, then and still known as "The Harleian Miscellany", which his widow sold to the British Museum. After the death of the Sixth and last Earl, the Brampton Bryan Estate passed to his eldest sister, Jane, Lady Langdale, on whose death in 1872 she left it by her Will to her remote cousin, Robert William Daker Harley, from the Beckjay branch of the family. It is by no means certain that the Sixth Earl and Lady Langdale were indeed Harleys, because their mother, the wife of the Fifth Earl, was notoriously promiscuous. Indeed, a footnote to the Complete Peerage states "She was a very beautiful woman, had so indifferent a reputation that her children were referred to as "the Harleian Miscellany" and her name was freely coupled with Lord Byron's and the Duke of Cumberland's among others".

William Harley must have been living at Beckjay before February 1563, when his eldest daughter, Elizabeth, was baptized in Clungunford Church. For the next two centuries, Clungunford Parish records contain countless references to the Harley family of Beckjay. William's eldest son, John Harley, baptized in Clungunford in 1569, lived there for 91 years and was a churchwarden in 1621. The Harleys filled such offices in many years until John's great great grandson, Thomas Harley of Beckjay who was frequently a churchwarden and an Overseer of the Poor for the Parish of Clungunford until 1768.

Just as the third son of the Brampton Bryan Harleys had had to earn his living by farming at Beckjay in Queen Elizabeth's reign, so the youngest son of the Beckjay Harleys, over a hundred years later, left his family farm and sought his fortune in Shrewsbury. Richard Harley had been baptized at Clungunford in 1658 and by 1691 was admitted a Burgess of Shrewsbury. His son, William, a watchmaker, was admitted a Burgess of Shrewsbury in 1753 and William's son, Samuel Harley, was a Burgess by 1767 and Mayor of Shrewsbury in 1784. Samuel's son, William, was also Mayor of Shrewsbury in 1814 and all three of William's sons were admitted as Burgesses, the oldest of whom was the father of the eventual heir to Brampton Bryan, on the failure of the senior branch of the Harley family in 1872. Six years after inheriting the family estates, Robert William Daker Harley, the descendant of the Beckjay and Shrewsbury Harleys married a daughter of Lord Rodney, who was descended from the Third Earl of Oxford and Mortimer, so that the link with the senior branch became much closer.

After the retirement of Thomas Harley of Beckjay as Overseer of the Poor of the parish in 1768, there are few mentions of the Harley family in the parish Registers. There are sad references, in the churchwardens' accounts for 1782 and 1785 to payments to Richard Harley of 5/- "in his illness". Richard was buried at Clungunford in January 1786. On 16 December 1773, the parish Register records the marriage of Benjamin Urwick and Sarah Harley and, for over eighty years, the Urwick family farmed the Beckjay land.

Benjamin Urwick's parents were Samuel and Mary, who had arrived in the parish of Clungunford in time for the baptism of their two youngest children in 1754 and 1758. Benjamin, born in 1746, was baptized elsewhere. One branch of the Urwick family was already established at Crowsmoor, near Long Meadow End, a mere three miles from Beckjay, while there were others at Felhampton, beside the road towards Shrewsbury, and at Great Hanwood, near Shrewsbury. It seems likely that Benjamin's parents had not moved far.

When taking over the Beckjay Farm from the Harleys, the Urwicks also took on many of the parish roles of their predecessors. In October 1787, we find the Agent for Richard Rocke's estate making payment to Benjamin Urwick, in his capacity as Overseer of the Poor for Clungunford and his son, Samuel, was frequently a churchwarden, a Trustee of the School and an Overseer of the Poor. Samuel's sister, Elizabeth, in 1796, entered into an Indenture of Apprenticeship with the then Churchwardens and Overseers of the Poor, whereby she agreed to take as her apprentice for the term of seven years Mary Luscott, a poor child of the parish, and to teach her "the Art of Housewifery". This system of apprenticeship was an essential feature of the Poor Law provisions, whereby each parish had to care for its own destitute people and instruct for adult responsibilities those children of the parish who had no adequate parents. In 1821, Samuel himself took Benjamin Bowen, aged 12, as such an apprentice.

Benjamin Urwick continued farming at Beckjay until his death in 1816, aged 70. His wife, Sarah, the last of the Harleys to be mentioned in the Clungunford Parish Registers, moved to Ludlow and died in 1825, aged 80. They had six daughters but Samuel was their only son. He married Elizabeth Walker of Stow, near Bucknell, when he was 39 in 1819. Samuel lived and farmed at Beckjay until his death in 1854, aged 74. In Kelly's Directory for Shropshire in 1856, his widow is recorded as the farmer at Beckjay. Samuel had expected her to continue to run the farm and, in his Will, he had left her not only all his household goods but also his "Cattle, Horses, Sheep, Pigs, Hay, Grain, Growing Crops, Implements of Husbandry ...... and all other live and dead stock", so that she should "carry on the Farming Business for her own use and benefit as long as she shall think proper". Beckjay Mill was being run by Richard Booth. With Elizabeth's death in 1860 at the age of 80, the Urwick connection with Beckjay ended.

Samuel and Elizabeth had one daughter, Catherine, who married, in 1852, Thomas Weyman, an ironmonger from Tewkesbury. They also had two sons. The elder, Samuel Walker Urwick was a farmer at Leinthall Starkes, near Wigmore, when in 1849, at the age of 27, he married in Clungunford church Catherine Louisa Lewis, the daughter of the then Curate of Clungunford, Rev. John Daniel Lewis. The younger son, William Walker Urwick was described as "Chemist of Beckjay" when in 1854, at the age of 29, he also married a local girl in Clungunford church. She was Fanny Blakeway, daughter of Charles Blakeway, farmer of Shelderton. They and their children subsequently lived in London, although their elder daughter, Elizabeth was buried at Clungunford in 1866, aged 11, and Fanny herself was buried there in 1871, aged 43, when she was described as "of Belgravia, Middlesex".

By 1871, the Census records that Thomas Turford, a bachelor of 45, was farming 240 acres at Beckjay and employing three labourers and a housekeeper. By 1891, the farmer was Thomas Myddleton, while George Miles was the miller at Beckjay Mill. However, another family was about to begin a century of occupation of the farm.

Daniel Ernest Davies, a youth of 19, who had trained as an Accountant, was sent by his father to take over the farm, a tenancy of which had been obtained for his elder brother, who had been thrown and killed when on his way by pony and trap to Beckjay from Ledwyche, near Ludlow. Daniel Davies married Edith Mary Price, then living at Marlow in the parish of Leintwardine, and they had three children, all born at Beckjay between 1909 and 1914. Daniel and Mary Davies lived at Beckjay Farm until 1954, when they moved to Aston-on-Clun, leaving their younger daughter and her husband and two children living at Beckjay, but, until his death in 1972, at the age of 91, Daniel Davies continued to be actively involved in the running of the farm.

Daniel and Mary Davies' younger daughter, Gwendoline married Ronald Barker in 1940 and her husband, who had trained as an engineer, had to learn farming skills in order to share in the farm work. They lived at Beckjay Farm after the war and their son and daughter were both born there. After their daughter, Mary, married Jim Bason in 1967, the Basons lived in Rectory Cottage, beside the church, where their two children were born. Jim Bason, who had himself been born close to Beckjay, at Rocke Cottage (formerly the Rocke Arms), had worked as a farm labourer for Daniel Davies since leaving Clungunford School at 15.

On Daniel Davies' death in 1972, the Lease of the farm, which was then 330 acres, ended, but John Rocke of Clungunford House, agreed to sell to the Barkers the farmhouse, 144 acres, two cottages and the farm buildings and with this reduced acreage they continued farming until 1976, when they retired. Jim and Mary Bason then moved into Beckjay Farm with their two children and they have since purchased further land to bring the total area to 202 acres. Beckjay has now been occupied and farmed by Daniel Davies' family for over 100 years.

The Harleys were only tenants of Beckjay Farm when they arrived there in about 1560. Most of the farmland around Beckjay had been owned for centuries by the de Jay family, who also had considerable property at Bedstone and at Jay, between Bedstone and Leintwardine. On the death of Sir Rowland de Jay, leaving only two daughters, Beckjay passed to his elder daughter, Elizabeth, who had married Robert Knight of Shrewsbury, and four generations later, in the eighteenth century, over 300 acres at Beckjay and near Abcott still belonged to the Knights of Henley Hall, near Ludlow, who had inherited through Richard Knight of Madeley and his son, Richard Knight, the ironmaster of Bringewood.

The Harleys did eventually buy some land at Beckjay. A Marriage Settlement made in April 1718, when Thomas Harley of Beckjay married Anne Brown of Skyborry, near Knighton, listed the property then settled, buildings and fields to a total of about 90 acres, including a house described as "a freehold messuage at Beckjay, lately purchased by Thomas Harley the elder from Robert Piggott". There is no indication as to which house at Beckjay was that messuage. The land on which the farmhouse stands was owned by the Knights.

Its south range (see **Colour Plate 20**) was built in the early eighteenth century, being added to an earlier stone building. It was built of attractive bricks, which tradition says were made on the farm. When the Urwicks farmed at Beckjay, they paid rent to the Knight family of Henley Hall and when Daniel Davies farmed there the freehold belonged to the Rocke family of Clungunford House. In the County Record Office at Shrewsbury there is a beautifully drawn map, dated 1809, of "The Estate at Beckjay and Abcott of Mrs. Elizabeth Knight",

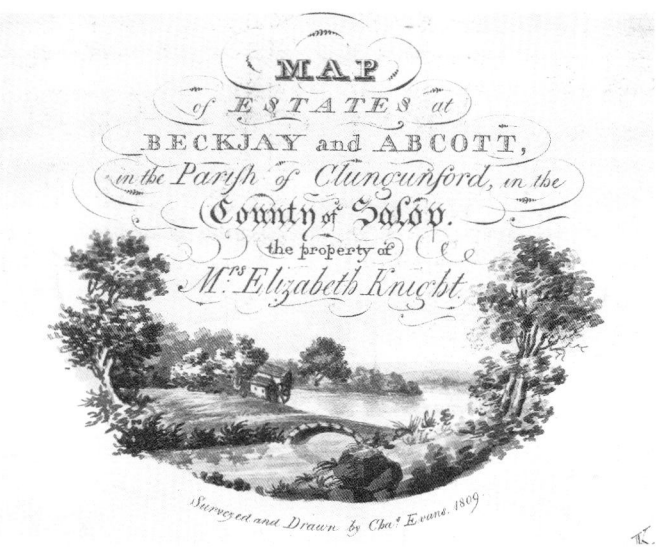

Fig. 34. *Title design of 1809 map of Beckjay Estate.*

illustrated by a charming drawing of a watermill. Elizabeth Knight owned 324 acres 2 roods and 18 perches of land. The tenants were John Cane, who farmed over 52 acres either side of the road towards Hopton Heath, Richard Langslow, who farmed over 70 acres of land north and west of Abcott Manor, and Benjamin Urwick, who had the remaining 201 acres 3 roods and 7 perches, including Beckjay Farm and also Beckjay Mill (see **Colour Plate 19**) which must surely be the watermill illustrating the map.

Elizabeth Knight was the last survivor of the five children of Ralph Knight, the youngest of the four sons of old Richard Knight, the Ironmaster of Bringewood. Her branch of the Knight family lived at Henley Hall, near Ludlow, and the land at Beckjay and Abcott was treated as an outlying part of the Henley Hall Estate, which had been entailed in the Knight family by the Will made in 1789 by her brother, Thomas Knight who died, unmarried, in 1803. Elizabeth Knight, as a prominent landowner, would not have been described as a spinster in Regency times and the only surprise in her being called Mrs. Elizabeth Knight is that she had, in fact, married Edward Baugh of Ludlow. On the death of Elizabeth Knight in 1809, the Henley Hall Estate, including the Beckjay and Abcott land, passed to a grandson of old Richard Knight's eldest son, Richard, who had established the Croft Castle branch of the Knight family. In order to inherit, the Reverend Samuel Johnes, younger brother of the famous Thomas Johnes of Hafod, added has mother's maiden name, Knight, as an extra surname. Thereafter he lived at Henley Hall and received the rents from the 324 Beckjay and Abcott acres.

The Rev. Samuel Johnes Knight was Rector of Welwyn, but he seems to have had scant dealings with his parish. When not at Henley Hall he spent much time at his mother's house in Portman Square in London. He and his mother had fallen out with his brother at Hafod and the author of the book on Hafod describes him as a clergyman "for whom treasure on earth was as much to be desired as a more problematical treasure hereafter". In the 1847 Tithe records of Clungunford, it is shown that Samuel Urwick was the tenant from the Rev. Samuel Johnes

Knight of the land which his father had rented from Elizabeth Knight in 1809, but mysteriously enlarged to 202a. 0r. 6p. On the death in 1852 of the Rev. Samuel Johnes Knight, who left only a daughter, the Henley Hall Estate and the freehold of the Beckjay and Abcott land passed to a grandson of Edward, the third son of old Richard Knight, namely Thomas Knight, who died the following year. His son, John Knight, was living at Henley Hall in March 1863 when he sold his Beckjay and Abcott land to John Rocke of Clungunford House. Despite the fact that three different branches of the Knight family had successively owned that farmland for the previous century, the Vendor's Solicitor felt able to confirm that "it was always part of the Henley Estate".

When, in September 1931, John Rocke's grandson, Evan Rocke, planned to sell the bulk of his Clungunford Estate and auction particulars were printed, Beckjay Farm was shown to be 261.987 acres and to be let to Daniel Davies at a yearly rent of £483 10s 0d. It was stated that the Tenant had been in occupation for about 30 years and that the holding had been consistently well farmed and was in capital condition. About 113 acres were well-cultivated, clean Arable Lands and the Pasture amounted to about 143 acres, which were well watered and included very valuable enclosures of rich feeding pastures, several with frontage to the river. The bidding at the auction failed to reach the reserve and the freehold of Beckjay Farm remained with the Clungunford House Estate until the sale of 144 acres to the Barkers in 1972.

BENTLEY HOUSE and SYCAMORE COTTAGE

The history of these two houses in the centre of Clungunford village is intertwined. Both properties belonged to the Baugh family for over a century, from at least 1643 until 1781, although it seems probable that Bentley House, itself, was not built until the Baugh ownership had ended. The Baughs had lived at Aldon Court, in the neighbouring parish of Stokesay, since 1578 and they continued there until the nineteenth century. They were related by marriage to the Herberts of Oakly Park, the Walkers of Ferney and other notable local families and several of them were Justices of the Peace for Shropshire. By 1643, a cadet branch of the family had settled in Clungunford, where, in May, the burials are recorded of the wife of Edward Baugh and also two of their children. In 1664, Richard Baugh was Churchwarden, but within a dozen years he had moved with his family to Alcaston, eight miles to the north. The Baughs never occupied their Clungunford property again. For over a hundred years, it was let to others. On Richard Baugh's death in 1682, it was inherited by his eldest son, who was Rector of Stoke St. Milborough, by whose Will it passed in 1708 to his younger brother, Lancelot, and then on to Lancelot's son, another Richard Baugh.

This Richard's son, another Lancelot, had a daughter, Harriet, who married Lewis Maxey. A parchment Indenture made "on the morrow of All Souls" in 1781 records an Acknowledgment made before the Court of King's Bench by Lewis Maxey and his wife that they had given to James Bridgewater "three messuages, three gardens, twenty acres of land, twenty acres of meadow, twenty acres of pasture and common pasture for all manner of cattle with the appurtenances in the parish of Clungunford". Although the transaction is described as a gift, it may well be that some compensation was involved. The property given to James Bridgewater was Sycamore House (now called Sycamore Cottage) and the orchard adjoining, together with a number of fields on the south side of the road near the river Clun and others close to the Crossways and near Watling Street. On these acres there were far more than three houses during the nineteenth century and later. It seems likely that Bentley House, a handsome stone house bearing a name common in the Bridgewater family, was erected during that family's ownership, although incorporating fragments of an earlier house, including an inglenook, and that the smithy and five thatched cottages, that stood until 1930 along the Chapel Lane edge of the orchard, were also built by the Bridgewaters. They had lived in Clungunford for some years already and the list of Churchwardens includes William Bridgewater in 1742 and James Bridgewater in 1751. In 1778, the Land Tax records for Clungunford show that James Bridgewater was tenant from the Baugh family, but from 1781 he was the owner.

James Bridgewater had married Sarah Price at Clungunford in 1760 and they had five children. In his Will, of which Probate was granted in 1794, he is described as a Yeoman. He made provision for his widow and left the balance of his estate to his elder son, William, but entailed, so that should William die without issue the property would pass to James' younger son, John, and his heirs. William never married and in his old age he let his farm to his brother's son, another John, who was then living at Bentley House and was farming the land in partnership with a William Jones. Clearly William Bridgewater was anxious that his nephew, John, should not be the sole beneficiary of his death, because, by his Will, made on 6 October 1849, he left to his sister, Margaret Bridgewater, who lived with him at Sycamore House, all his household goods and an annuity of £40 secured on all his land and property. Additionally, he left her for her life Sycamore House and its garden and orchard and the neighbouring cottages and smithy, so that after her death this part of his property would pass to his eldest sister's Lewis grandchildren. He left £100 to his niece, Sarah Langslow, whose son, John Langslow, Plumber and Glazier of Leintwardine, he made his principle Executor. The balance of his estate, Bentley House and its farmland, he left to his nephew, John, for his life only and thereafter to John's eldest surviving son, who was William Bentley Bridgewater. So it was that Sycamore House and the land and buildings adjacent to it, apart from the Methodist Chapel, passed to the Lewis family, while Bentley House and almost all the farmland belonged to their Bridgewater cousins.

Bentley House

On 1 December 1849, a mere four days before he died, William Bridgewater mortgaged the land and buildings which were destined for his nephew John and his heirs to John Carter of Ludlow, Tailor, for £500 but this amount of money was found to be insufficient for the payment of his debts and the implementation of his Will, because in 1853 a further £403 had to be borrowed on Mortgage from John Carter. His freehold of the Methodist Chapel was offered by auction at the Rocke Arms in 1851 and was eventually bought for £50 by William Bentley Bridgewater, who retained the ownership until 1899. The 61 acres of farmland that were mortgaged included about 12 acres between Bentley House and the river Clun, a further 8 acres at Mill Meadow, just below Beckjay Mill, and 41 acres in a compact block on the north side of what is now School Lane as far as the Crossways. The Mortgage continued to burden the property until, in June 1909, the 41 acres near the Crossways were sold to Evan Rocke, after which they became part of the farmland of the Clungunford Estate.

William Bridgewater's nephew, John, survived him by less than two years and died in 1851. According to the Statutory Declaration sworn by Thomas John Wolley in 1920, at the time of the final sale by the Bridgewater family, John Bridgewater's two eldest sons did not marry. William Bentley Bridgwater died in 1901 after over fifty years' ownership of the family property and his brother, Richard Wellings Bridgewater died in 1908. For many years, neither brother lived in the house and there was a series of tenants. In 1901, Thomas Jones ran the village Post Office there, but by 1903 it had been moved to Sycamore House and was run by the Lewis family. Both brothers had been among the Defendants to a Chancery Action in 1882 and that Action was still active when John Rocke's widow contemplated in that year taking a 14 year Lease of Bentley House, Bentley Cottage and about 11 acres of land between the house and the river. Even when the Mortgage had been discharged by the sale of the 41 acres, further financial problems arose and the remaining 20 acres, including Bentley House itself and the land down to the river Clun, were mortgaged again in 1913 by the last local members of the Bridgewater family, namely Ellen Bentley Bridgewater and Elizabeth Alice Evans. In 1920 they sold everything to Miss E.F.M.Wolley, who in 1932 sold on for £2,000 to Charles Vernon Everall (whom she had married) and his mother. The Everalls left in 1943, when they exchanged houses with Nellie Kathleen Hamar of The Mount, Clungunford, who subsequently married Cecil Edwin Purser, the retired publican of the Kangaroo at Aston on Clun. During her 34 years' ownership, Mrs Purser sold the three cottages and most of the remaining land, so that when Bentley House was bought in 1977 by Gordon Hayes it retained only the garden, orchard and paddock. In 1987, Gordon Hayes and his wife, Marion left to live in Cyprus and sold Bentley House to Clive Bruley. He sold again, in 1994, to Graham and Sue Lambert. Bentley House and its few remaining acres are used by Graham Lambert for an organic produce growing and retailing business, while Sue Lambert, a Doctor, has worked in the medical practices in Knighton, Clun and Bishops Castle.

Sycamore Cottage (formerly Sycamore House).
This house, now called Sycamore Cottage, has an ancient centre, incorporating timber that was felled during the winter of 1652/3, with additions on either side, which must have been built soon afterwards. The oldest part of the house was almost certainly built by Edward Baugh or his son and it is significant that its date is within a year or two of the building of The Rocke Arms and shortly before the construction of the first vehicular bridge at Clungunford, at the time that the new road was laid out, passing beside Sycamore House to the bridge and the Rocke Arms, eventually replacing the prehistoric route on the north side of the church, which led to the ford and Abcott Manor. The Hearth Tax records from 1672 show that Richard Baugh's house contained five hearths when only three houses in the parish had more, although the senior branch of the Baugh family at Aldon Court had ten hearths.

After the farmland was removed from Sycamore House in 1849, its income came from the rents of the smithy, where the Parish Hall now stands, and from the row of five thatched cottages. When Sycamore House passed from William Bridgewater's eldest sister, Mary, to her grandson, John Lewis, he worked there as a saddler, having been apprenticed as such in Knighton. His younger son, Thomas Edward Lewis, who was born in 1863, recorded his childhood in Clungunford, which seems to have been an idyllic place for a child to grow up. The saddlery business continued, but from 1903 John William Lewis was also sub-postmaster, the letters arriving before 7 a.m. and leaving at 6.30 p.m. by foot post between Clungunford and Aston-on-Clun, which was the nearest money order and telegraph office. By 1913, John William Lewis had ceased to work as a saddler and had added the business of stationer to that of sub-postmaster, in which combined role he continued until after 1934, when Miss Mary Lewis succeeded him. By then the letters came direct from Craven Arms. Before 1941, the Clungunford Post Office had been moved to the lowest house on Chapel Lane, where Miss Amy Clorley combined its work with that of a grocer. On the death of Mary Lewis in 1942, her brother, Thomas Edward Lewis, became the sole owner of Sycamore House. The smithy and the five thatched cottages had been sold in the previous fifteen years and were demolished to make way for the Parish Hall and the two pairs of Council Houses, which were not built until 1950. Before he died, aged 88, in 1952, he dictated to his daughter his reminiscences of his youth in a tranquil Clungunford that contained two grocers' shops and almost all the skilled tradesmen required to enable the community to be self sufficient. He recalled the excitement of going to see Ferney Hall ablaze, when he was eleven in 1875.

On the death of Thomas Edward Lewis, Sycamore House and its adjoining orchard passed to his son, another John William Lewis, who lived there with his family for two years before selling in 1955 to Mrs Pauline Wolley. She was the last of a long line of Wolleys to live in the parish of Clungunford and occupy most of its farmhouses at one time or another. She was the widow of Morris Wolley, who had lived and farmed for many years at Rowton Grange, while his father, Thomas John Wolley, had been, since 1891, not only the farmer at Clungunford Farm but also agent to the owners of the Clungunford Estate. The earliest mention of the Wolley family at Clungunford is in the Disentailing Indenture made in November 1771, by John Rocke, his wife and their elder son, Richard. It lists the acreage, rent and tenants of all his farms at Clungunford, but, unfortunately does not give their locations. George Wolley paid £56 rent annually for 107 acres. In the 1841 Census, Aaron Wolley is recorded as farming at Abcott and from 1850 he and Thomas Wolley were the tenant farmers at Abcott Manor and Abcott House. Even Shelderton was home to a Wolley farmer, Charles Richard Wolley, who was Rector's Warden in 1903 and 1904.

Mrs Pauline Wolley bought the redundant Methodist Chapel that was next to her house. It was to be demolished and the ground converted to a bowling green, just as her orchard was to be levelled as a playing field. In 1984, she sold Sycamore Cottage, as she had renamed it, to Peter Day, who resold it in March 1996 to Brian Taylor and Iris Groves.

THE ROCKE ARMS

Facing the west end of Clungunford bridge is a picturesque cottage, which for some years now has been run as a tearoom. (see **Colour Plate 22**) It is a very old building of stone, brick and half timbering and beside it is another building of brick and timber which was formerly a Cider House, for the cottage was a Public House for more than a hundred years. A main timber used in its construction was felled in the winter of 1653/4, indicating that the cottage, at the junction between the two approaches then being made to the bridge from the lane leading between Beckjay and Abcott, was constructed shortly before the bridge itself was built in 1657. In such a strategic position, it seems likely that it was a hostelry from the time that the bridge opened.

In a Return of Licensed Houses in July 1901, compiled for the local Magistrates, it is recorded that The Rocke Arms had had a full Licence for 95 years and that its trade was "roadside and agricultural". It belonged to the Squire as part of the Clungunford estate and the manager in occupation was William Bowen. It was said to have good accommodation and stabling for five horses and that there had never been any legal proceedings involving that Public House. This happy state of affairs was not to last much longer. In 1914, Evan Rocke, who was by then the Squire, closed the pub, because he had heard that it was being used by the Farmworkers Union for meetings of local dissident agricultural labourers.

The Rocke Arms can never have had a very profitable trade. It was not on a main road and its facilities were modest compared with The Lion at Leintwardine or The Craven Arms Hotel. The innkeeper in 1851, John Greenhouse, was described as a victualler also. In 1870, the innkeeper, Charles Rogers, was working as a miller, no doubt at Beckjay Mill. By 1891, the innkeeper, William Woodhouse, was also a carpenter. After the pub was closed, Miss Maud Herbert is recorded as having "apartments" at The Rocke Arms, but this use did not last long. Soon she married Ernest Bason and he was farming the orchard and 10 acres of pasture that are described in 1931 as being held with the house, and also the Glebe fields belonging to the Church and other land belonging to Bentley House. After Maud Bason died, her husband married again and continued to live there with his second wife and four children, of whom his three sons are still farming in the parish. He died in 1973. His widow stayed on there, selling cigarettes, tobacco and confectionary as an additional source of income until her death in 1985. Their children clearly remember when the river burst its banks in 1947 and the ground floor of the house was flooded, as happened, again, in January 2001. Behind the house in 1931 were a stone built Dairy, the Cider House with store over, a lean-to timber built Trap House, a brick built Cowhouse for four, two Pigsties and a stone built Stable for four with loft over. After 1985, the property was divided. The farm buildings continued to be used with the fields by Fred Bason while the house, by then called Rocke Cottage, was sold by John Rocke to George Mytton and his son, Reece. They restored the house beautifully and converted it into a charming tearoom with a lovely garden, most successfully continued and restyled since 1999 by Douglas and Annabel Hawkes.

The Arms granted to Richard Rocke in 1603 had included the punning design of three chess rooks (or castles). The crest was a martlet on a rock. A martlet in Heraldry is a bird like a swift, but with no feet. An old photograph from the time that the pub was licensed shows that the complete Arms of the Rocke family, shield and crest, were painted on the sign hanging outside, although in an advertisement for an auction sale in 1871 of two cottages and four small pieces of land at Abcott, it was stated that the auction would be held "at the Rocke's Crest Inn, Abcott". When the tearoom was opened, it was called after the crest alone, "The Bird on the Rock".

15

The break up of the Hopton Castle Estate

Most of the parish of Clungunford belonged to the Hopton Castle Estate until the last few years of the Commonwealth. Robert Wallop, keen adherent of Cromwell, divided and sold the large estate which had belonged for centuries to his de Hopton and Corbet ancestors. This sale proved the catalyst for the building of substantial houses at Ferney Hall and Broadward Hall and two large houses have since been built at Shelderton. It may be that Heath House had just been built before the dispersal of the estate, but, in any event, now that Hopton Castle was uninhabitable, a replacement was required for the owner of the residue.

FERNEY HALL

Ferney Hall is still in the Ecclesiastical Parish of Clungunford, although, after 1894, it was included in the newly constituted Civil Parish of Onibury. Until the last years of the Commonwealth, the Ferney, Shelderton and Broadward lands were all part of the Hopton Castle Estate, although within Clungunford parish. Ferney was then sold to Francis Walker. In the churchyard at Clungunford, close to the east window of the chancel, on the floor of which it lay for two centuries, is the cast iron memorial slab of Francis Walker, who died in January 1663/4. It bears his family's Arms, granted on 20 December 1660, namely Gules a cross fleury between four lions' heads erased argent, a demi lion crest and the motto "Loyall au Mort". There are two almost identical cast iron memorial slabs outside the east window of Burrington Church and another two either side of the altar in Onibury Church. All were originally on the chancel floors of their respective churches. These five cast iron slabs all bear the same Arms, made in a curiously hexagonal mould and only the names and dates of death of those commemorated are different. Following a 1658 cast iron slab, with no Arms, at Burrington to Mrs Joyce Walker, the five very similar slabs with Arms start with the Clungunford one of 1663, continue with the two at Onibury to Richard Walker (1666) and his wife, Mary (1673) and end with the two at Burrington to William Walker (1676) and Jane Hare (1678), who must have been a member of the Walker family.

The Walkers were ironmasters, enterprising men of the Seventeenth Century who laid the foundations for the industrial revolution in which Shropshire played such a leading role in the following century. Smelting of iron in those days, before the use of pit coal, required wood charcoal, burnt in small furnaces with bellows worked by water power. Bringewood, beside the river Teme was ideal for this purpose. Coppicing provided the charcoal and the iron ore was brought by teams of packhorses and donkeys from the Titterstone Clee and also through

Bewdley, while the calcium carbonate required for purifying the metal was readily available from the local limestone. From Bewdley, also, came members of the Walker family, who operated Bringewood Forge, downstream from where Downton Castle now stands and in the parish of Burrington, on the opposite bank of the river.

It was Robert Devereux, the 2nd Earl of Essex, Queen Elizabeth's young favourite, under whose auspices the forge at Bringewood was established in 1595 and he brought in the Walkers as his managers. Essex had a meteoric career and, when only twenty nine, commanded the English expedition to Cadiz, which was sacked in retribution for the Spanish Armada's attempt on England. Later, he plotted a rebellion, was convicted of treason and executed in 1601, at the age of thirty five. The Earl of Lindsay owned the forge before the Civil War, while the forests of Mocktree and Bringewood Chase still belonged to the Crown and a series of leases was granted to influential men, who thus controlled the local source of charcoal. Throughout these changes and the disturbed times of the Civil War, the Walkers continued to manage the forge. For three years until the death, in 1612, of Henry, Prince of Wales, the lease of the forge was granted to Sir Henry Wallop and the Walker family managed it for him. It was from Sir Henry's son that Francis Walker bought Ferney, over forty years later. By 1623, the forge was let for seven years to an earlier Francis Walker at £66.13.4. rent and he also paid £170.19.0. rent for adjacent land, but the Francis Walker who bought Ferney was not born until 1608.

From 1620 onwards, the Craven family had been building up a huge estate in South Shropshire. Lord Craven was a leading Royalist and his property was sequestered during the Commonwealth, but he recovered it and enlarged it after 1660. In the Herefordshire Record Office is a map made in 1662 by William Fowler on behalf of Lord Craven, entitled "A Survey of Mocktree Forest and Chase of Bringe-Wood". This excellent map shows in great detail the land close to Bringewood forge owned by Lord Craven and records the names of the tenants of each of the farms and fields. In 1662, Francis Walker, who was soon to be buried at Clungunford, was tenant of the 520 acre Deepwood Farm on the right bank of the River Teme, stretching from where Castle Bridge now stands to well below the present Forge Bridge. William Walker, whose 1676 cast iron grave slab is at Burrington, was the tenant of the Brakes Farm and 99 acres on the left bank of the river, but he sublet to others all except 8 acres on the river bank near where the Forge Bridge now is and a track leading to it from the Leintwardine road.. William Walker was also the tenant of a further 138 acres, called the Upper Radletts, on the right of the river and adjoining Francis Walker's Deepwood Farm. The 4 acres 2 roods on the right bank beside the present Forge Bridge, described as "The Furnace and Forge and land thereto belonging" were tenanted by Frazer Walker, but perhaps this should read "Francis Walker".

It is obvious from the 1662 map that not only did the Walker family have control of the "Furnace and Forge", but they also controlled all the land around them and the access from roads and tracks on both the banks of the river. The map also shows an earlier bridge or causeway where Forge Bridge was built a century later. The Walker family ceased to operate Bringewood Forge before 1698, when the forge and furnace were being worked by Richard Knight of Madeley, the far more famous ironmaster, whose family derived great wealth from ironworks in Shropshire and neighbouring counties. In the two following centuries the Knights purchased large estates at Downton Castle, Croft Castle and Henley Hall, all near Ludlow and much other land including Brand Hill in the parish of Clungunford, but Beckjay Farm came to them by descent from the de Jay family. By 1745, Richard Knight's cast iron slab was lying beside the Walker ones at Burrington.

Francis Walker was buried at Clungunford on 11 January 1663/4. Three days earlier, he made his last Will and then died. He appointed his son, Richard, as his sole Executor and residuary beneficiary. Despite his shaky signature, his Will declared, as was customary, that he was of sound and perfect memory. The Will is very informative. Francis Walker describes himself as "of Fearn Hall in the County of Salop", which was "lying in Corbetts Wood in the Lordship of Shelderton .... lately purchased from Mr Robert Wallop". He left that house and two cottages, that were also in Corbetts Wood but were let to John Onions and Meredith Pryce, to his seven years old grandson, Job Walker. He also left to Job such right as he had in the Lordship of Burwarton, a manor which was connected with the Bringewood forge under both Walker and eventual Knight management, because of its useful minerals.

The Testator's other grandson, Francis received only the rents from and the reversion to leases for named lives of three tenements in Shelderton. Cash legacies were left to servants in his house, to Clerks at Bringewood Forge and to others. He left £50 to four trustees "towards maintaining of the free school of Clungunford". The four trustees were Wrottesley Prynce (of Abcott Manor), Samuel Barkley (the Rector), Richard Bayley (of Broadward Hall) and Lane Harris (who lived at Abcott). He left £10 to the poor of the parish of Cleobury Mortimer, where he had leased from his son, Richard, "certain tenements and lands", no doubt used in connection with the transport of materials to Bringewood forge. He also left £5 each to the parishes of Clungunford, Pontesbury, Longdon, Longnor, Onibury and Burrington for their respective poor.

Francis Walker's son, Richard, his residuary legatee, lived at Wootton, a moated house near Onibury on Lord Craven's estate, beside the right bank of the Onny and only a mile from Ferney. It was built before 1634 and demolished in about 1840. Richard died soon after his father and was buried in January 1666/7 close by the altar in Onibury church. Job, to whom his grandfather had left Ferney Hall, was still only ten and it is unlikely that he ever moved into Ferney. In 1684, he is described as "of Wootton" in a Lease from Lord Craven of the Brakes Farm, "adjoining north to the ironworks called Bringewood Furnace and Bringewood Forge", which included the rights of "hawking, hunting, fishing and fowling within the Forest of Mocktree and the Chase of Bringewood". Both of these former royal hunting forests had been progressively reduced in area since the middle of the sixteenth century to provide fuel for Ludlow Castle and, to an ever increasing extent, charcoal for the ironworks at Bringewood, while local villagers deplored the loss of their customary estovers. A Rent Roll of 1689 in the Herefordshire Record Office states that Job Walker was then Lord Craven's tenant at Wootton. In 1712, Job was buried at Onibury and by 1715 it is recorded that his son, Francis, was living at Ferney. He married Elizabeth Hoare and, in 1725, was appointed High Sheriff of Shropshire.

On the north wall of the chancel of Clungunford church is a memorial to this Francis Walker, the Sheriff, and his wife, Elizabeth, daughter of Henry Hoare and their two children, Rebecca and Francis. It also records that the younger Francis Walker married Rebecca, daughter of

Folliott Walker, who was a cousin of his, and that they had four children, who all died in infancy. The younger Francis Walker died in 1776 and in October that year his widow, Rebecca, sold Ferney Hall to his young cousin, Frederick Walker Cornewall, who had just been elected to Parliament for Leominster. In 1783, the new owner died, at the age of thirty one and the Ferney estate passed to his younger brother, Folliott Herbert Walker Cornewall, who, in April 1787, sold the estate to Samuel Phipps of Lincoln's Inn. Rebecca Walker was buried at Clungunford in 1793, so ending the Walker family's long association with the parish. It is perhaps a pity that Folliott Herbert Walker Cornewall did not retain Ferney as his home, because he was a colourful character. He soon became Dean of Canterbury and then in quick succession Bishop of Bristol, Hereford and, in 1808, Worcester. In 1788, he succeeded his father as the owner of the Delbury Hall Estate at nearby Diddlebury, where he lived in style, keeping a pack of foxhounds and driving to and from his current Cathedral in a coach with four horses.

Until 1790, Ferney Hall had only a small area of land close to the house, but its Estate included several farms at Shelderton. In the County Record Office at Shrewsbury there is a fine pen and ink map of the Estate, made in 1782 by Joseph Powell for "Fred. Walker Cornewall". Almost all the land close to Ferney Hall was then common land. To the north and west were several areas of Shelderton Common. To the south west was Marlow Common and to the east was Duxmore Common. There were only rough tracks down Ferney Hill across the common land. In addition to the farmland at Shelderton, the Ferney Hall Estate included occasional fields at the top of the hill and a selection of strips in common arable fields.

The 1782 map is illustrated by a small drawing of Ferney Hall as it then was, showing a seven bay house of three storeys, of which the two bays at each end were in gabled projections, to the outside of which were attached very high chimneys. There was also a massive chimney stack behind the dormer windows of the centre. The house was of brick and appears to be of the late Seventeenth Century. The Shell Guide states that the park was laid out by William Kent. During the fifteen years after 1730, he was introducing to the surroundings of English mansions a studied informality, with frequent plantations, punctuated by architectural features. Because of the common land, Kent would have found little scope for exercising his talents and there is now no sign of his involvement, except, perhaps, a fine group of

Fig. 35. *Drawing of Ferney Hall on Joseph Powell's 1782 Estate Map.*

wonderfully gnarled Spanish Chestnuts of the right age on one of the areas of land to the north that did then belong to Ferney and the series of pools and dams in the adjacent dingle to the south.

However, in September 1789, the new owner, Samuel Phipps, consulted Humphrey Repton, who was not only an architect but had the previous year set up a practice under a title that he had himself invented as a "landscape gardener". Repton had studied the landscapes created by "Capability" Brown during the thirty years following the death of Kent. Brown's spacious and carefully composed landscapes of serpentine lakes and scattered clumps of trees were to be seen throughout England. Repton adapted Brown's Arcadian formula to achieve results more natural and picturesque, but the neat and clean surroundings that he advocated for his clients did not satisfy the aesthetic tastes of some of the more influential protagonists in what was at that time a fiercely contested discipline. In particular, they did not appeal to the adherents of the Pictureque.

Repton's proposals were usually described in a book bound in red leather, which he presented to his client. Such Red Books contained his beautiful water colour drawings of the panorama as he intended and moveable slips that showed the unimproved view. The Red Book for Ferney, now in New York, was delivered within a fortnight of Repton's visit. It opens with a sentiment calculated to appeal to the client. "The situation of Ferne (sic) Hall is by Nature so Beautiful that I must request your indulgence while I point out tho' at some length every possible improvement of which it appears to me to be capable". He went on

Fig. 36. *View of the front of Ferney Hall from Humphrey Repton's Red Book.*

to say that the proposals that he described in his Red Book were "trifles in point of expence, yet all tending to one great design, which may be made an amusing series of improvements for many years, employing a few Labourers only". The view, the foreground and the dingle could all be improved separately. He proposed opening up the front of the house by removing the outbuildings that obstructed it.

Sadly, no part of Repton's proposed improvements was adopted. The fact that so little land in the vicinity of the house belonged to his client must have cramped the style of a landscape gardener, but perhaps a more serious obstacle was the fact that Richard Payne Knight, the devotee of the Picturesque style in landscape design, had recently completed the building, a mere two miles away, of the externally undisciplined Downton Castle and was even then perfecting its wild and irregular setting. To make matters even worse for Repton, Knight actually owned much of Brand Hill, immediately to the north of Ferney, and could claim to be affected by any alteration in the view. Repton's proposals included the removal of the terraces which lay south east of the house down the hill towards Duxmore Common and their replacement by a vista of the type that within five years Knight was to ridicule in his didactic poem, "The Landscape".

Knight made his objections known and Repton replied by asking Knight to join with him in reviewing the ground and preparing a revised scheme. There is no record as to whether they ever met at Ferney, although Repton did return there briefly in October 1790. In 1795, Uvedale Price, of Foxley in Herefordshire, Knight's friend and rival in matters of taste, wrote to Repton as follows:-

> *I remember your being consulted about the improvements at Ferney Hall, a small place in the neighbourhood of Mr Knight, and whose most striking feature is a rocky dell near the house. I was extremely pleased to hear that you had asked Mr Knight's advice with regard to the management of that part, acknowledging that you had not been so conversant as himself in that style of scenery.*
> *This instance of your diffidence, and of your wish to draw knowledge from others, not merely to impress them with an idea of your own, was what first made me desirous of being known to you.*

Knight's views on landscape design were so opposed to Repton's over so many subsequent years that it seems impossible that they could ever have agreed a compromise. While Repton required careful maintainance of his exact composition, Knight advocated "counterfeit neglect" and his Whig politics inclined him to deliberate irregularity "Where ev'ry shaggy shrub and spreading tree Proclaim'd the seat of native liberty". The death of Samuel Phipps in 1791 ended Repton's involvement with Ferney, but his encounter there with Richard Payne Knight and his consequent acceptance by both Knight and Uvedale Price as a serious exponent of landscape design helped to launch his brilliant career.

Samuel Phipps owned not only Ferney but also Barmoor Castle, in Northumberland. He was a cousin, through the Sacheverells, of the Sitwell family of Renishaw, which then had three sons and a daughter. The eldest son Sitwell Sitwell, who was made a Baronet in 1808, inherited Renishaw and his descendants included the recent literary trio, Edith, Osbert and Sacheverell. Sitwell Sitwell's younger brothers were Francis Sitwell and Hurt Sitwell. From Samuel Phipps, Francis Sitwell inherited Barmoor Castle and Hurt Sitwell inherited Ferney Hall. All three brothers and their sister, Mary, are portrayed in a delightful conversation piece at Renishaw painted by John Singleton Copley in 1785, when the eldest brother was sixteen.

The Sitwell family owned the Ferney Estate until the Twentieth Century. Samuel Phipps had been buying land in the vicinity from the Knight family of Croft Castle as early as 1775, ten years before he bought Ferney Hall, itself and, indeed, before the death of the last Walker owner. In 1790, he had added more land at Shelderton that had formerly belonged to the Shelton family and he began the process of buying property at Bucknell to be treated as a disconnected part of the Ferney Estate. The Sitwells continued to expand their estate, both at Bucknell and close to Ferney and Shelderton. The Sitwell's influence at Bucknell is still indicated by The Sitwell Arms and in that village they often kept for their own occupation the house opposite the church, known as Bucknell Cottage, which, although larger than its name implies, was modest when compared with Ferney.

In 1818, the owners of land close to the Shelderton Common, which was on the south side of the top part of the road going up Shelderton Hill and on both sides of the same road after the top of the hill, arranged for the passing through Parliament of an Enclosure Act, whereby they divided the Common between themselves. The detailed Award was not completed until 1828. Those sharing in the division were Francis Hurt Sitwell (the son of Hurt Sitwell), Charles Bayley Unett (who lived at Broadward Hall), Richard Payne Knight (as owner of much of Brand Hill), and Rev Henry Cowdell of Shelderton. By this means Sitwell obtained most of the common land close to Ferney Hall. Later in 1821, a Deed of Exchange was entered into between Francis Hurt Sitwell and Charles Bayley Unett, whereby various fields that each of them owned near the house of the other were exchanged. Additionally, they rationalized the situation that had developed from the medieval common arable strip fields. There were three such fields close to the T junction at the foot of Shelderton Hill and another close to the left bank of the river Clun, downstream from Broadward Bridge. By 1821, the only strips that were not owned by Francis Hurt Sitwell or Charles Bayley Unett belonged to J. Humphreys, so that, when his rights had been bought out, the former strip field near Broadward Bridge belonged to Bayley Unett and the other three belonged to Sitwell. By these means, the owners of the Ferney and Broadward estates consolidated their respective properties and enabled more effective use to be made of the farmland.

The Sitwells did not always live at Ferney Hall themselves. Indeed, they were an unlucky family, with a series of early deaths and financial misfortunes. Hurt Sitwell had been only thirteen when Samuel Phipps died and he was not of robust health. Soon after attaining his majority and becoming the Squire of Ferney, he married Anne Hardy, but he spent much of his time at Bath and other places recommended by his Doctors. In March 1803, he died "of a decline" in Lisbon, aged only twenty five, leaving an only child, Francis Hurt Sitwell, aged two. The memorial in Bucknell church to Hurt Sitwell's widow, Anne, describes him as of Ferney Hall, but states that she lived for many years in Bucknell parish until her death in 1842. Their son was twenty four when he married Harriet Hoare, who was only twenty one. Her memorial at Bucknell says that she died in childbed a year later, only six days after the birth of their only child. Francis, himself, died in 1835, leaving their son, William Willoughby George Hurt Sitwell, an orphan, aged only seven, to be cared for by his grandmother for the next seven years.

A guidebook of 1822 to the Ludlow neighbourhood records that Ferney belonged to Mrs Sitwell and was occupied by General Lloyd. "It is placed on an eminence and commands a fine view of the extensive kind, towards the east, including Oakley Park and the Town and Castle of Ludlow, with the Clee Hills and other distant objects." In 1834, General Sir Evan Lloyd was still living at Ferney when his daughter, Alicia Mary, married William Oakeley of Oakeley, near Bishops Castle and in 1846 he was buried at Clungunford church, where there is a fine hatchment of his Arms impaled with those of his wife Alicia Eustace.

In 1853, William Willoughby George Hurt Sitwell became an officer in the South Salopian Yeomanry and was described as "of Bucknell", but soon afterwards, at the age of twenty six, he was able to move from Bucknell Cottage to Ferney Hall, in which his parents had never lived. In September that year, he married Harriet Harford. Tragedy struck yet again. Harriet died in May 1855, on the very day that their son and heir, Willoughby Harford Hurt Sitwell, was born. Having re-established the family at Ferney, the young father was taking a prominent part in local affairs. He was High Sheriff of Shropshire in 1855 and was soon a magistrate for both Herefordshire and Shropshire. He also established at Bucknell a pack of hounds drawn from the Belvoir Hunt and from 1854 to 1864 was Master of what was to become the Ludlow Hunt. The old house of the Walkers now seemed too primitive and a larger and more flamboyant mansion was erected on its site. The architect was John Norton of Old Bond Street, London. The rainwater heads bear the owner's initials and the date 1856 while the shield of the Sitwells' Arms is carved over the front door. Pevsner describes the architectural style as "intolerable neo-Jacobean", which he says "makes the neighbouring Stokesay Court appear chaste by comparison". William Willoughby George Hurt Sitwell married again in 1858 to Eliza Phillipson and by her had a second son, Francis Hurt Sitwell, and a daughter. These two children were the only siblings for an heir to Ferney at any time during the Nineteenth Century. Their mother survived until 1888 and their father until 1909. However a new disaster occurred.

William Willoughby George Hurt Sitwell was evidently living beyond his means and borrowed money on a series of mortgages of the estate. Luckily, he took out fire insurance with the Phoenix Assurance Company to provide for a maximum of £10,000 cover, in return for annual premiums of £23.5.0. The "dwelling house and offices communicating, heated by a hotwater apparatus (upon the low pressure principle) securely fixed" were insured for £3,000. Also covered were specified categories of contents and the stables and other subsidiary buildings.

In June 1875, the house was burnt down "by an incendiary", as Kelly's Directory of 1879 quaintly explains. The fire caused great excitement in Clungunford and Thomas Lewis, who then lived at Sycamore House and was aged eleven, went the next morning to see the house, which was still "in full blaze", with the staff and neighbours removing the contents into the stables and onto the lawns. The circumstances of the fire were more complicated than his memoirs describe. They are recorded in detail by the reports in the Shrewsbury Chronical of the Committal Proceedings in December 1875 and the trial at the Assizes in the following April of Mrs Jane Kingsland, Mrs Sitwell's lady's maid.

Although John Rocke of Clungunford was a neighbour and friend of the Sitwells and had actually helped remove the contents from the burning house, he conducted the Committal Proceedings at the Shirehall in Shrewsbury in his capacity as a magistrate. In the six months following the fire, police investigations had been exhaustive and many witnesses gave evidence. Many of the employees at Ferney described the prisoner's behaviour at the time of the fire. Other witnesses were friends of the prisoner, from Scotland and London as well as from the Ferney area, who had been sent by her parcels of Mrs Sitwell's dresses and other clothing belonging to the Sitwell family which they had been persuaded to buy. Jane Kingsland was obliged to admit that she had been selling clothes belonging to her mistress, but she alleged that Mrs Sitwell had given them to her, as was customary for lady's maids.

However, this argument was clearly incredible for some of the items that she had sold and she admitted larceny. Only the charges relating to arson were contested at the subsequent Assizes.

Evidence was given that Jane Kingsland, who was thirty three, had been lady's maid to Mrs Sitwell for seven years at the time of the fire. She had been taking and selling the clothes for several years and her fear of detection grew ever greater, but she had a young daughter for whom she had to provide. When Mrs Sitwell went otter hunting, she liked to wear a grey homespun dress, which the prisoner had unfortunately sold to a friend in London. When, on 9 June 1875, Jane was instructed to pack that dress in Mrs Sitwell's portmanteau for a trip to Builth Wells the following day, she panicked. First, she tried to persuade Mrs Sitwell not to go, alleging adverse omens connected with the planet Mars. On this tactic failing and finding that she was expected to accompany Mrs Sitwell on the journey, she feigned illness. That afternoon Jane alerted everyone at Ferney with cries of "Fire" and pointed to a closet where it was found that a small fire had just gone out. Jane then confirmed to Mrs Sitwell that the grey homespun dress was in the portmanteau and the next day Mr and Mrs Sitwell set out to Hopton Heath Station to catch the train to Builth Wells, where the absence of the dress would be discovered. In the early hours of 11 June, the butler awoke to find the house on fire and Jane fully dressed. A horseman was dispatched to Ludlow to summon the fire brigade and dozens of estate workers and neighbours helped to empty the house, which was a smouldering shell by the time the Sitwells could return.

Despite eloquent pleading by Jane's Counsel, to the effect that she had not at the time considered that she had stolen anything from her employers and therefore had no need to set fire to Ferney in order to confuse the evidence, the jury found her guilty and she was sentenced by the judge to penal servitude for fifteen years. Ferney was restored, with some changes to the original design but a similar overall effect. The insurance money was no doubt inadequate, but before long the Sitwells were able to return to their grand house, with its spacious reception rooms, its twenty three bedrooms and four bathrooms, all constructed in the most substantial manner.

Willoughby Harford Hurt Sitwell was fifty four when he inherited Ferney, on his father's death in 1909. He had been an officer in the 6th Dragoons and had been a County Magistrate for the Clun and Purslow Petty Sessional Division, for many years simultaneously with his father in an era when the Petty Sessions were still held in the Hundred House Inn at Purslow on the third Wednesday in each month. He was married in 1880 to Rose Brabazon and they had a son, Willoughby Hurt Sitwell, who was born the following year. However, when Willoughby Harford Hurt Sitwell died in 1913, it was clear that the Sitwell family could no longer afford to live at Ferney. Ferney Hall had been tenanted by Hugh Heber-Percy in the pheasant shooting season of 1911/12, with impressive bags and Kelly's Directory records him there in 1913 and 1917, but by December 1919 the Ferney and Shelderton parts of the estate, amounting to about 1,500 acres, were conveyed by the Sitwell family and their Mortgagees to Captain Harry Anthony Van Bergen, whose daughters have explained that he wanted to establish himself as a country gentleman and host glittering parties.

As soon as he had contracted to buy the estate, Van Bergen had to arrange to sell much of it in order to finance the purchase. In September 1919, before he had himself received the conveyance, an auction was held at the Craven Arms Hotel, when he agreed to resell nearly 500 acres, including Lower Shelderton Farm, Upper Shelderton Farm and three smallholdings in Green Lane and on Brand Hill, although he retained for thirty years at a modest rent the sporting and fishing rights on the two farms. His financial problems remained acute. In 1924, the year that he was High Sheriff of Shropshire, he attempted to sell by further auction almost all the remaining 1,000 acres that he had bought from the Sitwells. Offered at the auction were Ferney Hall itself and also May Hill, Saddle Hill, Swan Hill, Brandhill Farm, Coppy House Farm, Doctor's Coppice and Shelderton Rock. Evidently, he failed to find a buyer for Ferney Hall at that time because the 1929 edition of Kelly's Directory records that he was still living there. Indeed, he continued to exercise the right that he had reserved to shoot over the farms that he had sold and in 1927 and 1928 he also rented from Evan Rocke the shooting on the Clungunford estate.

The Van Bergen family lived in Ferney Hall for ten years, in gradually declining festivity and grandeur. They retained a cottage close to Ferney Hall, to which they could retreat when necessary, and from which they left for London in 1932. By 1934, Frank Cushney was living at Ferney Hall and his widow was still there in 1941. She was the last owner to live in Ferney Hall. With the surrounding land it was bought in 1952 by Frank Davis, who intended to demolish the house. He pulled down part of the back of the building and removed the lead from the centre of the roof, but then appeared to regret having made the house so vulnerable to the elements. He died in 1974, since when Ferney, still belonging to his daughter but no longer habitable, has become a splendid romantic ruin, among the remnants of its venerable trees and fine shrubberies. (see ***Colour Plate 23***)

HEATH HOUSE

Like Ferney Hall, Heath House is not in the civil parish of Clungunford. During earlier centuries, there have been times when it was treated as within Shropshire and Clungunford, but it is now in the parish of Leintwardine, Herefordshire. As recently as 1951, John Piper and John Betjeman included it under Clungunford in their Shell Guide to Shropshire, while the subsequent Shell Guide to Herefordshire ignored it. Until the division and sale of the Hopton Castle Estate during the Commonwealth, Heath House formed part of that Estate. It was built in the middle years of the Seventeenth Century, perhaps after the destruction of Hopton Castle in 1644, when a suitable new residence was needed for the owner of the Estate. It may be that the house was built for a Mr. Heath, although an alternative explanation of its name is that where it was built was formerly heath. The imposing mansion (see ***Colour Plate 24***) of two-inch-high mulberry coloured bricks now has sash windows in its main elevations, but originally had mullions and transoms, as on the two projecting wings of the north side of the house. The interior contains a massive and magnificent staircase of oak. It is sometimes suggested that it came from Hopton Castle, but new staircases of that type were incorporated in large houses until the end of Charles II's reign and it is probable that this one was made for Heath House. However, some of the panelling still in the first floor reception rooms could have come from a slightly earlier house.

When Robert Wallop sold the Hopton Castle Estate, Heath House and the core of the Estate passed to John Edwards, who proceeded to re-sell some of the land, including the 28 acres at Abcott which were bought for £104 in April 1658 by the Trustees of the Clungunford Charities. He also features in the March 1673/4 Will of Richard Bayley of Broadward Hall, whereby the first Executor was named as "John Edwards of Heath House in the County of Salop Gent". A few years later he had sold Heath House and the manor of Hopton Castle to Bartholomew Beale, Auditor of Imprests in the Exchequer, who died in 1684.

Barthomew Beale's descendants owned Heath House and the reduced Hopton Castle Estate until the last quarter of the Nineteenth Century. His grandson, Thomas Beale, was High Sheriff of Shropshire in 1734, when he was described as "of The Heath in the Shropshire Division of the parish of Leintwardine". The successive Beale owners of Heath House throughout the Eighteenth Century were J.P.s for Shropshire and, as such, feature in many documents concerning Clungunford. The connection between Heath House and Clungunford grew stronger in April 1812, when Rev John Rocke, the resident Curate of Clungunford parish and heir to that Estate, married in Leintwardine church Anne Beale, the youngest child of Thomas Beale of Heath House, grandson of the Sheriff. Anne's brother, another Thomas Beale, soon became one of the Trustees of Clungunford School and, as an influential landowner and magistrate, agitated with sufficient force for the bridge at Broadward to be first repaired and then replaced.

The Beales owned Heath House until after 1875, but in 1879 we find it recorded in the Post Office Directory of Shropshire, when describing Clungunford, that "Heath House, the residence of Sir William Henry Clerke, bart, is a very ancient plain building". It seems that the Beales let the house for a few years before they sold it. In 1886, Heath House and the Hopton Castle Estate was sold to Sir Edward Ripley, the second baronet, to add to the Bedstone Estate, which had been bought a few years earlier by his father, Sir Henry William Ripley. He had made a considerable fortune in the woollen industry of the West Riding of Yorkshire and in 1884 had built the many gabled, many coloured mansion of Bedstone Court. On Sir Edward's death in 1903, his widow, Eugenie, Lady Ripley, transferred to the more manageable Heath House, which had only 12 bedrooms. She lived there hospitably until her death in 1941, after which no member of the Ripley family wished to live in so large a house. Some of the contents and panelling were sold at auction and the house narrowly avoided the fate of demolition, which befell so many country houses in the 1950s, when the scarcity of staff and the burden of taxation made their maintenance appear impossible.

It was totally unsuited to conversion into flats, but so converted it was. The threat of disaster for Heath House and its wonderful staircase seemed only deferred until in the late 1950s, Simon Dale, an architect and conservationist, was captivated by it, bought it and moved in with his family. Already, there had been a foul murder there, when the Leintwardine doctor, Dr Beach, had been called out at night and was shot by the demented widower of one of his patients, as he turned into the drive. For some years, Simon Dale's wife and children lived with him at Heath House, but eventually they left, following his divorce in 1972. He continued there alone, as his sight was gradually extinguished. He became increasingly convinced that Heath House was built on top of a Romano-British structure connected with Arthurian rites. In January 1977, he tried to sell Heath House through Hereford Estate Agents. The Shropshire

Magazine, saying it was at Clungunford, gave a detailed description of it with an attractive photograph, but it failed to sell. The kindest and most gentle of men, by then almost totally blind, Simon Dale was beaten to death in his kitchen with an iron wrench in September 1987. Despite strong suspicions, no one was ever convicted of his murder. After changing owners twice more, Heath House should, once again, be assured of happier times.

BROADWARD HALL.

Broadward Hall is on the southern edge of Clungunford Parish and nearly in Herefordshire. (see **Colour Plate 21**) Although it appears to be a Regency Gothic building, with its picturesque battlements and decorative glazing bars, it is a much earlier house that has been altered considerably in the early Nineteenth Century. The Broadward land was sold when the Hopton Castle Estate was broken up by Robert Wallop.

Fig. 37. *Typical glazing bars at Broadward Hall.*

It became the home of the Bayly family, who soon began to spell their name as Bayley. As early as September 1658, the Deeds of the Clungunford Charities record that John Poyner, late of Broadward Gent. deceased, had bequeathed £3 for the benefit of the poor of the parish. John Poyner bought much land at Clunbury, Obley and other places in the district and it is likely that it was he who bought Broadward from Robert Wallop and lived there for the last year or two of his life. Whether he built the house or enlarged an existing house is not clear, but the cellars must be no more recent. John Poyner's daughter Eleanor, married Richard Bayly and the first mention of the Bayly family in the Clungunford Parish Registers was on March 17 1665, when Elizabeth, daughter of Richard and Eleanor Bayly was baptized. By 1666, Richard was Churchwarden and in the 1672 Hearth Tax records he was charged for seven hearths at Broadward, more than any other house in Clungunford Parish except Abcott Manor. In March 1673/4 he died. In his Will, which he made on 15 March 1673/4, he is described as "Richard Bayley of Broadward in the County of Salop Gent".

This Will provides a great deal of information about Richard Bayley's family, their Broadward home and his other property. He humbly commended his soul to God the Father, God the Son and God the Holy Ghost, trusting in a full and free pardon of all his sins and everlasting life and happiness. To each of his daughters, Anne, Sarah and Elizabeth he left £300, to be paid to them on attaining the age of twenty one or within two months of earlier marriage. To his son, Francis, he left £50, "to be employed for the placing of him to some trade or profession most fit and suitable to him respecting his inclination abilities and condition". Bequests of furniture were made to his daughter, Elizabeth and to his younger sons, Francis and Benjamin. Elizabeth was left "the redd bedd with all the bedding and furniture in the best Porch Chamber in my house where I now live". Francis was left "the Bedsteed and all the Bedding belonging to it and the chest all which now are in the Cockloft Porch Chamber in my house" and he was also given "the press and little table in the Outward Seller and the long table in the room between the Two Sellers in my house". Benjamin was given "the bed and bedding belonging to it now being in the store chamber and the chest that was his mother's".

Of the Testator's six children, probably only the eldest son, Richard, was over twenty one. Their mother had died already. The residue and bulk of their father's estate, including Broadward Hall itself, was left to Richard and his eventual eldest son, failing which to Francis similarly, failing which to Benjamin. In the Will, their father declared that it was his desire that all his children should inhabit and dwell together in Broadward until they should leave through marriage or employment or their portions and legacies under the Will should be fully raised and paid. Clearly the Testator feared that his children would fall out after his death. The Will provided that if Richard was not minded and willing to live and dwell with his siblings at Broadward, he should inherit merely the rents and profits of the land at Obley that had belonged to his maternal grandfather, John Poyner.

Much of the land referred to in the Will had been inherited from John Poyner, the Testator's father-in-law. Provision was made for his two younger sons, Francis and Benjamin, out of land at Hopton, Clunbury and Ledwich and there were entails in favour of their eldest sons. The Executors, who had to administer the arrangements between the Bayley children as best they could, were John Edwards of Heath House, Gent and Thomas Streete of Hopton, Yeoman.

Richard enjoyed his inheritance for less than eight years. When he died in 1681, his next brother, Francis, by then "a Doctor of Physic of the Town of Ludlow", inherited the property. Dr. Francis Bayley married Ursula, daughter of Ursula Cornwall, in 1692 and though this marriage land at Bodenham and Marden in Herefordshire came to the Bayleys. When he died in February 1728/9 she survived him, as did their son Charles, who was also a Doctor, and their daughter, another Ursula, born in 1696. Dr. Francis Bayley's memorial slab on the north side of the vestry of Clungunford Church, spells his surname without the "e", which his father had incorporated in the family surname over fifty years earlier. The memorial slab refers, also, to the death of his wife, Ursula, in February 1749/50, aged 75. His Arms of a chevron between three horses' heads and her arms of three martlets are engraved on the stone.

In Dr. Francis Bayley's Will, he refers to a Settlement that he and his wife had made of most of their property in 1700 and stated that, consequently, his wife and his son Charles are "already otherwise provided for". His Will was to provide for his "dear and most indulgent daughter, Ursula". He left his household goods, plate, jewels, cattle and other personal estate to be divided equally between his son and his daughter. He left his daughter, Ursula, £500 and also all his land near Broadward that was not already settled. Ursula thus became the owner of various areas of land in the Parish, including the wood at the top of Shelderton Hill, then and now known after her father as "Doctor's Coppice".

Dr. Charles Bayley married, in 1731, Mary Hill, the only child and heiress of William Hill, deceased, and his widow, Mary, of Court of Wootton, Wellington, between Hereford and Leominster. This Marriage was the occasion of a series of Settlement Deeds, whereby the various properties around Broadward and at Marden, Bodenham and Wellington were settled on the husband and wife and their progeny. Their only son, Francis, died in 1761. His fine memorial slab, beside the door to the vestry in Clungunford Church states that he was in the twenty fifth year of his age. It proclaims how this young man had "done his ancestors no shame, but served his friends and well secured his fame". The Arms on his memorial are, surprisingly, those of his heiress mother and not the arms of Bayley. Before the birth of Francis, twin daughters, Mary and Ursula, had been born in 1732 and another daughter, Letitia in 1733. Dr Charles Bayley was buried in May 1763, having lived long enough to see his youngest daughter, Letitia, marry Henry Unett in Clungunford Church in September 1762. The memorial slab to Dr. Charles Bayley and his wife, Mary, who followed him in August 1789, is on the south side of the vestry floor. It bears the Bayley arms with those of Hill on an inescutcheon.

The household at Broadward Hall during the Eighteenth Century must have been complicated in a fashion that is not often acceptable today. From the death of Dr. Francis Bayley, in February 1728/9, his widow, his unmarried daughter, Ursula, and his son Dr Charles Bayley lived together in the house, to be joined in 1731 by Charles' bride, Mary and soon afterwards by their four little children born between 1732 and 1737. Charles' mother died in 1749, aged 75. Meanwhile, Charles' sister, Ursula, lived with her brother and his family until she died in 1788, aged 92. She lies near the vestry door under another memorial slab, proudly stating her great age and displaying on a lozenge the same Arms as on her parents' memorial, namely the Bayley horses' heads impaling her mother's three martlets, an arrangement inappropriate for her. The Bayleys were somewhat casual about heraldry. She left money to her three nieces, who were then all in their late fifties, and property to the children of Henry and Letitia Unett. With her death in December 1788, followed by that of Dr. Charles Bayley's widow, Mary, in August 1789, the next generation of the family took over the management of Broadward Hall and the Bayley family property in Shropshire and Herefordshire.

Henry and Letitia Unett had three children, Henry, Charles Bayley and Letitia. The Unett family had lived for centuries at Freen's Court, close to the River Lugg at Sutton, between Leominster and Hereford. The next village is Marden, the home of Letitia's grandmother, Ursula, and only two or three miles away is Wootton, near Wellington, where Letitia's mother, Mary had lived and of which she had been the heiress. Land in each of these villages had come to the Bayley family at Broadward. Letitia's older twin sisters, Mary and Ursula, lived with them at Broadward and, under the terms of the various 1731 Settlements, as well as under the Will of their Aunt Ursula, they shared the family property. Neither of the twins married and they both lived at Broadward for over seventy years.

When one twin, Ursula, died in June 1804, she included in her Will special arrangements for the benefit of the other twin, Mary, that indicate that Mary was in need of particular kindness.

She left her Chaise and two horses to Mary and expressed her desire that Mary and her servants and attendants might be permitted peaceably to use and occupy the dwellinghouse at Broadward and have the use of its contents and outbuildings and gardens during her life. She provided money to pay for a particularly kind servant to be employed by her niece, Letitia (daughter of her sister of the same name) to wait and attend upon Mary and she stipulated that such carefully chosen servant should be paid not only the normally appropriate salary but £20 a year in addition – a considerable sum in those days. One must wonder what Mary's problems were: she died less than three years after her twin sister.

Under the terms of a series of Settlements and Wills made by the Bayley and Unett families, the Bayley family property in Clungunford and Clunbury and in Marden, Bodenham and Wellington in Herefordshire all passed to Charles Bayley Unett, the second son of Henry Unett and Letitia Bayley. His elder brother inherited the Unett property at Freen's Court, which was so close to the Herefordshire Estates that the Bayleys had acquired by their marriages. In 1807, Charles Bayley Unett was appointed a Justice of the Peace for Shropshire, which he remained for the rest of his life. In 1821, he exchanged with Francis Hurt Sitwell of Ferney fields and strips of land in the common fields, so that each of them could better consolidate their estates. In 1830, the Mill Meadow, until then a common field on the east of the river Clun, close to Broadward Bridge, was divided between Rev. Henry Cowdell, of Shelderton, Francis Hurt Sitwell and Charles Bayley Unett and, at the same time, the Clungunford to Leintwardine road, which previously turned down to the river two hundred yards above the bridge and then followed the river bank, was realigned so that it did not turn until it could lead straight to the bridge.

Charles Bayley Unett married, but he had no children. Indeed, in 1821 he took on two apprentices, John Powis, aged 13, and Henry Hammonds, aged 11, from among the poor children who were in the care of the parish. When he died in 1831, at the age of 54, he was buried at Clungunford. His Will appointed his wife, Rebecca, as his sole Executrix and left sums of money to various relatives and to his servants. Before leaving the residue to his widow, he provided £10 a year "to the servant who shall attend upon my sister, provided my wife approves of her conduct". This arrangement is explained by reference in a later document of 1854 to a legal application "In Lunacy, In the matter of Letitia Unett, a Lunatic, ex parte John Watts".

In 1843, after twelve years widowhood, Rebecca Unett had married John Watts, a widower from County Kildare, who came to live with her at Broadward Hall. When she died in 1846, John Watts continued to live there for a few years and took over the responsibility of caring for Charles Bayley Unett's sister, Letitia, who was in her late seventies. However, the ownership of the Broadward Estate was transferred to the grandchildren of Charles Bayley Unett's elder brother, Henry, who had died in 1807. That Henry's elder son, yet another Henry, who was born in 1789, had lived with his wife, Mary, at the old family home, Freens Court, until March 1844, when their financial affairs obliged them to go abroad, leaving many debts unpaid in Hereford. They wrote pathetic letters, which are now in the Herefordshire Record Office, before settling in Brussels. Their only son died abroad in 1846, but they had many daughters, five of whom were parties to a Conveyance when the Broadward Estate was sold in 1865.

After two centuries of ownership by the Bayley and Unett descendants of Richard Bayly, Broadward soon changed hands many times. In 1870, the owner was Arthur Crighton and by 1884 Rev. William John Crighton. By 1885, Kelly's Directory described Broadward Hall as "a castellated mansion, approached by a noble avenue, at present unoccupied". It was still unoccupied in 1891. J.C.Cyprian de Biddle Cope was the owner by 1895 : he came from Pennsylvania but also had strong connections with Italy, being a Marquis of the Holy See and a Baron of the Kingdom of Italy and having a house in Verona. He sold Broadward and its contents in 1900, when the Moreton family moved in. In 1903, Iris Moreton, aged three, laid an inscribed stone in the facade to the left of the porch. At that stage the wall over the porch was rebuilt as was the tower to the right of it. In 1913, the house and 124 acres were sold again to Harry Frederick Hamelton Hardy, who was living there in 1917.

Major Chase Meredith is recorded as the owner in 1922. He is still remembered in the district as Master of the Ludlow Foxhounds for many years and, subsequently, as Chairman of the Ludlow Bench. In 1943, Major Meredith sold Broadward Hall and the 124 acres of land to Bilston Corporation for use as a Childrens Home. In sale particulars prepared for Major Meredith, the house was described as "a fine stone-built residence of ancient origin and very thick walls". It had 11 bedrooms and 2 bathrooms and was lighted by acetylene gas. It had fine kitchen gardens, a tennis court and an archery ground as well as several cottages. Bilston Corporation carried out major repairs to the house before the passing of the National Health Acts by the post war Labour Government, following which it was decided to abandon the plan for a Childrens Home. In 1947, Bilston Corporation sold Broadward Hall and the 124 acres that had passed with it since before 1900 to Thomas Watkins, who had been Major Meredith's farm tenant of the land since 1940 and had lived with his family in the rear part of the house. Further land was bought before the property was transferred in 1964 to his son, Dick Watkins, who lives there still.

Mention should be made of the discovery in July 1867 of the Broadward Hoard of late Bronze Age artifacts, during drainage operations to the south of Broadward Hall and close to the boundary with Herefordshire. The implements and great quantities of animal bones were found about six feet below ground level. Although a significant number of the items were dispersed at the time, more than seventy are preserved in the British Museum. Many are parts of spearheads or swords, bright green in colour, badly corroded and mostly broken.

SHELDERTON

Like Broadward and Ferney, the Shelderton land belonged to the Hopton Castle Estate until the second half of the Seventeenth Century, when it was sold by Robert Wallop. Although subsequent documents sometimes refer to "the Manor of Shelderton" there was no such separate Manor. While the Ferney land was sold to Francis Walker and Broadward became the property of the Bayley family, the Shelderton part of the Estate was divided into smaller portions. In May 1656, Robert Wallop and his Trustees sold to Thomas Shelton of Ludlow, Yeoman, for £240 many fields at Shelderton, subject to various tenancies. Other sales were made to different purchasers and "the Smyth's Shopp" on the waste land was sold to Richard

Beene of Winchester, Gent., who sold it on for 50/- to William Lucas of Obley, Yeoman, in June 1659.

By March 1681, William Lucas, who had moved to Clunbury, and his son, William Lucas the younger of Stoke St. Milborough, had built up a considerable acreage at Shelderton. They sold about fifty acres for £360 to Samuel Barkley of Shelderton, Gent., a junior member of the family that owned the Clungunford Estate. These acres were scattered; some were uphill from Shelderton, at Swan Hill and Tately, but there were small areas near the river and, additionally, strips of arable land, totalling about twelve acres, dispersed in the common fields of Shelderton, on either side of the lower part of the road from Shelderton to Ferney and beside Watling Street to the north. Included in the sale was also "all that cottage, formerly a Smyth's Shopp erected on or nere the wast ground in Shelderton aforesaid". In 1689, Samuel Barkley mortgaged this land for £300 to the Rector of Worfield, the parish in the east part of Shropshire, where the Barkley Lords of the Manor of Clungunford had lived for a hundred years. The Barkley family bought more land at Shelderton and as late as 1782 the Plan of the Ferney Hall Estate (which then belonged to Frederick Walker Cornewall) shows that "Willm. Berkley Esquire" owned an area where Shelderton House now stands, several fields at Cross Horn and other scattered fields beside the river Clun and even on Brand Hill. Shelderton House, itself, was originally built in 1799, perhaps by him, but it has been enlarged and improved at various times since.

In 1816, Rev. Henry Cowdell was instituted as Rector of Cold Weston, where a tiny Norman Church stood across fields among a handful of farm dwellings on the slopes of the Brown Clee Hill. The area of his parish was a mere 419 acres and there were only 30 parishioners. The new Rector had graduated from Oxford that year and was only 23. He must have found it difficult to do justice to the needs of even so modest a parish, because he was soon living and farming at what is now called Shelderton House. It was during his time that the last vestiges of the mediaeval field system at Shelderton were swept away. There were three common arable strip fields beyond Watling Street close to his house and another just downstream from Broadward Bridge, in each of which he and other local farmers cultivated parallel strips with no barriers to divide them. They all also had the right to pasture their animals on the common land on both sides of the top of Shelderton Hill. Such conditions were scarcely conducive to any effort to improve crop or stock management.

Henry Cowdell was still farming in 1847, when the assessment of land ownership was made, preparatory to the calculations for the commutation of Tithes. By then, with his share of the spoils of the enclosure of the common lands, he farmed 202 acres at Shelderton Farm, including the fields that the Berkleys had owned in 1782, and 73 acres at Linches Farm, beside the river Clun and astride the present road between Clungunford and Leintwardine. His fields were mostly west of Watling Street, but he also had a long stretch of pasture on the top of Shelderton Hill, which had been part of the common grazing of Shelderton until the implementation of the 1818 Shelderton and Bucknell Enclosure Act. He was still living and farming at Shelderton in 1860, when he was clearly failing to perform his duties as a Member of the Committee of Management of Clungunford School and the other Members resolved that he should be asked whether he intended to resign as such. The 1863 Plan of the Ferney Estate showed that, by then, Lower Shelderton Farm and Linches Farm had both been bought by the Sitwells and consequently Henry Cowdell had been replaced as the farmer at Lower Shelderton by Richard Middleton. However, he remained Rector of Cold Weston until his death in 1875.

By 1782, the house, buildings and farmland of 375 acres at Upper Shelderton had become part of the Ferney Estate and between 1841 and 1877 they were let to Charles Blakeway, who not only farmed but also extracted lime from the quarries on his land. The 122 acres at Brand Hill, which had belonged to Richard Payne Knight in 1818, were subsequently inherited by his brother's grandson, Sir William Rouse Boughton Bart. of Downton Hall. 110 acres at Goat Hill, most of which in 1782 had been an outlying part of the Earl of Tankerville's Abcott Manor Estate and had passed with it to the Rocke family, belonged by 1847 to Rev. Owen Rocke, the Rector of Clungunford, and he still owned that farm in 1863. Further north along Watling Street, Rowton Grange and its 153 acres belonged in 1847 to Owen Edmund Hemming and was farmed by Timothy Bishop, while half of the 53 acres of Clungunford Glebe lay close to Cross Horn. Closer to Shelderton were fields and strips in the common arable fields owned by Thomas Mathews, who, on his death in 1816, left them to a son of Evan Humphreys, the former Rector of Clungunford.

After the sale of the Ferney Estate in 1919 by the Sitwell family to Harry Anthony Van Bergen, both Lower Shelderton Farm (tenanted by H.J. Marsh with 243 acres at an annual rent of £363.4.0) and Upper Shelderton Farm (tenanted by George Makelin with 219 acres at a rent of £312.3.0) were sold on by Van Bergan by auction at Craven Arms. Upper Shelderton, which was then an old and primitive stone farmhouse, contained a Hall, 2 Sitting Rooms, Kitchen, Scullery, Dairy, Pantry, 4 Bedrooms, 3 Attics and a Cellar and there was proud mention in the auction particulars of the fact that the Kitchen had a sink with water laid on. There were many Stables, Cowhouses, Pigsties, Barns and Sheds for all the different purposes of a busy mixed farm and there were three Workmen's Cottages. Lower Shelderton, a house over a century younger, had an equally comprehensive group of farm buildings and the farmhouse is described in the auction particulars as roomy and superior. On the ground floor, above Good Cellerage, it had an Entrance Hall with flagged floor, Dining Room, Drawing Room and Breakfast Room with a Large Kitchen, Dairy, Pantry and Scullery. On the first floor were 6 Bedrooms and a " Bathroom with hot and cold water supplies", while on the top floor were 3 Attics. With Lower Shelderton were four Workmen's Cottages. By the standards of 1919, it certainly was a "Superior House" as the auction particulars said.

At the auction, George Makelin bought the Upper Shelderton Farm, of which he had been the tenant for several years. William George Kirkham bought Lower Shelderton Farm, which he sold on in 1924 to George Puckle and Henry Gill, who farmed in partnership. The Puckle family lived at Lower Shelderton Farm while the Gills built the house at Little Common. In 1936, farming was in the doldrums, so the partnership sold Lower Shelderton to Reginald Noakes, who, after another 21 years, resold it, with land increased to 267 acres, to Elwyn Evans. Throughout all these changes at Lower Shelderton, the Makelins remained at Upper Shelderton Farm, until it was bought in July 1962 by Geoffrey Rollason, who transformed and enlarged the old stone farmhouse and created a large and beautiful garden, notable for its rhododendrons and azaleas.

In April 1983, Geoffrey and Philippa Rollason moved to Wiltshire. The house and garden at Upper Shelderton were sold to Graeme McKelvie, while the farmland was bought by Elwyn Evans to add to his Lower Shelderton Farm. Less than five years later, in October 1987, the Rollasons returned from Wiltshire and bought from Elwyn Evans the Lower Shelderton Farmhouse and all the land that had been held with both the farms. The house and surrounding buildings at Lower Shelderton, now called Shelderton House, were greatly improved and another fine garden was laid out. At Upper Shelderton, Graeme and Davina Mckelvie decided to move to a house with a less demanding garden and, in October 1999, it was bought by Adam Stanton.

Fig. 38. *Shelderton House.*

16

More Old Houses in Clungunford

Although several timber framed and thatched houses have been demolished in Clungunford village and at Beckjay within living memory, there are still a number of interesting old buildings surviving, in addition to those that have already been described. The oldest are beside the prehistoric drovers' road which, coming from Kerry and The Anchor, crossed the river Clun by a ford near Abcott Manor and continued eastwards on the north side of the church along the line of what are now Chapel Lane and School Lane to the Crossways and beyond. With the exception of Church Farm, the buildings on the present road towards the 1657 bridge and its 1935 successor date from after the middle of the seventeenth century.

The most picturesque house in Clungunford village is Glebe Cottage (see **Colour Plate 15**) formerly known as Rectory Cottage, close to the east end of the church and clearly of a great age. It is generally believed to have been the original Rectory, perhaps from the time that the church was built, but that post Reformation Rectors and their families wanted more rooms. The entrance front is of rubble limestone and faces north, on to the line of the old drovers' road. The house is T shaped and the southern extension is half timbered, ending in a stone chimney stack, surrounded by a rubble limestone outhouse, which used to contain a large copper boiler. In Archdeacon Owen's 1802 watercolour of the south side of the church, Glebe Cottage appears to be a single storey, thatched building, but this rendering of a peripheral element in the scene may not have been entirely accurate. However, the description of the house in 1928, by someone who spent ten days overhauling the church organ, describes the cottage as "a timber and thatch building, circa 1295". The house now has dormer windows to the upper floor and heavy stone tiles to part of the roof. Until a few years ago, Glebe Cottage had always belonged to the Church and when the Rectors lived in the Victorian Rectory and had a large garden it was the home of their gardener and his family.

Opposite the drive leading to the Victorian Rectory and close to the road is a timber framed house that was until recently two cottages. Their thatched roof has been replaced by tiles. It seems likely that this building, with its two steep staircases, dates from the second half of the seventeenth century.

Where the main road from the north enters Clungunford and crosses the old drovers' road, there is a timber framed house on each side. One is The Mount, a farmhouse apparently dating from the sixteenth century, which still has some of its original beams. Unfortunately, it is not possible to inspect it at present. Until the 1960s, the owners of the Mount farmed a smallholding on the north side of School Lane, but sheep have been replaced by six bungalows.

At the top of Chapel Lane, across the main road from The Mount, is a house that may have even older origins. On three sides it is timber framed, although partly covered in plaster, and only in the 1960s was its roof raised to provide for two full storeys. In 1848, it was a public house, the Cross Keys, owned and managed by William Anslow. He had previously been the miller at Clungunford Mill and was then running Beckjay Mill while also keeping his pub. After his death, his widow established a shop there and for nearly a hundred years it was a grocery and general stores, still remembered with fondness by some of the oldest inhabitants of the village, who used to call in there for sweets on their way home from school. Its address is still "The Old Shop". In the 1930s and 40s, Mrs Watkins kept the shop, while her husband owned carthorses for lugging timber. When electricity was brought to the village in 1937 and the wooden poles came by rail to Broome and Hopton Heath, his horses took each pole to where it was required.

Other old cottages remain along the drovers' route, both lower down Chapel Lane and at the Crossways, but several have been demolished during the last sixty years and some replaced by less picturesque but more comfortable homes.

Abcott House is a substantial brick farmhouse of the mid nineteenth century and between it and Abcott Manor are several very old cottages, formerly occupied by the waggoners, stockmen and numerous other employees of the two farms. At Beckjay a second farmhouse, known as Little Beckjay, retains a huge and very old chimney, the remains of two bread ovens and an oak panelled room. Across the lane is a cottage with thatched roof which may date from the seventeenth century and further on, beside the bridge at Broadward, is another picturesque old house.

There are a few more old cottages at Church Row, to the north of Clungunford church. Those cottages were once occupied by the village tailors, the shoemakers, dressmakers and others who catered for the needs of the village and in those days they were called Tradesmen's Row. Other old cottages are at Shelderton, at Little Common and in the outlying settlements at Hopton Heath and on Brand Hill, survivors from the time when the community was purely agricultural with the associated skills required to cater for its own daily needs. As the appearance of Clungunford and its hamlets make evident, many of the present inhabitants live in houses built during the twentieth century or in twentieth century conversions of barns, school or railway station.

17

Wildlife at Clungunford

When we came to live in the Old School in 1974, Clungunford was no longer one of the quietest places under the sun, as A.E.Housman described it in 1896, but the roads carried much less traffic than they do today. It was still reasonably safe for children to bicycle along the roads. The School had closed in 1961 and the classrooms had been used for various temporary purposes, including the storage of grain, which provided sustenance for numerous rats, who lived in the space between the floorboards and the earth beneath and emerged through holes near the skirting boards. Few of the windows retained their glass and there were many swallows' nests in a row inside the apex of the vaulted roof of the large schoolroom. When the windows had been reglazed for us, the swallows returned from South Africa, trying to reach their old nests. They battered against the glass, leaving their feathered imprints in the dust. Simultaneously, a mole entered through the back door and completed several circuits of the larger room, walking on the sides of its pink feet, before being guided out of the front door.

The former occupants of the building having been expelled by us, there was no lack of fauna close at hand in Clungunford. The liquid bubbling call of the curlew was then common in the spring, but is now less widespread in the parish. The resident barn owls and tawny owls now seem less vocal and are no doubt less numerous than a quarter of a century ago and it may be that the competition for their favourite food has been severe. There are more day time raptors, including Little Owls, which we have seen many times near Wetmore. Kestrels and sparrowhawks are frequent and there has been an explosion of the buzzard population, so that four can often be seen in the sky at once. Ravens and buzzards used to enjoy dogfights over our house, but ravens are now rare except on the high hills. Alas, honey buzzards have not been recorded at Ferney for over a century. Peregrine falcons are now back and once we saw a merlin beside Watling Street. An osprey flew over our house and the spread of the red kites has reached Brand Hill. Our little pool has had all too frequent visits from a statuesque heron and the occasional halcyon presence of a kingfisher. The resident coots and moorhens are joined from time to time by mallard, teal or tufted duck. The raucous and messy Canada geese are too numerous, but the family of mute swans who live on the big pool are exhilerating to watch in flight. Sadly, a spotted crake, wandering far from its normal haunts, died here ten years ago.

There are lesser spotted woodpeckers, treecreepers and nuthatches, great tits, coal tits, blue tits, willow tits and itinerant parties of long tailed tits, chaffinches, bullfinches, greenfinches and occasional troupes of goldfinches, blackbirds, song thrushes, mistle thrushes, wrens and goldcrests, confiding robins, crows, rooks, jackdaws, starlings, jays and far too many magpies, those smart and beautiful killers. Hedge sparrows, house sparrows and yellowhammers are holding their own. Willow warblers, whitethroats, chiffchaffs and spotted flycatchers return in fair numbers each early summer with swallows, house martins and swifts, seemingly ever fewer after their journey across Africa, while fieldfares sweep through from Scandinavia each autumn. In recent years, the number of flocks of seagulls reaching Clungunford appears to have increased and a cormorant has flown over our pool. Thanks to stocking by the shooting fraternity, there are always many pheasants, which often decorate the road on the lower part of Shelderton Hill while a few are in the habit of entering our house and flying up onto the windowsills. Unfortunately the pure albino cock pheasant, that was usually to be seen near Cross Horn, survived for only three seasons. A few grey partridges are still about, but there are now more red legs, although even they are not numereous.

There is no doubt that the total bird population of Clungunford has declined during the last few decades. The main cause is surely the change in farming methods and, in particular, the more intensive arable with little time for stubble or space for hedgerows and massive use of insecticides and other destructive chemicals. Fifty years ago the lapwing flocks in this area used to number dozens and even hundreds of birds, but the conditions under which they throve apply no more and, although a handful can still be seen from time to time, it is unlikely that their numbers will ever recover. The fate of that species is symptomatic of that of many others.

Many of the mammals in Clungunford parish are also finding survival a struggle. Farming methods and the increase in volume and speed of road traffic present great dangers to them. In the wooded hills to the east of Watling Street are red deer, Sitka deer and fallow deer, all of which seem to be flourishing. Badgers' sets are there also and the fecundity of the local stock is proved by the frequency of the badger corpses on the surrounding roads. Foxes are less frequently seen, alive or dead, but they still remain a threat to local poultry. Otters had almost disappeared over thirty years ago, although occasionally their spraints and their snow slides beside the river Clun showed a residue survived. Five years ago, a concussed otter, carefully lifted from the road near the top of Shelderton Hill, was able to slope away, continuing its short cut between the Onny and the Clun. A few years earlier, a dead pine martin was found in the wood on May Hill, although the nearest recognized habitat for that species is far away in North Wales. The red squirrel, which was abundant only fifty years ago and still also survives in North Wales, is no longer seen at Clungunford, where the grey squirrel has supplanted it. The polecat has fared better and has spread eastwards from Wales. Twenty years ago, we followed a frolicking family of five on our local stretch of Watling Street and last year a dead polecat was on the road near Little Common. Weasels and stoats are frequently seen, but there is no recent record of a local stoat in its winter coat of ermine.

Hares have declined in the district during the last thirty years and are now rarely seen. One reason may be that in 1971 and 1972 special hare shoots were held in February on the Clungunford estate, when 40 or 50 hares would be shot in a day, but, as with so many species of birds and mammals, the present intensive farming methods have had a devastating effect on their habitat. Nitrates from the farms upstream have even caused a serious decline in the trout and grayling in the river Clun, for which Clungunford was renowned until fifty years ago. Rabbits also are less numerous, although no doubt some farmers and gardeners still wish they were extinct. Hedgehogs are fewer and their continuing slaughter on the roads may soon eliminate them. Moles, on the other hand, do not face such danger and are still plentiful. The smaller mammals are successfully maintaining a sufficient food supply for the increased numbers of daytime raptors, the only really expanding section of the wildlife of Clungunford.

18

Clungunford 1559–2000
The Evolving Community

The Feudal System had not entirely ended in England when Queen Elizabeth I came to the throne. The Arundels' overlordship throughout the Clun valley had recently passed by marriage to the 9th Duke of Norfolk, who was to be attainted and beheaded for treason in 1572, when the connection of his family with Clungunford ended. The Lord of the Manor was then William Barkeley, whose descendants retained the position until 1709, although they never owned as much as a quarter of the parish. Most of the parish to the east of Watling Street, Shelderton, Broadward and many fields between Twitchen and Abcott belonged to the Hopton Castle estate, owned by the Corbet family. The Morris family of what is now Abcott Manor owned much land around it and also on Goat Hill. Beckjay, where the Harleys were farming, belonged to the Knight family and Rowton Grange and its land belonged to the Corne family. Church Farm and the Glebe were among other holdings that did not come within the area purchased by William Barkeley. At that time and until the nineteenth century ownership of any farmland in the parish of Clungunford almost always involved scattered and disconnected fields as well as strips in the common fields and the right to graze animals in the common pasture. The neat parcels of today did not apply.

Clungunford was a farming community, with its fortunes dependant on the vagaries of the weather, the health of farm animals and the price of corn, meat and all farm produce. Times of prosperity for farmers often coincided with times of war, although in late Elizabethan and early Stuart times, when England had no major wars, the growth in population caused such increase in agricultural prices that many houses in farming areas were rebuilt or improved, as clearly happened in Clungunford. With the rise in land values from the mid sixteenth century, landowners in England found the old copyhold tenure, with its customary manorial dues, less attractive than leasehold terms for a number of years or until the death of the last of two or three named persons, on the expiry of which an entirely new rent could be fixed. Copyhold tenants, themselves, found that the traditional fines payable to the manorial lord on a sudden succession could now be much more devastating than a fixed annual rent, even if the new system involved an initial entry payment. Consequently, there is scarcely any evidence of copyhold tenure in Clungunford during this period. Rents payable under the new leases could often bear some resemblance to the old copyhold dues, as when two capons at Lady Day or fifty bushels of barley at Michaelmas were stipulated. However, the greater certainty of tenure did encourage better husbandry.

Farming in the Clungunford area in the sixteenth and seventeenth centuries was mainly pastoral. As in previous centuries, sheep were dominant, not only for their famous wool and their meat but also for milk from the ewes, which was valuable for butter and cheese. The old Shropshire sheep were horned and had black or mottled faces and legs. They were extremely hardy and they could be left to graze on the common pasture in all weather. All but the smallest holdings kept cows and a horse or two. Horses on farms were seldom used for ploughing before the mid seventeenth century and were lighter animals, suitable for riding and pulling harrows and small carts. For heavier duty, oxen were still needed until the gradual adoption of carthorses, but only a large farm was able to maintain a full ox-team and smaller farms had to combine. Although horses needed to be fed corn, while oxen, when too old to work, could be sold as rather tough meat, the performance of horses was superior. A pair of horses could plough an acre in a day, which even four oxen could not. Farmers large and small kept pigs and poultry. With their pigs, many were able to exercise rights of pannage among acorns and mast in certain woodlands as well as feeding them on dairy waste and on peas and other fodder crops.

Most farmers grew some corn. In 1612, Speed described Shropshire soil as "a rich clay, abounding in wheat and barley" and by the end of the seventeenth century some clover and turnips were being grown. These crops were mainly for use on the farms, because they were difficult to transport by the roads and vehicles then available, whereas cattle, sheep and pigs could be driven along on the hoof, foot or trotter to fairs and markets in nearby towns or even further afield, using Watling Street or the old drovers' roads. Farming methods changed little between mediaeval times and the end of the eighteenth century. Many farm labourers were needed and a large proportion of them were hired at the local fairs to work for the following year or some lesser period. In Shropshire the daily rate of their pay scarcely changed between 1620 and 1740. In winter, it was apt to be 2d a day with food and drink or 6d a day without. In summer, it was a penny more, while for hay mowing it went up to 6d a day and for the corn harvest 8d a day, in each case with food and drink. The need for everyone in country districts to be able to grow the bulk of the food for their families was recognized by the Cottages Act of 1589, which stipulated that all cottages built after that date should have at least four acres of land. In Shropshire, this ideal was seldom realized and the Act was eventually repealed in 1775. There is no doubt that life was always precarious for agricultural workers.

It is impressive how the families who owned or tenanted the farms in Clungunford maintained them through the generations. The Corne family were at Rowton Grange for over two hundred years, as were the Harleys at Beckjay and the Bridgewater family farmed the Bentley House fields for over a century. Other families have handed their farms down from father to son as a matter of course. It is sometimes possible to tell what farming stock was transferred from one generation to the next by reading Wills and inventories of the assets of those who made them. Few are as informative as that described above of William Morris of Abcott, who died in 1549. Such inventories put a value on certain categories of assets. Francis Walker of Ferney was a prosperous ironmaster but he also farmed and the inventory of his assets, made in 1664, makes this plain. His farm animals, described as "all sorts of Cattell" were worth the large sum of £261.10.0, "Corne in the Barne and Corne on the Ground" were valued at £57.14.0, Hay was valued at £46 and "Instruments of Husbandry" at £14.

William Coston of Goat Hall, as the farm on Goat Hill was then called, described himself as a yeoman when he made his Will in 1697. He had taken a lease of his farm from Richard Prynce of

Abcott in May 1678 and the lease gave him the right to "dig, burn and take and carry away" limestone – an asset that many farmers along that limestone slope have exploited until modern times. His modest assets were worth a total of £92 and the inventory included Two Oxen, three Bullocks, four Cows, three young Beasts and two Horses (valued at a combined total of £27.5.0), also Sheep 40/-, "Swyne of all sorts"15/-, Implements of Husbandry 40/- and "Grayne in the Barne & Crop on ye Land" £7.5.0. Among his other assets were "Household Goodes of all Sorts" at £5, "Provision in the house" £3, "wearing Apparell" £4 and, engagingly, "Things Forgotten" 5/-. All these figures were written in Roman numerals, unhelpful to addition or subtraction.

Less affluent still was John Jones of Clungunford, who died in 1749. He cultivated a hemp plot and kept a breeding mare. He had a flock of 23 sheep and 4 swine rooted around the yard, while their predecessors appear in the inventory as 108 lbs of bacon at 3d a pound. In Clungunford parish during all these centuries, there were five or six farms of over 250 acres, rather more of between 50 and 200 acres and a number of smallholdings, while, no doubt, until well into the twentieth century almost every cottage had its pigsty and its flock of hens.

The three inventories mentioned above, from big, medium sized and small farms in the century before 1750 might just as well have applied in Clungunford a hundred years later, except that oxen would have been unlikely to feature, although some landowners and farmers preferred to use oxen well into the nineteenth century and George III, known to some of his contemporaries as "Farmer George", on coming to the throne in 1760, replaced with oxen all the draught horses on the royal farms. Changes in farming methods were taking place in East Anglia and the Midlands, but they made little impact in the Welsh borders. However, as in the rest of England, export bounties for grain, the effects of the frequent wars and population growth resulting from the Industrial Revolution led to increased demand for farm produce and a rise in prices, rents and land values. Landowners and farmers grew wealthier while the lot of the agricultural labourer scarcely improved. The most obvious hindrances to improved productivity were the persistence of the common field system and the splintered land holdings, whereby many farmers had fields scattered about the district, each one surrounded by other farmers' property, with problems of access, and stringent hedging requirements. While strips of arable land belonging to several farmers were interspersed in the same common field and their sheep or cattle were mingled in common pastures with those of their neighbours, there was little incentive to improve either crops or livestock.

In Clungunford, perhaps partly because the Rocke owners of the central area were living elsewhere throughout the eighteenth century, the necessary rationalization arrived particularly late. The fields of the Knight family, centred on Beckjay, of the owners of Abcott, of the owners of Heath House in the area between Abcott and Hopton Heath, of Ferney, Shelderton, Broadward and the Rocke family estate were scattered about like pieces of broken crockery and among them were portions belonging to Church Farm, Bentley House, the Glebe and other farming units. Inefficiency was inevitable as crops and barns, livestock and byres were separated by long stretches of rough track and the fields of others. Soon after 1807, Rev. John Rocke, by then the Clungunford Squire as well as its Rector, although living in Shrewsbury, decided to build up the family's Clungunford estate and to sell some of his property in Montgomeryshire. By chance, the Earl of Tankerville had decided to sell his land around

Abcott and at Goat Hill, so these were added to the Rocke properties, enabling greater rationalization. With his grandson's purchase of the Knight property around Beckjay and other accretions in the nineteenth century, each farmer on the Rocke family's Clungunford estate could have a coherent block of land. Meanwhile the Sitwell family of Ferney was acquiring neighbouring land, exchanging fields with the owners of Broadward and sponsoring the Enclosure Act of 1828, which brought to an end the 48 acres of strip fields and the 239 acres of common pastures between Ferney and Broadward Bridge. Enclosure often increased fourfold the value of the land enclosed, whether by creating bigger units than the small individual strips or by enabling crops to be more easily protected against foraging animals. New farming methods would be justified and even old methods would be more productive.

The pattern of life in so slowly changing a farming community was constant as each generation gave way to the next. Conditions were hard for almost everyone until well into the nineteenth century. Houses were small and primitive, work was incessant and the weather far more intrusive than it is today. There are records of many winters more severe than any nowadays. In the parish Registers is a rare comment "In this year 1607 was the great froste & sore winter that the fowles of the heavens pished". Whether they dropped dead from the sky is not clear. Until the building of the Thames embankment in Victorian times, the Thames sometimes froze over and fairs and parties were held on the ice, but there is no record of the river Clun freezing, although its floods could make a crossing impossible before the construction of the present bridge. However, in the first half of the twentieth century, skating and football on the pool at Clungunford was a frequent winter attraction and there are many records of children being unable to walk to Clungunford School because of snow and ice. On the short bicycle journey to Craven Arms in 1963, Brian Mellings' milk in a bottle could freeze so hard that the bottle broke and the thermos of tea had to be used milkless.

With no local hospitals, few doctors and only traditional medicines, occasional epidemics took their toll and the parish Registers record sad cases of several members of a family dying within a few days or weeks. Some stillborn babies were buried, some babies who had not been baptized and many others who had been baptized only a day or two previously. On 12 March 1699/1700 the Registers record "Martha & Mary twin daughters of Thomas Rowland (a wayfaring man from the Parish of Flint) & Margaret baptized", but sadly next day they were buried. Among other references to strangers to the parish were the baptism in 1600 of "Gilbert, son of a wayfaring woman", the burial in February 1621/2 of "a Mistrell's boy who was drowned" and the baptism in March 1630/1 of "David, son of a wayfaring woman". In none of these three cases is a surname given. The sequence of entries in the Registers continued year after year. Pauper burials were so described and the fees were paid out of the funds of the Overseers of the Poor. Both parents, if known, were recorded of children being baptized and illegimate children were so described even if the father's name was recorded. In 1792, 8 people were buried, of whom 3 were paupers. 10 children were baptized, of whom 3 were illegitimate, a smaller proportion than the national average today.

Infant mortality was frequent, but, even under the harsh conditions prevailing centuries ago in Clungunford, those who survived the dangers of youth could reach a great age. As the parish Registers recorded no baptisms before 1559, there must always have been scope for many years subsequently for the elderly to exaggerate their age, but, even allowing for this, there is no doubt that some people grew very old in Clungunford. In 1599, Commissioners from the High Court of Exchequer attended an Inquiry at Purslow, at which evidence was given as to whether or not Coston Manor had belonged to the Knights Hospitallers of St. John of Jerusalem before the Dissolution of the Monasteries, some sixty years earlier. The oldest inhabitants of Clungunford and Clunbury recalled what they remembered from the days of their youth concerning collection of rent at Coston, whether there was a cross on top of the house and whether it was a house of sanctuary from the law. Among the witnesses were Henry Maklen of Abcott and John Corne of Shelderton, both aged 90, Geoffrey Harries of Abcott, aged 86, and George Holland of Shelderton, aged 76. Reference was made to information given by George Macklen of Abcott who had died the year before. The parish Registers record the burial in October 1598 of George Makelen of Abcott "beinge of the age of CXIIII yeares". There were also many members of the family at Bedstone and Hopton Castle in the late sixteenth century. The fact that this surname was spelt in three different ways in the record of the Inquiry and in the parish Registers is no cause for surprise at a time when spelling was always haphazard. The second oldest person mentioned in the Registers was Walter Bodenham, buried in 1574, aged 107. After 1600, the Registers attribute no such immense ages to those whose burials they record, but as century followed century, many people in the parish reached their nineties and Clungunford remained a haven of longevity.

Among the families who have featured longest in the story of the parish, the name of Makelin, to give it its modern spelling, is remarkable. First mentioned in the thirteenth century, it reappears at intervals. When the Lay Subsidy tax was collected in 1524, one of the collectors for Abcott, in the Purslow Hundred, was George Maklede and one of the collectors for Shelderton, in the Munslow Hundred, was John Makelyn. It is tempting to assume that the Abcott man who died in 1598, recorded as aged 114, was the collector of Lay Subsidy at Abcott in 1524, when he was only 40. Three people with the surname Macklen were buried at Clungunford between 1565 and 1585 and members of the family appear regularly in the parish Registers until 1695, when Francis Maclean was buried. The Hearth Tax record for 1672 shows that John Macline of Beckjay paid 2d tax because his house had one hearth, so it must have been very small. For over 200 years, the family disappear from the records of Clungunford parish. In 1919, George Makelin bought at auction Upper Shelderton Farm and its 219 acres, which he had already tenanted from the Sitwells' Ferney estate for a few years. He and his brother also managed the Clungunford home farm for Evan Rocke, but the family's restoration to Clungunford was to be short lived because in 1962 George Makelin sold Upper Shelderton and moved to Leintwardine.

Other families which recur in Clungunford's history through the centuries but have now disappeared include (in a variety of spellings) Corne, Onions, Harley, Bodenham, Boor, Mullard, Millichap, Langslow, Blakeway, Wolley, Urwick, Anthony, Weaver, Jukes, Bridgewater, Bird and Howells. They were among the worthy folk on whom the community depended. Some were tenant farmers and yeomen who had small farms of their own. Others had essential skills, whether in agriculture, building or the other trades required in a self sufficient village. They rotated between them the duties of Churchwardens, Overseers of the Poor, Trustees of the charities and Parish Constable. Of course, the names of the local landowners also feature throughout, but until late Victorian times their role in the district was at a different level. The Barkeleys and the Rockes provided the Rectors of Clungunford for more than half of the last four centuries. The Walkers, the Sitwells, the Bayleys, the Unetts, the Beales and the Rockes were frequently Justices of the Peace and some of them were High Sheriffs, but it was only in the late nineteenth century that they became Churchwardens. When Charles Blakeway, the tenant of Shelderton Farm, died in 1877, he had completed thirty continuous years as Rector's Warden. The Sitwell owner of the Ferney estate succeeded him in that role for four years, after which for a hundred years the current Rocke owner of the Clungunford estate was usually one of the Churchwardens.

The 1841 Census recorded the age, occupation, marital status and number of children of all the inhabitants of the parish of Clungunford. It shows what a variety of specialist trades were available. Apart from the inevitable farmers and agricultural labourers, the squire, the rector, the curate and the schoolmaster, there were two or more painters, carpenters, dressmakers, stonemasons, blacksmiths, tailors and shoemakers, a gamekeeper, a wheelwright, a sawyer, a saddler, two Methodist Ministers, a publican and two millers. Richard Jukes of Clungunford, no doubt a member of the family of local builders, was well known in Methodist circles after 1825 as a Minister, hymn writer and poet. The Methodist chapels were on Brand Hill, where the Circuit Records for 1840 show there was a congration of only 8 members, and in the centre of Clungunford, next to Sycamore House. That congregation had 11 members in 1854, but there must have been a rapid increase because, in 1901, the chapel was replaced by a larger building with pews for 150 people. In 1970, that chapel was closed and was eventually demolished, to be replaced by a bowling green.

The blacksmith in Clungunford village was Richard Yapp, whose smithy was next to the Methodist chapel, on land belonging to Sycamore House. During 1841, the Rev. John Rocke paid him more than £10, and no doubt many horses were shod so conveniently close to Clungunford House. The other blacksmith was William Bathurst at Hopton Heath, who does not feature in the squire's list of expenses, unlike George Mold, the blacksmith at Clunbury, who may have been called upon to deal with a loose shoe or two when a problem occurred away from home. The Mold family are a dynasty of blacksmiths, still happily continued by Ron Mold at Kempton in Clunbury parish. Between 1909 and 1941, Frederick Mold worked in the Hopton Heath smithy while the Clunbury one was run by other members of his family.

John Greenhouse ran The Rocke Arms in 1841, but The Cross Keys was not then a licensed public house. William Anslow, who had been described as a shopkeeper in 1832, was working as a miller in 1841 at the Rocke family's Clungunford Mill, while the miller at Beckjay Mill was Daniel Jones. By 1848, Anslow became the owner and manager of the Cross Keys public house, at the entrance to Clungunford from Broome, but he was also able to act as the miller at Beckjay Mill, which was again the only working mill in the parish.

Domesday Book had recorded two mills in Clungunford. Fluctuations in the price and local production of grain determined the number of mills required. The additional mill at Broadward, which was recorded by 1300 but not in recent centuries, probably stood on the left bank of the Clun, downstream from the present Broadward Bridge, where in 1848 there was a field still

Fig. 39. *Exterior of old Clungunford Mill by Rev. Edward Pryce Owen 1833.*

Fig. 40. *Interior of old Clungunford Mill by Rev. Edward Pryce Owen 1834.*

called Mill Butts. Beckjay Mill was across the river Clun from Beckjay Farm and was long in the same ownership. Up to 1863, it belonged to the Knight family of Henley Hall and it was operated until the end of the nineteenth century. Higher up the river, close to the cottages then called Tradesmen's Row, was the other mill, called Clungunford Mill, which belonged to the Rocke family but was disused by the middle of the eighteenth century. In Richard Rocke's Rent Book, recording his income and expenditure concerning his Clungunford estate, he describes a programme of repair to "The Old Mill" in 1784. £1.5.0 was paid to Thos. Malpas for lugging stone and lime there, £2.15.6 to Wm. Jukes for mason's work, 9/2 to Wm. Williams for glazing and 2/8 to Richard Anthony for thatching. Other payments were for lath, for carpenter's work and for blacksmith's work. That year the Old Mill was in operation again, so that taxes had to be paid on it. Land Tax of 11/6, Shire Hall Tax of 2/10 and Church Rate of 1/-. It is difficult to fix the exact position of Clungunford Mill, which, like Beckjay Mill, was an undershot water mill. It had ceased operations before the visit to the village in 1847 by the representatives of the Tithe Redemption Commission and does not appear in their map. The mill wheel must have required a special channel fed from higher up the river where there are now only humps in the ground. The only indication on the 1848 map is the name "Mill Lane Head" for the second field on the right along the road from the village towards Broome. This would be the point from which a track once led to the mill and also to Tradesmen's Row, although it had been closed by 1847. The 1884 Ordnance Survey Map, however, shows the miller's cottage, beyond a small field on the east side of the river. That cottage was demolished many years ago, but some people still in the village were born there. The appearance of the mill can be imagined from the list of its component materials, but, luckily, the Reverend Edward Pryce Owen came to look at it in 1833 and again in 1834 and has left two delightful pencil and wash drawings, which are now in the Shropshire Records Office. By then, the weather-boarded and lightly thatched structure was again somewhat dilapidated, but it was still equipped for grinding corn. Cheap wheat imports from Ireland, Russia and North America, building up steadily after 1790, had made it redundant. The final blow to the chance of a good price for English wheat was the Repeal of the Corn Laws in 1846, by which date this mill was demolished.

When the parish was surveyed in 1847 for the tithe redemption calculations, it was found to contain 3619 acres. 1000 acres were arable, meadow and pasture were 2400, woods and plantation 200 and roads and waste 19 acres. Some suspiciously round numbers there. The annual rentcharges, in commutation of tithe were fixed at sums totalling £538.12.1, which was comparable to the amount that the Rector had been receiving from his parishioners each year, after allowing for the fact that he received no payment from the part of the parish that he owned and used himself. Despite its total dependence on farming, the population of Clungunford, as recorded in the census every ten years, rose from 436 in 1801 to 554 in 1841 and a peak of 647 in 1861, as the London and North Western Railway line, opened from Craven Arms to Bucknell the previous year, was extended to Knighton. The itinerant labourers who constructed the railway then moved on and in 1871 the parish population was down to 605, from which figure it has declined regularly at every census until its present level of about 240. The congestion in the cottages in Victorian times must have been intolerable by modern standards. In 1841, for instance, 87 people lived in the 17 houses at Abcott and 91 people lived in the 15 houses at Beckjay and Broadward. The 554 people in the entire parish shared 107 houses – an average of over 5 people in every house, when most of the houses were extremely small.

As the eighteenth century drew to a close, the new farming methods, that had long been practised on the lighter soils of eastern England, gradually spread to the Welsh borders. The benefits of rotation of crops became apparent, so that land would bear corn crops alternating with turnips, clover or peas and beans. Until 1840, the only fertilizers available to improve arable land were dung, night soil, marl and lime, of which there was a ready source in the hills on the eastern edge of Clungunford parish. After that date, superphosphates became available and Peruvian guano, Chilean nitrates and German potash were all imported in large quantities, but Shropshire's remoteness from the ports will have precluded these from reaching Clungunford until after the construction of the railway to Craven Arms in 1852 and thence to Hopton Heath in 1860. In the mid nineteenth century, the sickle gave way to the scythe, which could mow the hay and reap the corn in a third of the time. Reaping machines would not have been seen in Clungunford before the very end of Queen Victoria's reign, but improved ploughs, drills and rollers were being produced in Shrewsbury after 1868. Threshing machines, pulled and powered by traction engines, were readily available early in the twentieth century.

Fig. 41. *Threshing machine and traction engine.*

With extensive drainage incorporating the new cylindrical clay pipes and named varieties of seed becoming available for barley, wheat and oats, the yield of crops improved greatly, but the competition from imported grain still militated against arable farmers. With each major war, the need for home grown wheat became essential and prices rose, but at the end of the Crimean War and again in 1914 they slumped and the switch back to pasture resumed. It was only in 1945 that the Government decided to continue the wartime subsidies, extended later in different forms under the aegis of the European Common Market under its various titles. It remains to be seen how long Clungunford will maintain the present ratio between arable land and pasture, which is so different from that in centuries past.

As the common fields were coming to an end throughout England and more compact farming units were formed during the nineteenth century, the development of specialized breeds of farm animals was studied. Until 1860 the popular breeds of sheep in Shropshire had been the Southdown and the Leicester, but, in the circumstances prevailing, the purity of each strain must have been uncertain. After 1850, the Shropshire breed, whose forebears had long grazed the local uplands, was accepted as a separate flock, although no doubt containing much Leicester and Southdown ancestry. It was not until after the end of the war against the Kaiser that they were outnumbered in Shropshire by Clun Forest and Kerry Hill sheep. In due course, the Vaughans of Abcott Manor became renowned for their flock of the former breed and Donald Davies of Clungunford Farm for his flock of the latter.

Until well into the nineteenth century, cattle in south west Shropshire were a motley lot, generally similar to the longhorned stock of neighbouring counties. As with the sheep farmers, so cattle farmers were establishing new breeds to cater for particular conditions and needs. The Hereford breed, with their red bodies and white faces, whose herd book was established in 1845, became popular with beef farmers, but their milk yield was poor. In Clungunford until recently, all the farmers will always have kept some cattle, if only to produce manure for the fields. In the middle years of the twentieth century, there were herds of Herefords at Clungunford Farm and Beckjay. The Vaughans had Herefords at Abcott Manor, as did Bob Morgan at Abcott House until he changed to a dairy herd of Shorthorns. Jack Hamar at Bentley House had Ayrshires and the milk from both these dairy herds was collected in churns every day by lorry. At the former Rocke Arms, the Bason family kept a few cows and supplied the village with milk. Because of the restrictions now enforced concerning the production and sale of milk, such small scale enterprises are no longer viable and it seems unlikely that the residents of Clungunford will ever again be able to buy a pint of milk from a cow that lives among them.

New farm machinery introduced during the twentieth century greatly reduced the need for agricultural labour. Milking machines and tractors were a novelty in the 1940s, but within a few years they had become indispensable and had increased enormously the capabilities of one workman and probably enabled one or two others to be laid off. It will not have been easy for the older farm employees to adapt to the new conditions. The old skills were no longer valued. Round hayricks were out of fashion as were stooks. Soon, those skilled in managing sheepdogs as they walked sheep or cattle to market in Craven Arms, Ludlow, Knighton and Bishops Castle would see their animals being loaded into a lorry that they were unable to drive. Ploughing with horses was coming to an end. The waggoner employed by the Vaughans at Abcott Manor was virtually retired, but they put him on their new tractor, which he hadn't got a clue how to control. It continued through many a hedge as he shouted "Wo" at the top of his voice. With the introduction of quad bikes, even the sheepdog's employment is in jeopardy.

Fig. 42. *Ploughing with horses in Shropshire.*

Throughout all the changes, the life of the agricultural labourer has been arduous and usually miserably rewarded. These were the people whose families formed, until half a century ago, the largest part of the Clungunford community. Their housing was frequently cramped and primitive. Food, fuel and clothing for their often numerous children must have been a continual nightmare and, of course, there was no security of employment. If they lost their jobs, because of illness, old age, incompetence, insubordination or following some change in the circumstances of their employer or the price of corn, they almost certainly lost their homes as well. Probably the only refuge was the workhouse, or, more recently, the dole. Their pay fluctuated according to the fortunes of the farming industry, regardless of the cost of living and their needs. An average agricultural worker in Shropshire in 1875 was paid 12/3 a week. This rose to 16/- in 1894 and, thanks to the recruitment and the slaughter in the 1914-1918 War, by 1918 it was 46/-. Down again to 32/- in 1931, it was 35/- at the beginning of the next war in 1939 and had doubled to 70/- when the war ended six years later. Statutory minimum wages then played their part, increasing the weekly pay to £7.10.0 by 1950 and to £79.20 new money by 1983. Of course, by then the number of farm workers was far less and those who were left, using all the new machines and applying nitrogen, phosphates and potash liberally to the fields, were much more productive than had been possible only a few years before. Even after the improvement in agricultural wages during the last half century, they are still well below what industrial workers can expect to be paid. The received wisdom, which may sometimes have been correct, is that the farm worker can grow much of his own food and that the industrial worker deserves to be compensated because of the less salubrious conditions of urban life. Such arguments are unlikely to halt the drift to the towns of those of working age, a flow which, at least in the case of Clungunford, is countered by that of the retired.

The railway, the bicycle, the bus and the car have killed off the village tradesmen of Clungunford. Beckjay mill was demolished, the Rocke Arms closed as a public house, the smithy was pulled down and dressmakers and tailors went out of business. Until 1937, there were still a shoemaker, a stationer & post office, two grocers and another shop, but these dwindled away to a single shop & post office at Church Farm, which closed in 1985. The casual observer, driving through Clungunford, may think that its traditional farming community remains unaltered. Indeed, the three Bason brothers are still farming in Clungunford after half a century. (see *Colour Plate 26*) The fields are often larger and there are more crops and fewer farm animals, but the landscape is not greatly changed from a hundred years ago. The reality is very different. A recent survey has shown that half the present inhabitants of Clungunford have arrived during the last fifteen years. Many of the newcomers live in houses built or fundamentally reconstructed during those years. The survey did not consider the question of age, but it is evident that a large number of the recent arrivals and also of those who have lived in the parish most of their lives are aged over sixty five. Probably a lower proportion of the people in Clungunford are of working age that at any time in the past and, of those who are still working, many do their work outside the parish, just as all the schoolchildren go elsewhere for their lessons. It could be said that Clungunford is fast becoming a dormitory village, a place where people sleep but do not work, a place to which the old retire and which the young have to leave to get education or employment. Even farmers' children now find the prospect of taking over from their parents unattractive, with increasing regulations and diminishing returns.

How much longer will the farmland remain as it still is and will it depend on occasional visits from itinerant and insensitive contractors with massive machines and no commitment to the district ?

In the days before these fundamental changes, social life in Clungunford was very limited. There were fairs every year in Ludlow, Leintwardine and other towns and villages nearby, but these became less of a lure as other entertainments became available. In the 1930s, cinemas opened in Ludlow, Craven Arms, Bishops Castle and Church Stretton and all were accessible by bus or train. Race meetings at Ludlow would seldom have been attended by those at work in Clungunford, but the Saturday point-to points of the local Hunts at Brampton Bryan and elsewhere in the neighbourhood were a possibility. Coach trips to big towns, to the pantomime, the seaside and other tourist attractions became increasingly available, but for most people and particularly for labourers with large families the cost of travelling away from the village and paying there for entertainment was only rarely affordable.

Recreation in Clungunford has always depended on local initiative. The plate, commissioned in the village in 2000 to celebrate the millenium, listed some of the activities in the community, but there were others, as well. The opening of the Parish Hall in 1935 provided a venue, which had been so badly needed, although the Women's Institute survived from 1922 to 1991 on a peripatetic basis. The formation of the Clungunford Sports and Social Club in 1968 led to the enlargement of the building in the following year and subsequent improvements, together with the purchase of the neighbouring orchard and Methodist Chapel site and their conversion into a recreation ground and bowling green have now endowed the village with most useful facilities. Some of the former groups no longer exist. The Rifle Team, 2 Darts Teams, 2 Pool Teams and 2 Dominoes Teams, each of which used to represent the village, are no more and the Football Team, which took part in the South Shropshire League from 1956 to 1963, has also passed into history. However, in their place have arisen a range of new groups and enterprises, combining the skills and enthusiasm of all the diverse elements of the village, new and old. These include a Bowling Club, Wine Group, Gardening Club, Slow Ladies Walking Group and a Longer Distance Walking Group for those keen to walk 12 miles or more. There is a Bellringers Group, whose skills pervade the village every Thursday, a Kneelers Group, whose work adorns the church and the Village Choir, who sing in and out of church, while the Clungunford Players astonish their pantomime audiences by the range of their talents. As the Parish Council and the Parochial Church Council continue their ceaseless care for the Civil Parish and the church, a Village Design Statement has recorded the views of the inhabitants about Clungunford village and its satellite hamlets and indicated which aspects they would hope to see retained and which changed in future years. All these varied activities receive full coverage in the village newspaper, the Gunnas Gazette. Undoubtedly, Clungunford is humming.

Notes on the Chapters

Preamble:

(1) The Julian Calendar was established in 45 B.C. by Julius Caesar, providing for 366 days every fourth year, but this proved excessive, so that by the sixteenth century the calendar was ten days slow in relation to the seasons. In 1582, Pope Gregory XIII introduced the new, Gregorian Calendar, whereby ten days in October 1582 were deleted and future century years would only be leap years if the first two digits were divisible by four. Most of the Catholic countries accepted the Pope's new calendar, but England ignored it until September 1752, by which time the Julian Calendar was eleven days behind true solar time, so that 3-13 September 1752 had to be omitted in England. Until 1752, the English year began on 25 March, Lady Day, so that 1710, for instance, started on 25 March 1710 and ended on 24 March 1710, the next day being 25 March 1711. If a day between 1 January 1710 and 24 March 1710 is referred to in the book, it will be given the date 1710/11 to show that by our present calendar it would be dated 1711 and occurred after December 1710.

Chapter 1

(1) The named Tithe Map records two fields to the west of Watling Street as being part of Bottridge.

(2) The "jay" of Beckjay may mean "field", "gay" being an ancient word for field. This derivation is less obvious than the other Clungunford place names.

(3) The canons had sent a petition to Edward the Confessor on his death bed, saying that Spirtes' misdemeanours were not of their doing and requesting the return of the land granted to them in 1060. Unfortunately, the king died before the matter was resolved and that land, along with all Spirtes' other land in Shropshire and Herefordshire, was granted to Nigel the Physician, rather than to the cannons, after the Conquest. The profit from the produce of this land was originally intended to enable the cannons to carry out their duty of care to the poor and the sick.

(4) T.R.E. is short for "Tempus Regis Edwardi" or "in the time of King Edward", that is, before the Norman Conquest.

Chapter 2

(1) This map is based partly on information gained from the feudal surveys, the Liber Niger and Kirby's Quest, in particular, as well as on the records of the Purslow and Munslow Hundred Courts and partly on information provided in the Tithe map of 1848, particularly through it's later listing of old field names. Certain eighteenth century maps have also proved useful, because they show which families owned certain pieces of land and, since we know the descent of these families from medieval times, we are able to ascertain how this land was divided in the Middle Ages. Land to the west of Abcott and that bordering on Coston must have been moved from the fief of the de Halberdynes to that of the de Hoptons at some point in the thirteenth century and for this reason the edge of that fief is shown as marked with diagonal zig-zags.

For the purposes of this map we have assumed that the fields near Beckjay, which were owned by the Knights in the eighteenth century were the same fields, which Elizabeth de Jay took as part of her inheritance when she became Mrs Knight in the fifteenth century. Although she had a son, Edward, who died in 1505, leaving a Will (surviving in the Family Record Centre), he had no children and left his estate to his sisters, one of whom married into the Ireland family. It seems that Elizabeth left the land at Beckjay to some member of her husband's family.

(2) Later in the century they seem to have had some problems because by 1307 they are recorded as having a tenant, Nicholas Reygate, in the Manor of Jay. When the Clarenceaux Herald came to Shropshire in 1623, the Ireland family showed him a collection of early documents concerning the de Jay family, from whom they had inherited them. These documents are now lost, but the Herald copied them and included the copies in the de Jay entry in his 1623 "Visitation of Shropshire".

Chapter 3

(1)This is the earliest reference concerning Abcott, which has come to light so far.

Chapter 4

(1) The Walter de Hopton who had died in 1305 had left a small boy as his heir, so the king appointed a guardian, Hugh de Neville, to look after the boy's affairs. This Hugh may, or may not, have been a reliable guardian, for in 1337, when no longer a minor, the Walter de Hopton of the day had to pay the Nevilles 2000 marks for his inheritance at Shelderton. Presumably this was to release a mortgage, which Hugh de Neville had raised on Walter's land. Possibly this had been useful to the estate during the time of sheep murrain following the years of bad harvest, but more probably, it had been useful to the boy's guardian. In the next generation, after the death of Walter, the minor in 1367, there was an Inquisition as to the ownership of Shelderton and Broadward. Walter left no sons and his daughter, Elizabeth, having married a de Charlton, her son John de Charlton was declared Walter's heir. However, this was challenged by another Walter de Hopton, probably a nephew. The second Inquiry, held at Shrewsbury in 1369, still maintained that Shelderton and Broadward belonged to the de Charltons, so, in order to return the estate to the male line, Walter de Hopton and his wife Joanna bought the it back from his uncle. This Walter was Sheriff, King's Justice, Cattle Rustler and a Member of Parliament, who was given an allowance of fourteen pounds to cover his expenses while away from his Hopton estate on parliamentary business in 1363.

(2) All this is set out in documents recording the assessment for the "Feudal Aid " on the Knighting of the Black Prince. Roger de Halberdyne is listed as one of those liable to pay, but in the second document, which details the amounts due from each individual, he is said to have handed back his fief.

(3) A deed concerning Clungunford, dating from 1373, has been published in the Transactions of the Shropshire Archaeological Society, II:IV. This somewhat strange document refers to a transfer of Tately Farm, which John Makelyn, son of Hugh Makelyn of Abcott, had granted to Henry de Broom subject to one third part of it reverting to John's widow, as a dower, when he died. Meanwhile, John owed Henry twenty pounds in silver currency. By this, 1373, document Henry said that, if John's widow were to reclaim her third of Tately, he would immediately insist on repayment of his silver. This sounds like a threat, especially as the document originally had a seal, which suggests serious business. However, a third of Tately would not have been worth twenty pounds of silver coinage in those days, so Henry was, on the face of it, being generous. The lack of pottery sherds points toTately having been uninhabited at this date, so the portions of the farm mentioned relate only to the land there. No house is mentioned. What is certain is that there was by this date a competent trained lawyer in the neighbourhood, who produced a professional document, which was sealed at Clungunford. It also shows that the richer members of the community were using money, rather than barter. This is another early record of the Makelin family, who have one of the longest family histories recorded in the parish.

Chapter 5

(1) There is considerable confusion in the pedigrees of these families as to whether Elizabeth and Joanna Burley were the daughters of William or his brother, John. Most of the genealogists make them the daughters of William's brother, John. However, the reference in the Patent Rolls to their inheritance of Clungunford makes it quite clear that they were the children of William, Speaker of the House of Commons.

Chapter 6

(1)These rare Hundred Court records have survived only because Clungunford was a tiny part of the estates of mighty barons, whose muniment rooms were carefully looked after for centuries. Had the estate of Clungunford been an entity in itself, there would be fewer surviving records. As part of the Hundred of Purslow, the village records belonged to the Arundels and their heirs, who sold out to the Walcots, who sold to Clive of India, whose son married the heiress to Lord Powis. These fragile medieval, parchment "rolls" were kept in the former land agent's house in Lydbury North until the second half of the twentieth century when they went to the SRR. Few of them survive in a robust enough state to be handled, but those that do provide insights into village life in the fourteenth, fifteenth and sixteenth centuries. No doubt the archivists at Shrewsbury will be able to tease out more detail from these fragile documents and will eventually publish them when they are catalogued. In the meantime, we must make do with the more robust specimens, like the unusually well preserved one illustrated here.

(2) Preserved in the More Papers at SRR.

(3) "John Harford, esquire and John Farley, yeoman" who, according to the Patent Rolls, paid the crown a large sum of money in 1553 for a great many parcels of land all over Hereford and Shropshire, all of which had belonged to monasteries. Among these parcels were two in Abcott. One was described as being "in the tenure of William Morris, which had belonged to Wigmore Abbey". Unfortunately, Wigmore does not have a cartulary and the patch of land at Abcott was too small to be recorded in Henry VIII's valuation of that monastery's possessions so we do not know when this land was given to Wigmore. William Morris, who must have started the negotiations, was actually dead by the time of the sale, so the document must refer to his son, Thomas, who was his heir at Abcott. In 1540s, when their house was built, the Morrises were still tenants of the crown, following the Dissolution of the Monasteries. Presumably they felt very confident of their ability to buy the freehold of the land soon.

The other parcel was "a messuage and half a yard of land in Abbecote, Salop, in the tenure of …..Harryson….which had belonged to Haughond Monastery". This was the fifteen acres which Simon de Halberdyne had given away in the thirteenth century. There is every reason to believe that the Morisses bought this land also and it is possible that the "messuage" was the predecessor of the present Manor

(4)In the middle of the century the Stringfellow family from London were active in Shropshire in this field. The first, Robert, a collector of Tonnage and Poundage taxes from the London docks, seems to have funded his purchases by failing to hand in to the king all the tax he had collected. Evidently he was rumbled and ordered to repay the crown, thus accumulating a huge debt. His son, Richard, inherited not only the properties but also the debt. It is the discharge of this debt, which presents an odd series of documents concerning the ownership of central Clungunford in the 1550s and 1560s and recorded in the Patent Rolls.

(5) Half the Burley inheritance in central Clungunford had come down, through the female line (via the Trussels) to the Earl of Oxford, who did not want it. Therefore it was given in "fee farm" in 1557 to Richard Stringfellow. A seventeenth century abstract of the deeds concerning the sale by the Earl of Oxford in 1556-7 exists in the SRR.

Stringfellow had to make it over to the crown and to agree to pay what was in effect a rent for it for twenty one years to help clear his debt. In the midst of all this, William Barkeley arrived on the scene. In 1558 he bought the other "moitie" of central Clungunford for three hundred pounds from Sir John Littleton, who was the heir of William Burley's other daughter. No doubt the deal was fixed by Richard Stringfellow, who then managed a deal whereby the "moitie" he had obtained from the Earl of Oxford was also "released" to William Barkeley in 1559. In the following year, the crown agreed to release Stringfellow from his debt for a sum of money, which he was now able to pay.

List of Colour Plates

1. Domesday Book. E31/2/2 Detail Courtesy of P.R.O.
2. View from Clunbury Hill in 2001. Photo by Alex Ramsay.
3. St. Cuthbert's Church, Clungunford. View of south side in 1802. Watercolour by Archdeacon Owen. Courtesy of Justin Coldwell.
4. St. Cuthbert's Church, Clungunford. View of north side in 1802. Watercolour by Archdeacon Owen. Courtesy of Justin Coldwell.
5. St. Cuthbert's Church, Clungunford with Rev. Barney Bell in 2001.
6. St. Cuthbert's Church interior in 2001. Photo by Alex Ramsay.
7. Sheep. Luttrell Psalter. 14th Century. (f.163v) Add 42130. Courtesy B.L.
8. Ploughing with oxen. Luttrell Psalter. (f.170) Add 42130. Courtesy B.L.
9. Watermill. Luttrell Psalter. (f.181) Add 42130. Courtesy B.L.
10. Reaping. Luttrell Psalter. (f.172v) Add 42130. Courtesy B.L.
11. Abcott Manor from the south. Photo by Alex Ramsay.
12. Chimneys at Abcott Manor.
13. Half timbered east gable of Abcott Manor. Photo by Alex Ramsay.
14. Watercolour of Clungunford in 1802 by W. Pearson. Courtesy of Robin Parish.
15. Glebe Cottage, formerly Rectory Cottage. Photo by Alex Ramsay.
16. Clungunford Farm with Bowes Rocke and family. Photo by Alex Ramsay.
17. Rowton Grange. Photo by Alex Ramsay.
18. Church Farm. Photo by Alex Ramsay.
19. Beckjay Mill in 1855 by William Curtis. Courtesy of Jim and Mary Bason.
20. Beckjay Farm with Jim Bason. Photo by Alex Ramsay.
21. Broadward Hall. Photo by Alex Ramsay.
22. The Bird on the Rock Tearooms, formerly The Rocke Arms.
23. Ferney Hall in 2001. Photo by Alex Ramsay.
24. Heath House.
25. Clungunford House on Silver Jubilee Day 1977.
26. Fred, Bert and Jim Bason farming in 2002.
27. John Rocke as High Sheriff in 1971. Photo courtesy of Bowes Rocke.

Notes.
1. P.R.O. denotes Public Record Office and B.L. denotes British Library.
2. All photographs of paintings in this list were taken by Alex Ramsay.
3. Photographs not attributed were mostly taken by the authors.

List of Black and White Illustrations

33. Donald Davies with champion Kerry Hill ram.
34. Title design of 1809 Map of Beckjay Estate. SRR 1141/Bdle 115.
    Courtesy of Messrs Phillips, Solicitors of Ludlow and SRR.
35. Drawing of Ferney Hall on Estate Map of 1782. SRR 1141/Box 90.10.
    Courtesy of Messrs Phillips, Solicitors of Ludlow and SRR.
36. View of Ferney Hall in 1789 from Humphrey Repton's Red Book.
    Courtesy of the Pierpont Morgan Library, New York.
37. Typical glazing bars at Broadward Hall.
38. Shelderton House.
39. Exterior of old Clungunford Mill in 1833 by Rev. Edward Pryce Owen.
    SRR 6001/201 Courtesy of SRR.
40. Interior of old Clungunford Mill in 1834 by Rev. Edward Pryce Owen.
    SRR 6001/201 Courtesy of SRR.
41. Threshing machine and traction engine.
42. Ploughing with horses in Shropshire.

Note.

B.L. denotes British Library, V&A denotes the Victoria and Albert Museum and SRR denotes the Shropshire Records and Research Centre in Shrewsbury.

Index

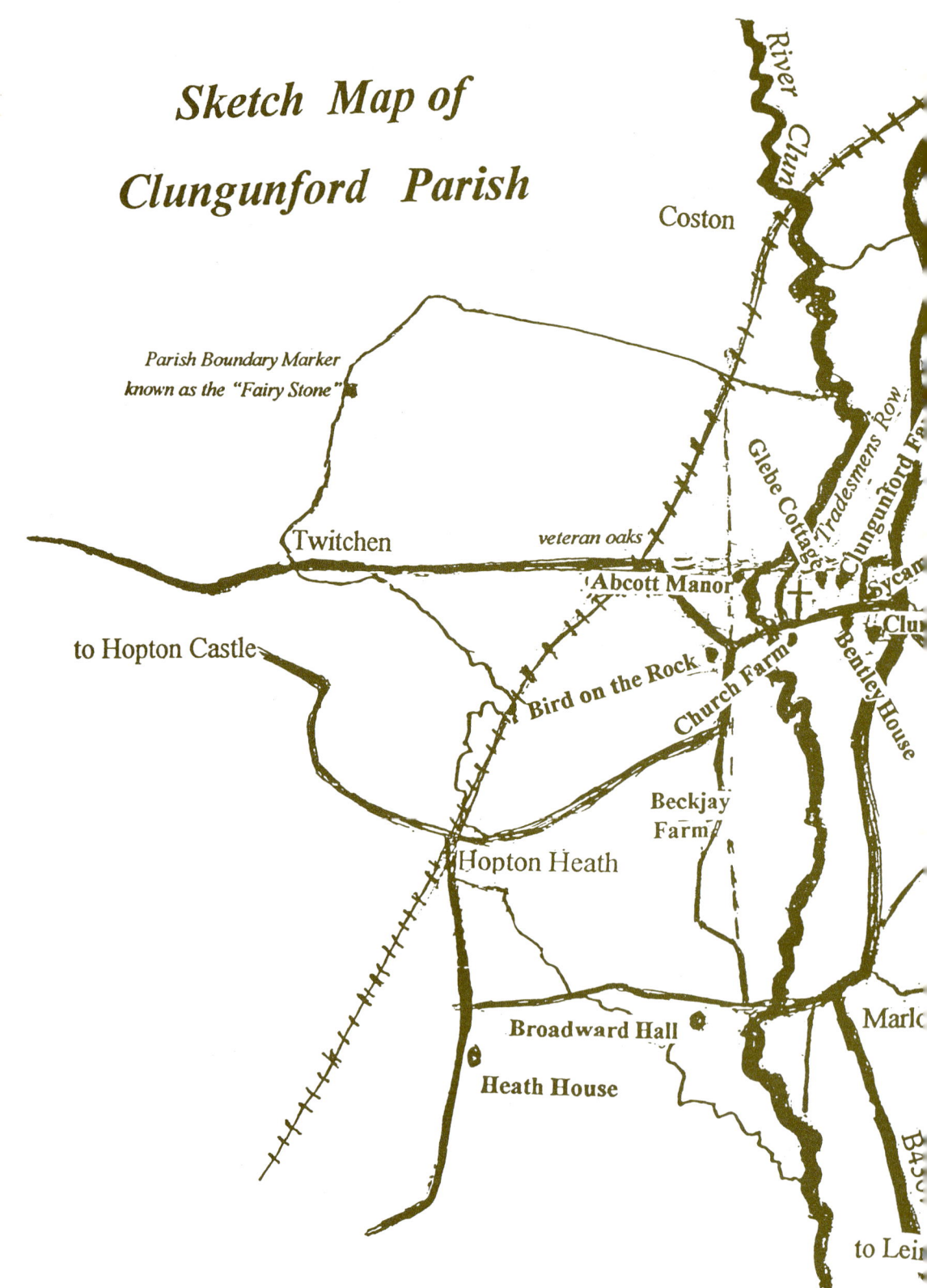

Sketch Map of
Clungunford Parish

Coston

River Clun

Parish Boundary Marker
known as the "Fairy Stone"

Tradesmens Row

Glebe Cottage

Clungunford F

veteran oaks

Twitchen

Abcott Manor

Sycam

Clu

to Hopton Castle

Bird on the Rock

Church Farm

Bentley House

Beckjay
Farm

Hopton Heath

Broadward Hall

Marl

Heath House

B43

to Leir